An Unreasonable Woman

An Unreasonable Woman

In search of meaning around the globe

Shirley Deane

Press 53
Winston-Salem

Press 53
PO Box 30314
Winston-Salem, NC 27130

First Edition

Cover design by Kevin Morgan Watson

Author photo by Paul M. Jackson
www.paulmjackson.com

In order to protect the privacy of some individuals, some names have been changed.

Printed on acid-free paper

ISBN 978-1-935708-11-7 (Paperback)
ISBN 978-1-935708-21-6 (Hardcover)

Dedicated to Lenita, my late mother,
who made all things possible

“The reasonable man adapts himself to the world; the unreasonable one persists in trying to adapt the world to himself. Therefore, all progress depends on the unreasonable man.”

George Bernard Shaw
Man and Superman (1903)

An Unreasonable Woman
In search of meaning around the globe

PART 1

1

DURBAN, SOUTH AFRICA

Early January, 1976

My taxi pulled up to Regency Court at sunrise. I climbed out, humming a show tune from my Manhattan youth. A two-week holiday had ended, the air was clear and cool, and the SCHWEPPES sign that ran vertically down the façade of my russet brick apartment building sparkled in the early morning light.

I lived next to the "C" in the sign, Apartment 114 on the eleventh floor. Few tenants spoke to me, but that didn't matter. My book mattered—a *Who's Who of Black South Africans*. The first, ever. My vacation was the reward I gave myself for hundreds of hours of risky interviews. Now, relaxed and refreshed, I would transform those tape-recorded interviews into a manuscript.

The stark black arrow in the lobby, pointing toward the rear of the building, reminded me of the first visit of the blacks on my Board of Directors. The supervisor had caught them in the passenger elevator. "Hey, kaffirs!" he roared. "Use the cargo lift! Back there!"

I stood rigid with silent rage as my guests left the passenger elevator and trudged toward the back. A professor of medicine, a newspaper editor, an attorney, a minister, a schools inspector. Herded like sheep by a man who never made it out of eighth grade.

"Don't fret," one of the board members said later. "We're used to it." I wasn't used to it then, and never got used to it.

Now, in the eleventh-floor hallway outside my apartment, I glanced over the balcony railing. Behind the apartment building, the "boys," as they were called, sat chatting and smoking outside their wood and iron shacks. Their services came with the rent. Every morning they came to my place in knee pads, scrubbed floors, sinks and tub. I'd wanted to do it, but the supervisor insisted it was "the kaffirs' job."

The key turned, and I stepped in. The sound of the deadbolt pulling out of its socket beneath the solid wooden door brought a smile to my face. Once I locked myself inside that apartment, I was safe. Nobody could break in.

A narrow corridor led to my living room door, also locked. I unlocked it, and turned the knob. Neat and clean, just as I left it.

I parted the gray drapes and opened the windows overlooking Berea Road. Noisy, heavily traveled, not a tree in sight. Mohamedy's and Moosas' general stores across the street. A few yards up, the Caltex petrol station. Near the entrance to my building was the exit from a highway to the north and the pastel suburbs of the west.

My décor suited me. A dark green sofa crouched along one wall of my living room. An old upright piano nearby leaned forward as if begging for a pianist. A metal filing cabinet hugged the opposite wall near a maple desk with a manual Olympia typewriter. A gray easy chair sat in front of the window. Close by, my pride: A bookcase.

My pride lay not in its pine boards and sagging bricks, but in the contents. Ninety-two reels of tape enclosed in square plastic boxes. The history of my life in sound.

I had been in show business, playing jazz accordion on radio, TV, and in night clubs in New York and Chicago. At twenty-seven, I left America to perform in Europe, Africa, and the East, recording performances, impressions of celebrities I'd met, and experiences while driving a Land Rover alone from London to Kathmandu. One day I would transcribe those tapes for a book. But first, I'd write the Black Who's Who.

I unlocked my file cabinet where I'd stored the interview cassettes during my two-week holiday. My Indian secretary would transcribe them. She had a new Royal typewriter, two new ribbons, and a potion called "white-out" that magically repaired typing errors. I pulled fifty tapes from a file drawer, put them in a carry bag with a ream of typing paper, inserted new batteries in my Philips recorder, and left.

Rani Naidoo lived in Tin-Town, an impoverished Indian township outside Durban. Most South African Indians were descendants of farmers who had come to the country a century earlier to work as indentured laborers on Natal's sugar plantations. They occupied third place on South Africa's color scale. Whites first, "coloreds" next (they had some white blood), Indians third, Africans last.

A narrow, unpaved road led to the small shack with a tin roof where Rani lived with her aging mother. The pretty twenty-year-old waited on the porch. Olive skin, black eyes, no make-up. A thick braid hung to the waist of her sari.

She greeted me with palms together, led me inside, and served tea in the living room. We sat at a square table set beneath a window that overlooked a playground. Small boys in tattered shirts and shorts screamed as they threw balls to one another.

Rani cleared the table, picked up her typewriter and my recorder. She had used a Philips on her last job, and knew how it worked.

"I'll type fast," she said.

"Don't forget to double space."

I headed back to town, ate lunch at the Royal Hotel, drove to the top of Smith Street and turned down Marine Parade for a slow drive along the Indian Ocean. At the sight of the Edwards Hotel, I recalled the story about Eartha Kitt's visit to South Africa for a performance.

When Kitt arrived, she stood at the hotel entrance and pointed toward the sea. "That's the Indian Ocean?" she asked a porter.

"Oh no," the porter told her. "That's the white ocean." He pointed left. "Indian ocean five kilometers down."

I'd often heard liberal whites say, "South Africa will come right, it won't be long." I believed it because I wanted to believe it. Because I loved South Africa. I loved the rugged coastline, the scent of mimosa, the Drakensberg Mountains, the defined Indian and African cultures.

Ten years had passed since I'd arrived. In my first year, I

volunteered services to the Indian community. Delivered food to families in "Tin Town." Typed thirty fund-raising letters a day on a Remington manual typewriter. Packed pills into tiny bottles at a free clinic for Indians and Africans. For the next seven years, I raised funds for an African girls' high school. It was during my seventh year at the school that I saw the all-white *Who's Who of South Africa.*

Next morning, I drove to the CNA building in Johannesburg to ask the editor why he'd left Africans out of a *Who's Who of South Africa.* "South Africa has twenty million blacks and five million whites," I reminded him. "Blacks gave their sweat and blood to make South Africa what it is."

The man stared at me from pig-like eyes. "I detect an American accent," he said.

"You detect right, sir."

"Why do Americans always poke their noses in other peoples' business?"

"Forget it, sir. I'll do my own *Who's Who*." I stomped out.

Back in Durban that night, a forgotten spirit rekindled. I was three years old, ecstatic at my birthday party. I was twenty-seven, standing on the deck of the *M/S Oslofjord*, waving farewell to Mom, Dad, and Manhattan. A wild adventure about to begin—working my way alone around the world. Six years later, climbing into my new Land Rover in Birmingham, England. Ready to drive around the rest of the world. Alone.

Now, the same rush. The surge of life force that signaled the start of adventure. This time, to engrave the acts and attainments of South Africa's majority into a historic record. To fill the unforgivable void left by the white *Who's Who.*

I penned my first line that night: *Dedicated to South Africa's twenty million Blacks, and to the five million Whites who say, 'I know them,' and believe they do.*

2

DURBAN

Later that day

The shrill ring of the telephone pierced the stillness of my living room.

"It's me, Rani," my secretary said. "I've been calling you for two hours."

"Sorry. I stopped for lunch, and took a slow drive home. What's up?"

She burst into tears. "There's nothing on those tapes!"

"What do you mean, nothing? They're recorded interviews. All of them."

"There's nothing. I tried them all. Nothing."

"That's impossible! Never mind, I'll be right over."

I drove fast. Rani probably pressed "record" instead of "play," and did it with all fifty tapes! Why didn't I transcribe them myself? Stupid to trust someone else. All that work, lost! Driving through KwaZulu, one of eleven homelands that the government allocated to blacks. Plodding through non-viable strips of land that cut through the country like ribbons. Driving in low gear on rutted dirt roads. Skirting free-roaming cows and chickens. Interviewing farmers, businessmen, educators, musicians, teachers, nurses, ministers, sportsmen, actors, doctors.

Some didn't speak English, and I couldn't speak Zulu. A translator had to be found who lived in a wood and iron shack "up that way," where all the shacks were made of wood and iron. All that! For nothing?

Rani waited on the porch, red-eyed, her long hair loose.

"Don't worry," I said. "We'll fix it."

Half a dozen cassettes lay on her table with the recorder. I picked up one labeled *Elles Manqele*. Her house in Mapumulo was "the one with a red roof." Every house in her area had a red roof.

The matron worked at a hospital with forty-five beds and a hundred and fifty patients. She'd adopted fifteen children because Africans had no orphanages. Did post-mortems after tribal faction fights. Built a kitchen herself out of sheet iron in a hospital where the old kitchen doubled as a birthing room.

I inserted the cassette and pressed "play." The tape rotated silently.

"Her voice. Where is it? Where's Manqele's voice?" I couldn't hear it, just a peculiar pulsation sound like a metronome thump every few seconds.

Rani's tapered fingers quivered as she covered her mouth with the flap of her sari. I put another tape on. The widow of Chief Albert Lutuli, winner of the Nobel Prize, who lived in a fifty-year-old, iron-roofed house off a potholed dirt road in Groutville, and cooked on a paraffin stove. She told me that when she and the Chief were finally allowed to travel abroad, a full year after the Nobel was awarded, they flew to Norway with Dag Hammarskjold, and had an audience with the King of Norway.

Lutuli couldn't believe her eyes. "Norwegians looked at me as if I was a human being instead of kitchen help."

"Damn," I screeched. "Where the hell is her voice?"

I pulled it off, and put on Robert Mazibuko, a farmer in the Valley of a Thousand Hills. One great rolling hill after another along the Umzimkulu River. He told me how his trench composting system had transformed the once barren valley. He'd taught his people how to prevent soil erosion and make the most of their small farms.

But Mazibuko was silent. Just that periodic pulsing sound.

"Could you have pressed "record" instead of "play?"" I asked Rani.

"Oh, no. No. I know how the Philips works."

I put on Buthelezi's tape—Gatsha Buthelezi, chief minister of the KwaZulu government, president of a national cultural liberation movement, traditional prime minister of the Zulus, advisor to the Zulu king. He'd been to the United States as guest of the State Department, met President Nixon, visited universities, been a guest of the United Kingdom and German governments and nine African countries, and gave Pope Paul a geography lesson on kwaZulu. He straddled many cultures with ease, often appearing in traditional dress, moving like a predator with leopard skins swinging across his powerful thighs. Yet he wore a yarmulke in a synagogue, and in the U.S., he appeared in Texas regalia with a Stetson, string tie, and belt buckle.

I hosted a surprise party for his birthday one year, invited his friends, Harry Oppenheimer, chairman of South Africa's largest diamond mine, the press, and the diplomatic corps. Days earlier, Buthelezi had met with Prime Minister John Vorster, pressing for more land for his people. When I played, "Don't Fence Me In!" on my accordion, he stood and sang, "Give Me Land, Lots of Land Under Starry Skies Above." With a Texan accent.

Buthelezi had spoken for two hours at our interview, but his tape was silent.

I picked up Matron Mqwebu's tape. I'd interviewed her in a cramped, shabby, bustling hospital in Melmoth, where she was also administrator, fundraiser, and bookkeeper. She showed me beds under beds, a hundred and fifty for three hundred patients. She started the first "mobile clinic," walking from home to home.

Mqwebu had told me about the rainy day when a local woman, carrying her baby in the customary sheet-sling on her back, waited for a bus in her area. The government didn't build bus shelters for blacks. The downpour was torrential. When the bus arrived, and the woman boarded, she turned her baby around. The baby was lifeless, drowned by the rain. Mqwebu announced that if local men wouldn't do it, she'd build bus shelters herself from cast-off timber and metal.

Every story I heard was a chronicle of endurance. Many made me cry. But Mqwebu's story was gone.

"I'm stumped," I told Rani. "They're all like that?"

"All."

"Something's wrong with the machine. Don't worry. I'll take it to Philips. They invented the thing, they ought to be able to fix it. We'll get those voices back."

The time was four-thirty. Philips would close at five. I drove at top speed, parked in front of the service entrance and entered a large repair room. Behind a U-shaped counter, a stocky man in a white smock checked the clock above the door. "Sorry, we're closing," he said.

"Please, sir, it's urgent. Just five minutes. Please."

I placed the Philips and my bag of tapes on the U-shaped counter cluttered with recorders, radios, headphones, cassettes, batteries, cables.

"What's the problem?" he asked.

"My tapes won't play. They were fine when I gave them to my secretary. Something's wrong with the machine."

He plugged my Philips into a socket, picked up a tester tape labeled "Sinatra," and folded his arms. There it was, the Voice, singing, "My Funny Valentine." Sure, moving, mellow, like I'd always heard it.

"Nothing's wrong with this machine," he said.

"I don't understand. Why don't *my* tapes play?"

He picked up a tape that I'd marked Gcabashe, a common Zulu name. No sound.

"See?" I said. "Nothing but those damned pulsations."

He put on Msimang's, then Ndlovu's. Then he turned the machine off and put the tapes back in the bag. "Those cassettes were erased with a powerful magnet," he said.

"A *magnet*? That's impossible. I don't have any magnets in my flat."

"No. *You* don't."

"I don't get it. What are you trying to say?"

"You're American, aren't you?"

I heard the unvoiced corollary. *So what have you been up to?*

As I walked out, I saw his image through the glass door in front of me. The stare, the folded arms, the raised chin.

I sat stiffly behind the steering wheel. Offices had closed, the city was emptying itself. White men and women hurried toward their cars, bound for the surrounding posh suburbs. Africans headed for the black bus terminal where buses would take them to their match-box sheds in KwaMashu or Umlazi township.

From my parking place a block below Regency Court, I trudged up the inclined street. The evening was warm, but I trembled.

I unlocked my outside door and my living room door. *They'd* been here. Who are *they*? Humans who spoke Afrikaans and worked for SB, Special Branch. Or the reviled, feared BOSS, Bureau of State Security. They had been in my living room. Keys would have posed no challenge. They opened my locked doors, and poked around. Maybe in my bedroom, maybe the bathroom. They opened my locked file cabinet, and with a powerful magnet, waved their smutty hands back and forth until they wiped those tapes clean.

What else would they do? Or was this their first and final act? Bugger those bastards! They don't know that they're dealing with the chutzpah kid. They'll never get me down. I'll redo the interviews. Duplicate my tapes. Transcribe them myself. Photocopy my manuscripts. They'll never stop me, those Nazis!

Pieter Botha, the Defense Minister, had sympathized with the Nazis during World War II, opposing South Africa's partnership with the Allies. Maybe that qualified him for his job. *You tried, you buggers. But you won't win!*

A bottle of red wine from the vineyards of the western Cape stood on my kitchen counter. I filled a fluted glass, brought it to a side table in the living room, and eased myself into my recliner.

I turned toward my bookcase. Toward the ninety-two reels of my life's history.

"*Oh, no!*" I shrieked. "No! Not that! Not the history of my life! *God Himself would have stopped them!*"

3

DURBAN

Later that night

The sun had set, the room was dark, the drapes still open. How long had I sat on that chair, not daring to try the tapes on my shelves? What if those bastards had wiped them clean? Erased my history?

I lingered near my window, peering down at the bare darkness of Berea Road. Mohammedy's and Moosas' stores, and the Caltex petrol station had closed hours earlier. No one walked the street.

I drew the drapes, turned on a floor lamp, and pulled a reel from the first shelf. I had to know. Tape eleven, it said. *My Greek radio show in Chicago, 1952.* I threaded it on the spindles of the Gründig, pushed "play," and leaned back in my easy chair. The reels rotated.

Now, in this spot, I'd hear my name. *Shirley Denos*, the announcer would say. (*Deane* wasn't Greek enough for that show.) Here, I would play a four-bar intro to Gershwin's "The Man I Love," and sing the words. In Greek.

> *Kapia Mera, tha fani, aftos pagapo*
> *Kai tha eenai megalos kai theenatos, aftos pagapo*

I only heard the bleep, bleep, bleep of the pulsation sounds. But maybe I'd hear something in a few minutes. The reel rotated while I thought about the show, about my accent sounding so natural that listeners assumed I was Greek. It was the same in all languages because of my musical ear.

Mom and I learned that I had perfect pitch when she bought me an accordion for my eighth birthday, and brought me to Joe

Biviano, who taught on West Forty-Eighth Street in Manhattan. The bald, handsome man tested my ear. "Shirley has perfect pitch," he told Mom. "But unless she practices right, and uses her left hand like a pianist, she'll end up a polka player. *Oompah-pah, oompah-pah.*"

Every day for two hours, Mom sat beside me in our ground-floor apartment in Queens. "Play C scale with your right hand…Good. Left hand…No good. Again… Better…Both hands at the same time…No good…Up with the right, down with the left, same time…No good. Again..."

Tape eleven was soundless. Damn. I stopped it, rewound, pulled it off and threw it on the rug, the loose end scattering like brown confetti. *"Bastards!"*

I pulled tape twenty from my shelf, my first TV show in New York. I was sixteen when I auditioned for the show in the Roseland Building on Broadway and Fifty-Second Street. Booking agent Marvin Spear, a bloated man in baggy trousers and red suspenders, picked up a pad from his desk, held aside a curtain to the audition room, and lit a cigar.

"Let's hear it," he said.

I strapped on my accordion and played "Dark Eyes" with rapid finger movements, "My Funny Valentine," and "Lullaby of Birdland" with hefty jazz beats.

"Never heard a squeezebox like that," he said. "You sound like George Shearing. Hope you got a sexy gown."

"Why? I'm a musician, not a stripper."

"Don't matter if you're a poet. Show business is show business. When you play a squeezebox, the only thing that shows is the bottom, so make the most of it. Get a fishtail kind of thing. Like this." He sketched a mermaid.

"I can't walk in that."

"You don't need to walk. You'll stand in one place. How's your repertoire?"

"Classics. Semi-classics. Jazz. Swing. Blues. Every song on the Hit Parade."

"Good. You'll need a union card. You can't even play a bar mitzvah if you don't belong to Local 802. Minimum age is eighteen."

"Oh! I'm only sixteen!"

"Fake it. They won't bug you for an ID. They need the dues."

I went to Local 802 wearing heavy makeup and a hat with a veil. "I want to join," I told the secretary.

"Your age?"

"Eighteen."

I passed a musical test, paid my dues, got the card and a directory listing thirty-eight thousand musicians.

Tape twenty rotated, but I heard no music from the TV studio where I played under lights so bright that I couldn't see the audience. No "Carnival of Venice." No "September in the Rain." No applause. Only the bleeps. *Bleep bleep bleep*. I pulled off the tape and flung it at the wall. It bounced off the sofa and landed on the floor, scattering more confetti over the rug.

My life had been a battle. A battle now, a battle then. As a teen, I dreamt of living like Dr. Albert Schweitzer, running a small clinic on a rubber plantation in Malaya. Like him, I'd make my life my argument. But my mother had other ambitions.

The day I registered at NYU, the Admissions Counselor asked what I wanted to study. I turned away from Mom. I hadn't dared tell her before.

"I want to qualify for medical school," I said, "so I can live like Dr. Schweitzer."

"Live like Schweitzer?" my mother jeered. "You're a musician. A composer."

"So is he."

"You're not him."

"I want to be."

Mom gave the counselor the look.

"Medicine is a long course," Rosenthal said. "And costly."

Mom nodded, leaned back, a half-smile on her lips. "True, Miss Rosenthal. And girls don't need it. A simple college degree is enough."

Rosenthal understood. Enough to hook a good Jewish husband. But marriage didn't interest me. I couldn't see myself cooking, washing shirts, going to furniture sales. I didn't know why, since girls didn't attract me. My blood tingled when Elliot, my first date pressed himself against me, blowing warm, moist breath on my ears as we danced to "Stardust" at Tavern on the Green. But when I thought of marriage, I pictured a prison.

"Anyhow," Mom told the counselor, "Shirley's already a professional accordionist. She plays clarinet, she composes. She's a natural, born with perfect pitch."

"Then Music Education is her best option," the counselor said.

"I don't want to teach music," I told them. "I want to live like Schweitzer."

"That's not an option," Mom said.

Rosenthal swiveled around and wrote my name on her form. "The School of Education will be proud to have her," she nodded.

I sat with closed eyes on the subway back to Queens. One day, I'd find another way to live. A way where the inside dictates what the outside does. Not parents. Not bosses. Not society.

During my first semester, I dreamt that I gave birth to a baby girl, and stood over her as she lay in a carriage. Her wide-eyed gaze filled me with terror. I yanked the blanket over her head to avoid her stare, but she suffocated. The dream depressed me.

Dr. Voss, a psychology professor in his sixties with a deeply lined face, listened in his cluttered office as I recounted the dream. He'd analyzed many.

"The message is clear," he said. "What do you aspire for?"

"To live like Schweitzer."

"What are you doing about it?"

"Trying to forget it. Mom says it's not practical."

"Your effort to forget is killing your spirit."

I left his office, too choked to speak. I got As and Bs, but never stopped feeling like I took the wrong direction at a fork in the road, and just kept going.

I threaded reel sixteen, labeled *Tea for Two*. I'd recorded it on contract with a Mexican band at The Deck in New Jersey. One night at break time, the drummer motioned me to follow him out the back door to an alley. A little guy with pants two inches too short, and pink socks that sagged above his shoes.

Nicky unfolded his hand to show me a long, thin cigarette. “Pot,” he whispered. “Greenest stuff you can get. Right out of Mexico. Try.”

I’d never smoked, but he said it was easy. “Just breathe in. Hold it as long as you can. Then breathe out.”

I felt dizzy. Back on stage, the accordion looked like a piano. I couldn’t figure out how to strap that contraption on my shoulders. A sax man helped, and I fingered an A-flat intro to “Tea for Two.” After one chorus, I began to play improvisations that stunned me. Never had I played like that. Surely, the gods and goddesses were gazing down in awe.

When we finished our song, the manager stomped up to the stage, his eyes on me. “Chris’ sakes!” he barked. “You played nineteen choruses of “Tea for Two!”

That was the last time I smoked pot. That was the last time I heard my awesome rendition of “Tea for Two.”

From the top shelf, I pulled a reel labeled *The Waldorf*, and placed it on the spindle. *Let this one play, God.* Maybe the bastards only wiped out a few reels, and left the rest. Maybe I can still hear that Friday night at the Waldorf, my first club date.

I sat back and listened. Listened to my thoughts.

A porter had carried my accordion, amplifier and tape recorder to an elevator across the spacious Waldorf lobby with its draped walls and potted palms. On an upper floor, he led me along a wide corridor to a large convention hall, empty, except for a waiter arranging hors d’oeuvres and liquor on a table.

I plugged in my amplifier and recorder on the other side, set the accordion down, and brought my garment bag to the ladies’ room. In my fishtail gown, I tried to sit on a velvet padded bench, but couldn’t. My tiny steps back to the hall reminded me of the way aging patients shuffle their feet along hospital corridors.

I played softly. Well-dressed executives glanced my way, then turned toward the table for a drink. They paid no attention to my music, so I played my favorites. “Falling in Love with Love.” “There Will Never be Another You.” “Every Time We Say Goodbye.” What a fabulous job! Fifty bucks to play the songs I love!

By 8 p.m. the men’s voices grew loud. They staggered toward

me, collars open, ties loose and skewed. "Hey, sweetie. Play 'I've Been Workin' On the Railroad.'"

I played it, they sang it. Four choruses.

"Hey, cookie, 'Let Me Call You Sweetheart.'"

I played, they sang. A few of them swayed so close to me, swinging their glasses to the beat with such vigor that I feared they'd spill their drinks on my keys. I moved backward. They moved closer, almost pinning me to the wall. Their voices got louder with "'Won't You Come Home, Bill Bailey.'" They began to gaze at me in a different way.

"Wow. Black hair and blue eyes. Lookit 'er bedroom eyes!"

"Yeah. Bedroom eyes. She's got 'em."

They crowded closer, their whiskey breath hot on my face, their cigarette smoke in my nostrils. "Hey, beautiful. Doesn't it pinch? *Ha, ha, ha*."

They roared. "Her squeezebox pinches. *Ha, ha, ha*."

One hour to go, but I couldn't stand it. "Break," I called out, and put the accordion in the case. I went to the ladies' room where I wanted to scream out loud, smash the mirror with my fist, and see it shatter to bits.

The Waldorf reel ended. Soundless, all of it, except for bleeps. I pulled it off the spindle and threw it at the far wall. It hit the file cabinet, rolled onto the desk, and fell to the floor, bouncing over the rug like a scrappy old vine in a dead forest.

I flopped into my chair. Gone. Everything gone. Music I composed. Words I wrote. Concerts I played. My history. My mind wouldn't accept it. Words repeated themselves: *Impossible. It didn't happen. Couldn't have happened.* I felt like a bomb had exploded within me, and left a crater in my chest. For an hour or two, I stared into that pit with closed eyes, conscious only of its nothingness. Of a vacuum in which there were no memories, no loss, no grief. Just one vacant pit.

The phone rang. I checked the clock. Midnight! Some fool is calling me at midnight? I picked it up.

"Bloody American bitch," a male voice shouted. "You won't get out of here alive!"

He hung up.

4

DURBAN

Mid-January, 1976

A steady downpour pounded the windows of the law office of Duchesne Grice. His father had founded Shepstone & Wylie law firm in the late 1800s, driving to and from work in his Rolls Royce. When he died, his son sold the Rolls, and bought a Ford.

Grice chaired the Board of Barclays Bank and the Institute of Race Relations. He served on a dozen corporate boards, and chaired my *Who's Who* board. Soft-spoken, unruffled, respected by men, adored by women. All that a woman could want, I thought, sitting across his desk that day. Happily married, his secretary had assured me.

I told him about the erasure of my tapes, and the threatening calls.

"That's a bad sign," he said. "We'll have to see Colonel Steenkamp, Chief of Security Branch."

"But they're probably the guys who did it!"

"Precisely why we should see him. Let's show him what we're doing before anything else happens. Draft a few pages from the notes you have."

Depression settled over me in Steenkamp's stuffy office on the third floor of a dilapidated building. The scrawny man nodded toward two chairs in front of his desk. Would we like tea, he asked. No, we told him. Then he left for a few minutes.

I fingered his diary. "No surprise," I whispered to Grice. It was nailed to his desk.

"What's this all about?' Steenkamp asked when he returned.

Grice told him about the book, the zapping of my tapes, the abusive calls.

"We undertook this work," Grice said, "because such a book could generate pride and self-respect among Africans. And it would give us whites an insight into their struggles to attain what they did against all odds. Let's show you what we're doing."

I handed the colonel a hastily typed page about a farmer who told me that he'd been an ancestral worshipper, and converted to Christianity when he heard the parable of the five wise and five foolish virgins. And a page about a nurse who set up training programs in food preparation to prevent kwashiorkor among children.

"Why, this is marvelous!" Steenkamp said. "I had no idea anybody was doing anything like this. We could certainly use this data!"

The man was a fake.

"Miss Deane," he asked, "who do you think would do this? Zap your tapes and disturb your sleep with abusive phone calls?"

"Your office, sir."

Grice nudged my leg.

"Sorry, sir," I said. "But that's what I think. Who else would do it?"

"There are several possibilities. BOSS, for one—Bureau of State Security."

"Surely, Security Branch and BOSS work together," I said.

Grice nudged my leg again.

"Oh, not at all, Miss Deane, not at all. If you only knew! And it's not just BOSS. It could be the CIA."

"The CIA? What would they be doing here?"

Steenkamp laughed without opening his mouth. "You'd be surprised, Miss Deane. The CIA is omnipresent."

He was right about that.

"Colonel," Grice said, "we want to be perfectly open. We're doing nothing to offend anybody. We want to help Africans, whites, all South Africans."

"I know that," Steenkamp said.

"We hope you'll see that no more incidents of this kind occur," Grice said. "Miss Deane can accomplish this challenging feat provided these tactics cease. Please don't misunderstand. I believe your office had nothing to do with the erasure of Miss Deane's tapes."

"You're absolutely right, Mr. Grice. Don't worry. We'll investigate your reports. I assure you, this will never happen again."

We rode the lift in silence.

"I don't believe a word Steenkamp said," I told Grice in his car.

"Let's give him a chance," he said. "He may be sincere. Meanwhile, we'll tell the Board at our next meeting."

The eight men on my Board sat around Grice's desk on a sultry Friday evening. Three whites including Duchesne, and five blacks. We ate biscuits and drank tea while they exchanged news. I wished they'd carry on so I wouldn't have to tell them about the erasure. I dreaded it. Dreaded the effect it would have on the other two whites—Dr. Conrad Strauss, manager of Standard Bank; and Percy Thomas, the witty, retired secretary of the Chamber of Industries. Most of all, I dreaded its effect on the five blacks.

Obed Kunene was the youngest, the editor of *Ilange*, a black newspaper. A smartly dressed man who often said that if he could get whites out of their ostrich syndrome he'd tell them that all blacks wanted was to be treated as human beings. Not pariahs in their own country.

Bill Bhengu, a small, shy man who stacked his law office desk with green and brown folders (brown for non-paying clients), had toured the United States and noted with surprise that American whites could adjust to a non-privileged status.

Schools inspector Edward Moumakwe herded cattle as a child in return for rations to feed his siblings. Those privations fueled his drive to convince students to become architects of their own destiny.

Dr. Ephraim Mokgokong, a modest man with an easy-going

approach to life, was the first black South African to earn a senior degree in gynecology, accepting with good will a far lower salary than his white counterparts.

Reverend Sikakane, the elder of our Board, had founded an ecumenical center, an oasis in a desert of segregation, where whites coached black candidates for matriculation, and blacks gave whites crash courses in Zulu. "We're not beggars waiting for crumbs to drop from the table of our self-styled masters," he'd often say. "We know only one master, and it's not the government of South Africa."

The blacks had met for many months to agree on criteria for selection and to select the men and women who qualified. Our criteria differed from other directories because few South African blacks had degrees. Most lived in rural areas where the government didn't build schools. Blacks pooled resources to build their own schools and hire their own teachers who were unqualified under official standards.

Readiness to sacrifice self in the interests of the black community became the chief criterion. Leadership qualities and personal achievements followed. Our directory would feature personality portraits, bio-data, and full page photographs of Africans from our province of Natal.I would raise funds, interview, and write the book.

Editor Kunene worried. "Many men have tried to do a black *Who's Who*, but they failed. Some were snatched from their homes after midnight, and never seen again."

"The government will never take chances with an American," I assured them. But the men sat grim-faced as I reported the erasure, abusive calls, and our visit to Colonel Steenkamp.

"Don't worry," I told them. "I'll redo the interviews. Besides, I took detailed notes. I won't need to re-interview everybody."

In the glare of the ceiling light, the ebony faces had turned ashen. The white faces, pasty.

Strauss, a large man, was not given to small talk. "Friends, this sounds like it's not going anywhere. If the political powers have done all this at the start, how will we complete a Who's Who?"

"I wouldn't like us to give up," Grice said. "I think we stand a good chance."

"Those rogues will do anything to prevent the book," Bhengu said.

"Don't worry," I told them. "The culprits who wiped out the tapes thought it would discourage me, but it didn't. They won't do anything else."

The *Who's Who* appeared in my mind's eye on the shelves of book stores and in libraries throughout South Africa. I accepted its reality just as I accepted the reality that I'd travel the world alone when my friends doubted I could do it. They doubted that anyone could do it without money. But I *had* to, so I did. What I *had* to do, I would. The secret police might hamper me, but they could never shake my resolve.

On the way to the restroom, I heard Bhengu say that he'd never met anyone with my pluck.

"We need to pray for her safety," Sikakane said, and led the men in prayer.

That night, I left my phone off the hook.

5

NEW YORK

1947-49

Dense clouds of cigarette smoke filled the musicians' union hall, a giant room packed with men who milled about, chatted, made notes on pads.

An agent tapped my shoulder. "Saw you on TV. You were great!" A cigar stuck to his lower lip as he handed me his card:

Walter Bloom
Musical Entertainment Agency
48 West 48th Street

"What's your repertoire like?"

"Standards, pops, classics, semi-classics, Latin, jazz. Whatever you want to hear."

"I got a deal. A new club opened at the Dixie Hotel on Forty-Second off Broadway. They want an accordionist six nights a week: 6:40 p.m. to 1:40 a.m., Saturdays to 2:40 a.m., Mondays off. Indefinite. What do you say?"

"The pay?"

"A hundred fifty bucks a week."

"I'll take it. I need to audition?"

"Y'already did, on TV. Oh, that fishtail gown. Hope you got three or four."

"Sure," I fibbed.

"Walter Winchell will catch you the first week. Play good."

On opening night at the Dixie, my face crimsoned when the bouncer lifted me to the podium because I couldn't climb in my fishtails. I played "A Foggy Day in London Town" and "Autumn in New York," but nobody listened. They drank, talked, and ate.

A few days later, Bloom called. "You're a hit, kid. You saw Walter Winchell's review yesterday?"

"Yes."

"What do you mean, 'Yes'? You should be celebratin'. Who gets reviews like that? What'sa matter?"

"I don't like the place, Mr. Bloom."

"Walt."

"I don't like it, Walt."

"What don't you like?"

"They don't listen to my music. They drink, eat, talk."

"That's showbiz, kid. People wanna drink and eat and blab, and they wanna hear nice sounds in the background."

"And the songs they ask me to play—'Mairzy Doats' and…"

"Kid, listen ta me. Thousands of musicians are huntin' jobs in this town. For a job like you got they'd be oilin' my palms and kissin' my ass. For Chris'sakes, you're makin' a hundred-fifty bucks a week. Indefinite. Who gets contracts like that? For Chris'sakes, and you're only a kid."

"I guess it's the area, Mr. Bloom."

"Walt."

"It's the area, Walt. I'd rather play the east side than Broadway. You know, Park or Madison Avenue."

"You wanna play the Copacabana?"

"I wouldn't mind, Mr. …Walt."

"Listen kid. Ya don't *start* at the Copa. Ya *stop* there."

Show business was the cross I bore to be free. My parents wanted me to marry. I was their only child, their only hope for grandchildren. But I didn't want to live that way. "Plan for marriage," they told me. "Or pay your college fees yourself."

Paying my way freed me to transfer from Music Ed to Washington Square College, so that one day I'd qualify for medical school. But freedom eluded me; the Dixie owned me. I wore the clothes and drank the booze and played the songs it wanted. Nobody asked for classics or jazz. They wanted to hear, "How Much is That Doggie in the Window?"

I wrote a song about my plight. My fishtail gowns rubbing my knees together. Swallowing smoke when I sang. House rules demanding I drink with lonely men. But I never sang it at the Dixie. I sang it for myself: "I'm a Lump of Clay the Market Molds."

One night, I pretended that someone asked me to play a semi-classic. I played "Dark Eyes." Poured my soul into it, played with closed eyes. Used all the switches. Piccolo, flute, violin, clarinet, bassoon, bass. The accordion sounded like an orchestra.

When I opened my eyes, the manager was standing in front of the podium staring at me, his arms folded at his chest like he'd caught me gambling in the back room.

"Whad'dya think this is? Carnegie Hall?"

One evening at the Dixie, minutes felt like hours. At 2 a.m., I locked up my instruments and dragged myself to the Eighth Avenue subway station where the two-thirty train had come and gone.

A stench of vomit sickened me. I shifted to the other end of the platform that was empty except for a drunk who couldn't pick his head up. Near the bench was a sign about a C train which reminded me of the "C" I got in sociology. I'd slept through the exam.

The E train pulled in at 3 a.m., and chugged its way to Roosevelt Avenue as the darkness in me deepened. *I'm a machine. Put a nickel in, and out comes music and a smile.* I detested show business, and dreaded going back to my parents' apartment.

At Roosevelt Avenue I waited longer than usual for the local to Elmhurst. By the time I climbed the subway steps to the street, I was seething inside. Other college kids didn't have to work like this. Why did I?

I unlocked the outside door to my building, dragged myself down the long corridor to the far wing, climbed the staircase to the second floor, inserted the key, and unlocked the apartment door. My mother stood in the foyer in her pajamas.

"How dare you come back an hour late?" she hollered. "What will the neighbors say?"

"Neighbors! Neighbors! That's all you think about—what will the neighbors say? They don't mind if I come home at three, but they'll be shocked at four? They're waiting up for me? I'm having fun at the Dixie? I'm having fun sleeping four hours a night?"

I stepped toward her, my fists clenched. I wanted to grab her neck and wring it. She walked backward in the foyer, past the telephone corner, her wide eyes glued on me. I was six inches from her and I could have suffocated her like she suffocated me.

She held up a hand to fend me off. The other hand searched behind her for the knob of her bedroom door. She ran into the bedroom, slammed the door and locked it, stood on the other side, unmoving, breathing loud. She saved herself, and she saved me. The apartment was silent except for my father's snores. Wide awake, I showered, dressed and left, stepping outside like a stranger to myself. I never knew I could feel so much hatred toward my mother.

I took the subway to Central Park where early morning sun warmed my body and soothed my brain. I could almost smile, though I still felt the power of my rage. At a phone booth, I rang my friend Bart to ask him to meet me for breakfast.

From my table at the back of the Automat, I watched him move through the turnstile door, a short man with a receding hairline, his eyes searching the room for me.

Bart was the son of Polish immigrants who had settled in Chicago and supported the family by tailoring clothes. The purchase of a violin for Bart's tenth birthday was a sacrifice they never regretted. He was a genius, his teachers said. Nimble fingers, a sharp ear, a deep, round tone.

He played in a symphony orchestra, eager to leave when rehearsals ended, seldom speaking unless spoken to. He loved to play for himself and for me, not for audiences. He liked to stroll the ocean front, chatting of letting things happen rather than making them happen. Of the futility of war, and the grim years he'd spent in Germany in World War II.

He listened as I told him about the previous night, his brown eyes never wandering from mine. "I see only one solution," he said. "Marry me."

"I'm afraid I'll mess up marriage."

"You won't. Whatever you want to do, we'll do together."

"Let me think about it."

"Take your time, hon. I'll wait. Like the moon waits for the sun."

One Saturday morning deep in February, I sat at my bedroom desk in front of a stack of textbooks that I couldn't have gotten through if I'd read all day. I'd missed too many classes. Life seemed purposeless, like I lost my compass.

I couldn't live with Mom anymore, and I couldn't continue studying at NYU and working nights. What options did I have? Just one: Marriage. Bart was gentle, and I loved him in a way. Mom didn't want me to wed a poor fiddler, but that didn't matter. Marriage would be a reprieve from the life I was living. A halfway ticket to freedom.

On a hot and humid summer day, I inched up the aisle on my father's arm. *This is spiritual suicide*, my mind repeated. But I kept walking.

6

DURBAN

February, 1976

Something gnawed at the back of my brain like an insect that couldn't find its way out. I'd finished my local interviews, was preparing to re-interview the rural blacks, and had given myself a day off. Free and easy for a day. My phone hadn't rung for two days. In fact, nothing menacing had happened. Yet the feeling of freedom eluded me.

I strolled along West Street, attracted by new fashions in store windows. A-line skirts, fitted tops, swimwear. An evening gown pulled my eyes, a fishtail similar to what I'd worn in show business. Sleeveless, sequined straps. I stared at it, then froze. Behind me, a huge shadow stood still. The shadow of a man, a big man with a large head.

I moved on with my face turned toward the store windows, and stopped. He moved, stood behind me again like a frame. An ominous frame. People passed by. I saw them through the window, but no one thought his frame unusual. Something was wrong, awfully wrong.

John Orr's Department Store was a block away. I hurried toward it, walking fast, checking store windows. The shadow kept pace. The space between us narrowed. I walked faster, it walked faster. I began to run when I saw the entrance to John Orr's. I raced through an open door and darted toward the ladies' room. The man's footsteps in back of me sounded like an animal.

Inside the rest room, I panted. A young woman brushing her long, auburn hair asked, "You all right?"

"I am. Do me a favor, please. There's a man outside, a bad man who followed me. When you get out, ask a clerk to call the store policeman. Tell the policeman that a man with bad intentions, maybe a killer, is waiting outside the ladies' room. Waiting for me to get out."

"Oh, of course, I'll do it. But you think he'll hurt me?"

"No. He's not after you, he's after me. I don't know why. I don't know who he is. I only know he's a menace."

A few minutes later, I heard loud talk in Afrikaans. The big man and a store security guard. "Out," two guards shouted.

When the noise subsided, I opened the door. He was gone, but my heartbeat quickened. A guard asked, "You know that man?"

I shook my head.

"What did he want?"

"Don't know," I said. "He chased me for several blocks. I was scared."

"Want to make a police report?"

"No," I said. "Just leave it."

I rang Grice, asked him to meet me at the store café, and waited at a back table. How brazen that man was whose face I didn't see! How he dared to follow me in broad daylight with so many people around. To wait outside a ladies' restroom for me, unconcerned about who saw him. That meant that he didn't fear the police. Maybe he worked with them. Oh, God! *Maybe he works with BOSS*!

I tried to describe the shadow to Grice. How gross it was, how it made me feel.

"That chap may have nothing to do with the harassment campaign," Grice said. "He may be mentally ill, just out of Creedmore Hospital. But I'll inform Colonel Steenkamp.

"Your face shows strain," he said. "What do you do to relax?"

"Nothing."

"Music would help. Still play your accordion?"

"Nah. Too big. Too heavy."

"You have a piano."

"Too loud. Neighbors complain. I'd like to learn classical guitar."

"The son of a client of mine teaches in his home," he said.

"I can't afford to buy a guitar."

"He'll lend you one. Wayne's a fine chap. Has a British wife and two small kids."

Grice drove me home the long way, around his Lambert Road home. I didn't know why he kept it, since he and his family lived in a suburb.

"I'm worried about the safety of my manuscripts," I told him.

"I'll get you a large safe deposit box at Barclays Bank," he said as he drove up Berea Road to my building.

Once more, I drove through the Zulu homeland to re-interview some of the rural Africans. Amaria Ndhlovu, principal of a primary school in Madadeni, told me she became hoarse from our first interview. She reminded me that the most significant statement she had made during our first meeting was that all of Madadeni, with its two hundred thousand blacks, was purchased from *one* white farmer.

Back in Durban, all I had to do was transcribe my tapes, write, raise funds, and learn classical guitar.

Wayne's sunlit music room overlooked a garden permeated by the sweet scent of pink, yellow and white flowers that South Africans call *Yesterday, Today, and Tomorrow*. We sat on a divan. Wayne, in jeans and a black T, murmuring notes as he played a Bach sonata on his guitar. At times wild, at times tame. I longed for his command over the guitar, but I was starting late.

He taught me a scale. I liked the feel of the instrument. Plucking strings with my fingers and cradling the guitar on my lap instead of strapping a thirty-pound accordion on my shoulders. He loaned me a guitar and said he'd teach me once a week.

Wayne, his wife, Tessa, and I rocked on swings in their garden, while their four-year-old son played "Three Little Pigs" on a kids' guitar, and the two-year-old sang. Talk veered to recent detentions of Africans and Indians, to the book I was writing, and the erasure of my tapes. They were like old friends. Liberals, musicians, vegetarians like me. They invited me to a party that weekend. "All left-wingers," Wayne assured me.

I left with good feelings about myself. I'd always thought that when we say we like someone, we mean that in their company, we like ourselves.

At home, I took out the guitar, parked myself on my piano bench, and played a C scale. *I'm going to love this.*

Wayne called at ten that night. Hysterical, sobbing. "Don't come here again, Shirley! Never, never come here again!"

His words struck my heart like hammers that minced my inner world. Bulldozed all the comfort I had felt. Scrambled it into rubble that left me feeling as worthless as dirt.

"Why?" I whispered. "What happened?"

"A man called when you left. He said, 'If you see Shirley Deane again, your sons will be dead that day.' Oh, God, don't show up, please. And don't call. Tessa almost had a nervous breakdown. Give the guitar to Grice. Don't come here again. Never, ever!"

I bawled like a woman gone mad. Again, the phone rang. Maybe it was Wayne to say that he didn't mean what he said. He was just kidding. It's okay to visit, to take lessons, to go out with him and Tessa.

But the Voice spoke. "Bloody American bitch. You won't get out of here alive!"

"Bastard! Fucking bastard!"

I slammed the receiver into its cradle, and onto my ring finger. Blood oozed from beneath my nail. Tears drenched my face.

7

NEW YORK & CHICAGO

1949-52

Marriage felt strange, like our walk-up Manhattan apartment was a theater, and I was playing a role in a limited run. But the script seemed wrong. I had to cook. Me, cook. I had to wash Bart's shirts. Go to furniture sales. Everything I dreaded all my life. I moved around in a daze, asking myself how it happened.

"Cook us some chicken for tonight," Bart said one morning on his way to a rehearsal. Chicken! I could barely fix toast without burning it, let alone chicken. My mother never taught me. She hated to cook, other than pot roast. Our vegetables came from cans, our desserts from a bakery. Me, cook chicken!

I asked the poultry man at the A&P how to cook it. "Broil it," he said.

The bird had feathers but that probably didn't matter. I put the whole beast in the oven like it was, and turned on "broil." Within minutes, a nauseating stench came from the kitchen.

A neighbor from below rapped on the door. "Somebody died?" the Italian woman asked, holding her nose. I shrugged helplessly and nodded toward the smoke billowing like thunderclouds from the kitchen. She put a handkerchief over her nose and mouth, walked into the kitchen and opened the oven door.

"Mama mia! Mama mia!" she shouted. Grimacing, she shut off the stove, ran out and down the steps. At the bottom, she fixed her eyes on me. "You must clean out the bird! *First* clean. *Then* cook!"

When Bart came home, he scoured, scrubbed, mopped. "Let's eat out, hon," he said. "And don't cook chicken anymore. I really don't like it."

Bart didn't say so, but I wasn't the wife he'd wanted. Not in the kitchen. Not the living room. Not the bedroom. He was gentle in bed but I loved him like a sibling. Passion would happen by itself, I thought. It didn't.

"I can't force myself anymore, Bart," I told him in bed one night.

"What's wrong, hon?"

"I don't know."

"Don't worry, you've been through a lot. The problem will sort itself out. Want to learn chess?"

We played in bed, night after night. Game after game. Chess became my passion.

After our divorce, Bart returned to his Chicago roots. I moped around the apartment like a fish that had squirmed free of its hook but forgotten how to swim. I'd married to get out of my parents' apartment, and divorced to get out of marriage. For what? To eat, sleep and work? Surely, life meant more than that. But whoever I asked, had no answer.

I returned to gigs to pay my bills. The first one, a party at the Plaza for a bank chairman's birthday.

Guests were drunk by eight. Men crowded me, their boozed breath in my nostrils. One tried to rock the accordion back and forth to "My Blue Heaven." I wanted to quit early, but I needed the money. On a break, I went to the restroom and composed a song on a paper towel:

"The Fiction of Corporate Dignity"
Dignified at six, loose collars at seven,
At eight they want to sing, My Blue Heaven
When the clock strikes nine, if they haven't yet dined,
Their question, Doesn't it pinch, just blows my mind.

On the way back, I dared myself to sing it, but I didn't.

"Here she is. Hey darlin', how 'bout 'The Bells Are Ringin' for Me and My Gal?' Look it 'er bedroom eyes."

At ten it was over, but I didn't want to go home. I wanted to play good music. A drummer had told me about a club on 125th Street in Harlem that had good jam sessions. No strict rules about time, he said, but lots of groups sit around waiting their turn to jam.

I headed north. I'd never been to Harlem, and wondered if they'd let me in. No women, they might say, or no whites. Or worse. Who in hell would bring an accordion to a jazz club? Maybe I was mad, going alone to Harlem, but I wanted to shed the Plaza vibes and play what was in my heart.

Street babble hushed as I stepped out of my car. Four guys on the corner glared at me while they passed a joint around. I opened the trunk, took out the accordion and amp, and wheeled them through the door of the club like I was booked.

Dense cigarette smoke and loud chatter filled the neon-lit room. A five-piece band played on stage. Men gaped as though I were an apparition. Nobody offered me a seat.

At a table near the door, two guys drinking beer shared a joke. When they saw me they stopped, their beer glasses halted halfway to their lips.

I pointed to an empty chair. "May I?"

"Lady," the bald one said, "this place is for—"

Before he finished, I sat.

"Whaddya doin' here?" the young one asked.

Men at nearby tables pushed forward to hear. "Hey, this place is for nigguz, lady."

I waved off his words with my left hand, and rubbed the skin of my right. "Paint, man. That's all it is. White paint."

"Hah! Ya hear that?" He poked a guy at the next table. "White paint, she said!"

"Whaddya doin' here, missus?"

"I came to jam."

"You? Jam? Jesus."

A bouncer in a suit and tie strode toward me from the back of the room. I feared he'd throw me out. No single women, he'd say. Or no whites.

The musicians on stage ended their set, nodded to a group at a front table, and began to pack up their instruments. I jumped up, rolled my cases to the stage, stepped up, pulled them up, plugged in the amp, put the accordion on, and turned to the bass man and drummer. "Hey guys, you mind staying for one tune?"

The drummer's lips parted, but no sound came out. A guy with drumsticks at the front table, halfway out of his chair, said, "A whitey here? With a squeezebox? C'mon! This ain't no place for…"

"Please, let me play one tune. Just one."

"Let 'er play one," someone yelled from the floor.

"Okay, one. She can play *one*."

"Christ!" a guy at the back belted out. "Whitey and her squeezebox! Shit, man. Here comes the 'Beer Barrel Polka.'"

I'd quieten them down with my old trick. With the amp volume way up, I played a smashing chord on the high register, cascaded down to the base of the keyboard, and stopped. Someone yelled, "Holy shit!"

"'Birdland,'" I called to the bass man, and beat out a solid four-four intro to "Lullaby of Birdland." The room swung. I was on, I was in, I was home. Heads shook like, how can it be? A woman. A whitey. A squeezebox.

The bass man and drummer backed me up like four arms coming out of my shoulder sockets. After the second chorus, the bass man took a sixteen-bar solo. I echoed his phrases with the same notes on my bass. The drummer took sixteen bars, and we backed him up like we'd played together for ten years.

The audience shouted. "One more!" The group at the front table said they'd wait.

I played a French tune in Bach style, heavy on bass, piccolo on treble, then a strong rhythmical intro to "April in Paris."

"Sounds like Shearing," a guy in front said.

"One more, lady," someone said.

With a strong jazz-blues beat, I sang a song that Joey Williams recorded with Count Basie.

Well alright, okay, you win, I'm in love with you.
Well alright, okay, you win, baby what can I do…

Everybody sang. I could have played forever, but it was time to go.

The bass man and drummer carried my accordion and amp to my car. Drummer Amos said, “Never heard an accordion like that.”

“I won’t forget tonight,” Noah said. “Like we been jammin’ together for years.”

“Could we work together?” I asked.

“A white chick with a nigga rhythm section? Ain’t gonna happen in my lifetime.”

“Why not? Maybe we have what it takes to change things.”

Noah’s eyes danced. He was tall with a round upper back that came from hunching over his bass. I wished I could rest my head on his chest and tell him that the world humiliated me, too, but I didn’t dare. I didn’t need to turn around to know that a hundred eyeballs were bursting out of their sockets. On corners. Pressing against the inside windows of the club. Peering through the cracked windows of a house across the street. It would have made headlines.

I drove home at ease with myself. The Plaza had tied me into knots. Harlem untied the tangle.

Bart called from Chicago. A producer needed an accordionist for a Greek TV show. Was I interested?

I packed, hitched a U-haul to my car and drove west. Bart had furnished a one-bedroom apartment for me on the second-floor of a high-rise on North Humboldt Boulevard. Gray shag covered the floors. Forest green drapes hung on the windows. He’d bought a sofa bed, a table and chairs.

Greek TV in Chicago was like a circus compared to New York. Ten seconds before the red light turned green, with my fingers poised on the first notes of my theme song, the director shouted commands to me in Greek that I couldn’t understand. But when red turned to green, I played, sang, and spoke, in Greek.

The thirteen-week show seemed more like a parenthesis in life than life itself. More parentheses followed. The Hotel Sherman for six months with a jazz guitarist and bassist. My own television show sponsored by National Clothing Stores, televised outside the State and Lake Theatre.

Chicago was cold that winter. I wore heavy sweaters and long gloves with finger-tips cut out to feel the keys. Julio Maro, a tenor who had worked for Arthur Godfrey before he worked for me, sang my theme song—"Hello Young Lovers." I should have felt proud, but I felt nothing. I earned well. I lived well. I drove a new Chrysler sedan that I'd bought for three thousand dollars in cash. Yet everything seemed trivial, until I read an ad for Piper Cub lessons at Waukegan airport.

Up we went on my first flight in a Piper Cub. I sat behind instructor John as he flew figure eights around pylons, did partial and full stalls, power-on and power-off landings. I'd have to do it all to get a license. I panicked when he went into a spin, my fingernails digging into his back until he glided out.

Two months later, I was ready to fly solo. I checked the cotter pins around the aircraft, climbed in, taxied down the runway, pulled the stick back and took off. At eight-hundred feet, I flew into the pattern around the airport, circled several times and came down, landing as I was taught, on the first third of the runway. Very easy.

After several sessions practicing take-offs and landings, John said I was ready to leave the airport traffic pattern. The sky was clear that sunny spring morning when I pulled the stick back and took off. At eight-hundred feet I set the throttle for sixty-five miles an hour so the plane would cruise on its own.

My God! Infinite space and I was alone in it! *This* was freedom. No boundaries, no obstacles. All my life, I'd wanted freedom. Now that I had it, I longed to press it into permanence. But how? The fuel would only last for three hours. Infinity, curtailed by the size of a fuel tank.

Trucks dominated the traffic on the forty-mile drive back to Chicago. Perhaps real freedom exists only in the sky.

One morning, John asked me to do a three-point landing. He

stood near the runway with my logbook and pen in hand as I took off, flew to eight-hundred feet, circled, and came down. I taxied almost to a stop, but when I glanced at John, he gave me a thumbs-down signal. My landing was bumpy.

I powered up to try again, without realizing that I didn't have enough runway to get up. I pulled the stick back to take off, and when the nose rose into the air, I saw them. Two power poles ahead, separated by a distance narrower than the wing span! My heart pounded. I didn't know what to do. I couldn't think. I pulled my feet from the rudders, and placed them flat on the floor. I folded my hands in my lap, and closed my eyes. All would be over in seconds. *Sorry, Mom. Sorry, Dad. Sorry, John.*

I listened for the crash. Waited, listened. Heard nothing but the drone of the engine. I opened my eyes. Where were the poles? I turned around. They were far behind me. Intact. The plane was intact. I was intact. What happened?

When I landed, I sat in the cockpit like I awoke from a nightmare. John raced up. "Who the hell gave you permission to stunt fly?"

"I wasn't piloting. My feet were on the floor. My hands were in my lap. My eyes were shut. I don't know what happened."

"What crap you givin' me? You banked the plane inches from the poles. You were tryin' a stunt."

"I didn't, I swear. I let everything go. I was too scared to think."

"For Chris' sakes! If you didn't bank the plane, who the fuck did?"

"I don't know."

"I'm askin' you, if you didn't bank it, who in hell banked the fuckin' plane? God?"

I couldn't answer.

In my log book, John scribbled, *God banked the plane. Deane missed the poles by six inches.*

In bed that night, I could still feel the moment when I let go of the controls. Feet flat on the floor. Hands in my lap. Eyes closed. All would end in seconds. But a *force* took over. Was that God? Nobody could tell me.

8

DURBAN

Early March, 1976

Good thing you drive on the left side of the road in South Africa. Berea Road was a wide, heavily traveled artery. Had driving been right-sided, I'd have spent ten minutes crawling up the Berea to make a U to town.

My green Toyota, parked in front of my building with the wheels turned into the curb faced a steep incline down toward the center of town. It had just been serviced, washed and polished. I laid my attaché case in the trunk, and was off to Barclays Bank to store the typed pages in my safe deposit box.

I climbed in, turned on the ignition, released the emergency brake and started down the Berea slope. Put my foot on the brake but felt no resistance. Pressed it to the floor. Nothing. Pulled up the emergency brake. Nothing.

A school bus had stopped for a red light at a right angle in front of me. *Oh God, stop this car!* It didn't. It gained speed as it slid down the road. I reached the corner with a few feet between my car and the school bus. The tires screeched as I swung the wheel sharply to the left, missed a parked car by a few inches, and missed the bus by a foot.

With my car still in the center of the lane, drivers behind me honking, I leaned back, eyes shut. My body trembled. I couldn't budge. Pedestrians gathered, and a policeman came. A woman said, "She must have had a heart attack. Call an ambulance."

The Toyota service station was packed. I'd sue, I roared at the mechanic. "You serviced my car last week, and I almost killed a busload of kids." I ranted on and on. Customers, technicians, clerks stared. When I quit, the mechanic spoke. "Someone disconnected your brakes."

A hush fell over the station, like in a film. Cars hoisted, mechanics beneath them holding oil-soaked rags and lubricant cans, staring. Poised like a moment frozen in time. Like those moments I'd stood with my accordion, eyes fastened on a TV director's raised index finger. The red light, the count-down in seconds. Five-four-three-two-one. The second when the light turned green always felt like a parachute jumper's leap into space. The second when I knew my face had appeared on screens.

Someone disconnected my brakes.

"You're lucky, very lucky," the mechanic said. "Somebody up there is watching over you."

I'd heard that three times. In Chicago when my Piper Cub banked between two power poles. When I reached the Pakistan-India border in my Land Rover. And now. I might not be so lucky a fourth time.

The men on my Board seated themselves around Grice's desk at lunch time, devouring meat and chicken sandwiches from the Royal Hotel. A cheese sandwich for me. Not with crusts like American sandwiches which I preferred, but the dignified, crustless kind.

Grice told them about the shadow that followed me into John Orr's. The telephone threat to kill my guitar teacher's sons. The tampering with my brakes.

The eight men sat like stone statues, their dour faces criss-crossed with bars of sunlight that flooded the room through open blinds. Strauss said in a voice too loud for the small room, "The handwriting is on the wall. Can't you folks see it? This book will never be."

Thomas, the funny man, said, "Yeah, I see it. But you know, I belong to the PFP."

The PFP was the Progressive Federal Party, the official opposition party in the white parliament. Thomas meant that he could bring up in Parliament all unjust, criminal actions taken toward whites. But he knew, we knew, the whole world knew that the PFP was just a travesty created to convey the impression that South Africa was a democracy. To South Africans, PFP meant *Pack for Perth.* The first sign of a blood bath, and whites would be off to Australia.

Mokgokong, the gynecology professor, weighed the consequences. Weighing was his habit. *Should he save the mother or the baby?* He weighed and worried. Was it worth the chance? He thought not.

Moumakwa, the schools inspector, had imaged the book on bookstore shelves. Whites thumbing through it, surprised that blacks are as human as whites. But the book wasn't worth what I'd endured. He'd vote to quit.

Bhengu would do anything to help, but what could he do when black lawyers had no clout? He feared that nothing could combat South Africa's security police.

Sikakane, who had skirted the laws of apartheid at his ecumenical center, knew what you had to put up with to pursue a dream. A book about blacks would teach whites about his people. But if something happened to the writer, whose fault would it be? His.

Grice knew that a black *Who's Who* would validate his efforts of decades to bridge the white-black gulf. But my safety mattered more.

Editor Kunene, clad in a dark blue suit with a loosened red tie—clever, young, determined to see blacks take their rightful place in South Africa—said, "It scares me, the whole bloody thing. I recognize the pattern. It's right out of the *Manual of Harassment.*"

"A manual?" I asked. "You mean a published book?"

"Published by the CIA," he said. "Sold to Intelligence in countries friendly to the United States."

"Oh, shit!" I blurted. "Sorry, gentlemen."

"First, they obstruct the plan," he said. "Then, the steps: Psychological harassment. Sleep intervention. Alienation of friends. Endangering life."

No one spoke. Thoughts translated into drawn-in cheeks and cocked brows. Then the questions. Did Kunene have the *Manual*? (He didn't.) Could they see it? (They couldn't.) What's next? (Kunene didn't know. *The Manual* was a confidential document that he'd glimpsed years earlier.)

"Well?" Kunene craned toward me. "Do we pitch the project?"

"Pitch it?" I asked. "The book is like a train on a track. Can a train stop in the middle of a track? No. It can only stop at a station. We didn't get there yet."

"We're gambling with your life!" Thomas said.

"They won't do any more," I told them. "They've used up their tricks. Even if they took my life, what would they achieve? You guys have access to my notes and the pages I've written. You can finish the manuscript yourselves, and publish it. How would knocking me off help them?"

I didn't confess that I feared what the government could do next. That my fear was palpable, but I dared not surrender to it, or it would stifle my freedom.

Fear was rife in South Africa. Every day, the English language press reported right wing terrorism. Tear gas canisters fired into protest meetings. Journalists' homes petrol bombed. Windscreens smashed, even Alan Paton's. One of the ugliest incidents was skinning the pet cat of a retarded child, the daughter of a liberal minister. Someone tied a blue ribbon around the cat's neck, and left its body on the family's doorstep.

My determination to complete the Who's Who might have been a virtue, or it might have been a fault. I didn't know which. I knew only that I could not stop. Twenty years earlier, friends had tried to talk me out of a plan they called insane, impractical, unattainable. Who can work their way around the world with no money? I'd be raped, murdered, or both. Stuck penniless in the communist corridors of East Berlin. Lost in Africa. Devoured by cannibals.

Their logic could not compete with the power of my vision. *I* didn't hold the vision; the vision held me. Trekking the Black Forest. Relaxing on Mykonos. On safari in the Congo. Listening to Imams in Baghdad. Strolling Cairo's streets. The world was my home. I was ravenous for it. Not for its tourist sites, but its life.

Once, in the staff lounge of New York's Bellevue Hospital, I tried to explain the power of inner vision to a psychiatrist friend. A small, lithe man with black eyes, clad in an ink-stained white smock. He knew what I meant, he said. "That's positive thinking."

"Oh, no," I told him. "Positive thinking works from the outside in. Inner vision works from the inside out."

The doctor shrugged. He didn't understand, nor did I. The world scenes projected themselves on my mind. Moscow, the Black Forest, the Congo, and Cairo were like upstairs rooms in the house I lived in, rooms I hadn't yet seen. I was convinced that the images reflected my future.

I asked myself how anyone can know what is going to happen before it happens. That's impossible. Yet, those scenes carried a force that I couldn't doubt any more than I doubted my existence.

That same power of vision—this time, a completed African Who's Who—prevailed against all logic and sense in South Africa.

"Gentlemen," I told my Board, "we must not allow the South African government to scare us into submission like they've done with others. If we quit, we'll have played into their hands. Why should we do that? They're rats. I've met plenty, from Chicago to Lahore. Rats don't scare me. The more they do, the madder I get."

The room grew silent.

"Gentlemen, the *Who's Who of Black South Africans* will be written."

9

CHICAGO

1953

I performed on radio and TV, and in Chicago's Gotham on Rush Street, a classy opera supper club where mezzos sang arias from *Rigoletto*, and I played excerpts from *Scheherazade* on accordion. I flew a Piper Cub, and drove a new Mercedes. But something was missing.

I'd been married, but loved Bart like a sibling. I had crushes in high school and at NYU, but was never really in love. I didn't know what love meant. All I knew on the day that I climbed the steps to the Chicago Judo Club was that something was missing. I thought it was exercise.

Inside, on a wall near the door, an oak plaque read: *Nikolaos, the Conqueror*. Nick stood in front of the workout room, motionless in his white judogi and black belt. Unsmiling, his arms folded across his chest, he peered down at his students like a beardless god.

"I've come to learn judo," I told him. He pointed to a bench. "Wait there." I took a seat, judged him to be ten years my senior. Thirty-four or thirty-five. No wedding ring.

In the beginning, I took judo lessons for exercise. Before long, I was coming for Nick. For Nikolaos, the Conqueror.

My yellow belt test was in two weeks. "Nick, can you give me some personal coaching?"

"Sure," he said. "I'll come by your place tonight."

We worked on break falls, safety and balance, shoulder and chest holds, throws and pins. He stood behind me, gripping my waist and arms so I couldn't move. I thought he'd embrace me, but he let me go. "Enough," he said.

He sat on my easy chair, his stocky legs outstretched on the footrest. I set a bottle of scotch on my glass cocktail table. "May I pour you a drink?"

"I don't drink."

"If you don't like to drink, what do you like?"

"Judo and Greek mythology." He checked his watch. "I have to be at Hector's, my club on South State Street. My younger brother works the day shift, and I take over at eight." He pointed to the bottle. "That stuff is no good for you."

"You sell it in your club."

"Business is business."

One evening, Nick invited me to Hector's. We rode in his silver-blue Buick while I tried to read an article on judo, but it was too dark. Automatically, I reached for the glove compartment because that's where I kept a flashlight in my car. I opened it.

A silver pistol gleamed in the dark. "*Jesus!* What's that for?"

"Protection."

"From what? From whom?"

"Anybody. Like judo. Judo is for protection. That pistol's only a twenty-two caliber."

I couldn't make sense of the man. A hunk of masculinity, yet he makes no pass. A bar owner, yet he doesn't drink. Judo and Greek mythology occupy his mind and life, yet he totes a gun.

The sign for Hector's glittered with brazen neon lights. He seated me at the bar where his younger brother waited on two drunks.

The outside door opened. A young woman with frizzy red hair entered, carrying a camera, light meter and flash. Nick led her to a table in back. They whispered, he handed her something, and she left.

"Who was that?"

"A photographer. She makes the rounds every night."

"Your girlfriend?"

"I don't have time for things like that," he said.

He told me about his mother, an invalid. He'd moved in to take care of her when his father died. "In Greek tradition, that's the duty of an elder son."

Nick was such a good man.

When we got back to my building, he drove to the side and through an alley to the back entrance.

"Why not park in front?"

"Tenants are nosy," he said. "The less they know, the better."

I reached up to kiss him goodnight, but he pulled back. "Why kiss in the car? Let's go upstairs."

In my bedroom, I donned a black lace nightgown, and turned off the lights. Nick strode in nude.

Two hours later, I said, "Now I know what *sex* means."

Nick laughed. "Now you know what *Greek* means."

We made love every night, but he never stayed over. One evening he said he needed a vacation. "How about spending it with me, Angel? We can go to the Ozarks in Missouri."

"But your mom, Nick. How will she live without you?"

"My brother will care for her."

On a cool morning in October, we sat on the veranda of our motel apartment. Nick took my hands in his.

"Angel, I want you for my wife. We could marry in February. I'll sell Hector's, we'll travel the world, then decide where to settle."

For the first time in my life, the word "marry" didn't sting. It meant living with a man I loved. Seeing the world that I longed to know.

"But your mother, Nick. How can you leave her?"

"My brother will move in. In Greek tradition, we help each other."

"I love you, Nick."

"I love you, Angel."

He drove to town, returned with an engagement ring, and slipped it on my finger.

Back in Chicago, my new Chrysler coupe was due for service. I called Nick. "My Chrysler won't be ready till tomorrow, and I have to play the Hilton tonight. Can I borrow your car?"

"Sure, Angel."

Nick drove to the Chrysler service station. His brother waited in a car behind him. Nick got out, kissed me on the cheek. "Remember, park behind your building. Neighbors get nosy."

He stepped into his brother's car. When they took off, I opened the glove compartment, relieved to find it bare.

At the Hilton that night, I played until 10 p.m. At 11, I reached my apartment building, parking in front so I could wheel my accordion and amplifier into the elevator.

I was donning my pajamas when the phone rang. Sure I would hear, *Hi, Angel*. But the voice was a woman's.

"Is Nick there?"

The question, the husky voice, startled me.

"Who is this?"

She hung up. The phone lay frozen in my hand. I had heard that husky voice before. It was the woman who lived in the apartment above me—Pam. She must have seen Nick's car outside. But so what?

I pulled on my robe, stomped up the stairs, and rang the bell. The name on the door read Pam White. It opened a crack, and a pale woman peeked out. Her head bobbed. I stepped in. The apartment stunk from cigarette smoke. Empty beer cans littered the floor. She sat on the sofa, head down, hands clasped in her lap. I took a seat across from her in an overstuffed armchair.

"Why did you call me?"

"I saw Nick's car out front. I know you're a musician, and you live downstairs. Nick told me you were working on a green belt, that it would be a feather in his cap if you got it, so he helps you early evenings before he goes to Hector's. When I saw you park his car I got curious. Why were you driving it?"

"It's none of your business, but mine is being serviced."

"But why would he lend you his car?"

"Why not? We're engaged; we're getting married in February. And what's it to you?"

"Oh no. No," she shook her head. "Nick and *I* are engaged. We're getting married in March."

I stretched out my left arm and pointed to my engagement ring. "See?"

Pam held out her ring finger, the diamond there. Staring at the stones, we acted like dumb fortunetellers who couldn't read their crystal balls.

Pam sobbed. "How could he cheat me this way?"

"How often do you see Nick?" I asked.

"Every day. He comes over when he closes Hector's, stays the night, and drives me to work in the morning."

"Stays the night with you? Not with his mother?"

"He loves me," Pam sobbed. "I'm the only woman he ever called Angel."

"He calls me Angel, too."

"I don't believe it."

"I'll prove it."

I dialed his number.

"Hector's." It was his voice.

"Hi, Nick." I put the receiver to her ear. I knew he answered, "Hi, Angel," because her face paled. I took the phone back.

"Nick, I only have a minute, I'm still working. Just called to say hello. I'll see you tomorrow, love."

Pam was still crying but I had to tell her the rest. "We went to Missouri together, Pam. That's where he proposed."

"Bastard! He told me he went to a judo match in Jefferson City."

Pam started to dial his number. I put my hand over hers. "Wait. I saw a red-haired woman in his club one night. I think he's involved with her. Let's find out before we talk to him."

Back in my apartment, I called nightclubs that had freelance photographers. "Have you got a red-haired camera girl there?"

A brusque male voice at the Bluebird said, "Yeah, we got one. Name's Marna Jacobs."

At midnight, I parked Nick's car around the corner from the Bluebird, went to the bar and ordered a Manhattan. The redhead was snapping photos at tables. When she strolled near the bar, I waved.

"A guy who was here one night sent me to talk to you," I told her. "You took his picture. He'd like to have lunch with you sometime."

"Can't. I'm married. I have a kid."

"Oh. My friend will be disappointed. Your husband doesn't mind you working nights?"

"No. We don't live together. I'm an orthodox Jew. He's Greek. We married in court because I was pregnant, but my parents won't let us live together till he converts."

"It must be tough to live apart from your husband."

"Not really. He comes for breakfast every morning." She giggled. "And sex. I teach him Hebrew and Torah. One more year and he'll be accepted in the faith, then we can live together."

"What does he do for a living?"

"Teaches judo in the afternoon. Runs a club at night." Marna picked up her camera. "Gotta make the rounds."

"Hey, would you meet with me sometime? I'd like to learn about the Torah."

She wrote her name, Marna, and phone number on a triangle-shaped napkin.

Heading back to the car, it became clear.

Drives Pam to work at eight every morning.

Goes to Marna's. Eats breakfast. Screws. Studies Hebrew and Torah. Eats lunch.

Goes to the Judo Club. Comes to my place. Eats. Screws.

Goes to Hector's. After closing, goes to Pam's. Screws. Sleeps.

Drives her to work.

In my quiet apartment I tried to imagine the dark heart of a man who lived three lies with three women. He was more than a cheat. He was a madman hiding behind a mask of sanity. I should have forgotten him that second, but I couldn't. I had to see his face when the three of us marched into his bar.

In the morning I called Pam. "I'll be at your apartment at eight-thirty tonight. We'll drive to a pub near Hector's to meet the redhead."

At 3 p.m. I called Marna. "Marna, I met you last night. There's something about your husband…"

"What about him?"

"Something you need to know. I can't tell you on the phone. Can you meet me tonight at 9 at Teddy's Bar & Grille? It's on the corner just up from Hector's."

"All right. But this better be good."

"And please, Marna… keep this quiet until we meet."

I drove Nick's car to the service station and called him. "My car is ready, Nick. I'm leaving yours outside Chrysler. Your keys are at the service desk."

"Okay, Angel."

"I won't be home this evening. I'm playing a cocktail party. I'll stop at Hector's when I finish."

"Okay, Angel. Love you."

I reserved a booth at Teddy's Bar & Grille for 9 p.m. At 8, I picked up Pam. She pumped me in the car. "Who's the redhead? How old is she?"

The bar was packed. Pam sat across from me with her back to the door. Marna strode in, unsmiling, joined us.

"What's this all about?"

"Sit down Marna. Marna, Pam."

Pam scowled, crouched in the corner, staring.

I ordered three glasses of Scotch and began. "I met Nick at the judo club. He came to my apartment a few times to help me with judo holds. One evening he brought me to Hector's—the night you walked in, Marna."

"I thought I'd seen you somewhere. Nick said you were an accordionist scouting for a job. Why didn't you tell me this last night?"

"I'll explain. I fell in love with Nick."

"Many women do," she said.

"We got intimate."

"You got *intimate?* I don't believe that. He loves me; I'm his wife."

Pam swiveled. "His *wife?* You can't be. I'm engaged to him. We're getting married in March."

"You're *what*?"

"Wait, please," I urged them. They screamed, people stared, and I feared what was coming.

"For God's sakes," I said, "please let me tell you what happened. We fell in love and went to Missouri for a week."

Marna jumped up. "You went with him to the judo match?"

"That was no judo match. We went away to be alone, and he proposed. We're getting married in February." I held out my left hand to show her the ring.

"She and you are engaged to him? I don't believe a word of it! I know Nick. He's true to me. He's my husband. He fathered my kid."

Pam turned. "You got a *child* by him? Then how come you don't live with him?"

"Marna's an orthodox Jew," I said. "They can't live together until he converts."

"Converts to Judaism? I don't get it," said Pam. She thrust her arm toward Marna. "Don't you see," she pointed to her ring. "Nick gave me this. I'm his Angel."

"Nick gave you the ring? Calls you Angel? No," Marna said. "I'm the only woman he ever called Angel."

"He calls all of us Angel," I told her.

Marna stood. "I'm gonna see him. Gonna find out what the hell this is all about."

"Wait Marna, please. Let me finish. You said he goes to your place in the morning, studies Hebrew, makes love, eats lunch. Then he goes to judo. After judo he comes to my place, makes love, goes to Hector's, closes shop. He comes back to our building, parks in the alley, and spends the night with Pam."

"Spends the night?" She pointed to Pam. "*With her?* No! He sleeps at his mother's house. She's an invalid."

"He sleeps with me," Pam sobbed.

"Listen to me, Marna. Every morning, he drives Pam to her waitress job. Then he goes to your place."

Marna gazed straight ahead, past me. Suddenly she got it. Like an electric shock, she got it.

"Bastard! I'll kill him. I'll hang him by his balls. I'll put him behind bars for the rest of his life. Engaged to both of you. Screwing the three of us. Married me. Fathered my kid. Made false promises. Next year we'll do this, we'll do that. Damned fucking bastard."

We left the bar, turned toward Hector's, strolled in, single file. Marna, Pam, me.

The club was empty. We sat at the bar, side by side. At the end of the room, someone shoved a chair back, and moved toward us with slow, heavy steps. Nick. He stepped behind the bar, moved up to where we sat, glaring at us like we were a mirage. Then he burst into thunderous laughter.

Marna shrieked. "*Shtik! Drek! Bastard! Fucking liar!* You'll suffer for this."

The more she hollered, the louder he laughed. Pam stood, and pushed him. "You lied to me. Lied. You said I was the only woman you loved. The only woman you called *Angel*."

Nick laughed like a lunatic.

"How can you do this to me?" Pam cried.

The women screamed while I eyed him wordlessly. Slowly, I slid the engagement ring off my finger, laid it on the bar, and flicked it. It hit Nick's stomach, and fell to the floor. He stopped laughing.

"Goodbye, Nick."

I drove slowly along Lake Shore Drive. I needed the quiet of the lake and the dark of the night. How strange I felt. Not at all shaken like Marna or Pam. Not mad, just empty. Void. The shock had purged my heart of feeling. The shock was not that Nick had three women; it was the illusion on which I'd based my all-consuming love. *An illusion in my mind.* That realization stripped me bare. What a bizarre emptiness I felt!

An hour later, I reached my building. Uneasiness settled over me when I unlocked my door. A ray of moonlight fell on my gray shag rug. A shadow cut across it. Nick stood in the middle of the room, his gun pointed at me. His eyes were cold. "I'll give you one last chance to change your mind."

I felt nothing. No fear, no loss, no hate. That *something* that falls in love and believes in make-believe was gone. My voice rose from the void in my guts. "Get out!"

He stood unmoving. Then he laid his pistol on the glass cocktail table. "Goodbye, Angel," he said.

I sat in the dark a long time, then ripped sheets and pillowcases from the bed and threw them in the trash. I sprayed the mattress with Lysol and scalded glasses he drank from.

Next day in the library I found the word for the madness that appeared so sane.

> *Psychopath. Characteristics: An absence of guilt and anxiety, habitual liar, inability to form meaningful relationships or learn from experience. Often intelligent, impulsive, charming. Can make a good impression. Hard to diagnose, masked by the appearance of sanity. Can't behave responsibly. Many murderers are psychopathic. No treatment exists.*

I cleared my apartment, packed my Chrysler, and headed for New York. I'd go back to NYU, and one day I'd work in a clinic in the East.

I learned a lot in Chicago. My chief lesson was not that I couldn't trust men; it was that I couldn't trust my own mind. I thought Nick was God's gift to mankind. I painted my own reality. Invested it with thought, feeling, desire, and planned my life around it. Built castles made from the sands of Greek shores and the seas of the Far East. Bliss was Nick. Delight was Nick. Nick was my life.

Next time, I'd know better.

Back in New York, at dinner in my parents' apartment, Mom served pot roast, and Dad poured red wine.

"So that's it," I summed up. "Nick and I would eat supper, make love, he'd go to Hector's, come back to Pam's apartment, sleep with her, drive her to work in the morning, then make love to his wife."

"Oh, my!" Mom repeated, pressing her cigarette stub hard into an ashtray.

Dad beamed. *"My God!"* he said. *"The man is a genius!"*

10

DURBAN

April, 1976

Grice's words echoed crisply in Colonel Steenkamp's office.

"Colonel, we reported the harassment so you could take measures to stop it. You promised you would. But instead of stopping, it got worse. Abusive calls. Threats. Tampering with Miss Deane's car. Endangering her life. What's going on?"

"I'm so sorry, Mr. Grice. I have no idea what's going on, who's doing what or why. And such a worthwhile project! I'll talk with BOSS, Bureau of State Security, and arrange for an officer to take over. They're better equipped to handle these matters."

Major Dan Van der Merwe from Bureau of State Security fidgeted on my sofa, his eyes darting from my file cabinet to my piano to my reels of tape. I couldn't shake my conviction that he'd been there. That he'd wiped out my tapes and life history.

"What's this all about?" he asked in a robust Afrikaner accent.

"I'm sure you know what it's about, Major."

"Colonel Steenkamp told me a little, but I want to hear the whole story from you."

Again, I went through it. The erasure, calls, threats to my guitar teacher's sons, tampering with my brakes.

"That's all?"

My mind flinched. I longed to tell him that I didn't trust him. That the role I was forced to play, pretending to believe that he would protect me from further harm, caused me to lose respect for myself. But I had no option. He could kill me, strangle me. I imagined headlines in *The Daily News*: "Deane slipped on a banana peel, and fell out the window of her eleventh story flat."

"Shame," some would say—a common South African rejoinder. *"A young woman. American, you know."*

"Your question doesn't merit an answer," I told him.

His brow cocked up. "I'll get my men on it. Who do you think is responsible?"

"BOSS and Security Branch." I could almost feel Grice's leg nudge mine.

"Why, Miss Deane, would you think that BOSS had anything to do with this?"

"Only BOSS and SB could unlock my doors and file cabinet."

"Miss Deane, let me educate you about locks. Only nine basic locks exist in the world. That's all. You don't have to work for a security agency to open them. Any good locksmith can do it. Now, the colonel gave me the job of investigating this matter to see who is responsible, and to stop them. Have you any personal enemies, Miss Deane?"

"No one who'd harass me like this."

"Do you fear anything?"

"Why ask that?"

Van der Merwe leaned back, crossed one leg over the other. The weight of his jacket shifted, and a pocket bulged. A recorder, perhaps? A gun?

"We want a complete profile on you, Miss Deane. Then we'll have an idea of who might want to harm you."

What did I fear? The only fear I could think of was roaches. I'd feared them from childhood. "Cockroaches," I told him.

Van der Merwe laughed hard. "We'll watch over you, Miss Deane," he said. "Don't worry. We'll find the culprit."

I loathed myself when he left, and I loathed him for causing my self-hate.

A week after the Major's visit, I left my apartment at 11 a.m., carrying my attaché case. Again, bound for Barclays Bank safe-deposit box with pages of my manuscript. The air was clear, the skies cloudless as I fiddled with my keys to open the door of my car.

Through the driver's window I saw something crawl on the wheel.

A roach! More movements. Giant black roaches climbing over one another on the front and back seats, the windshield, wipers, doors.

I panicked, ran to the African workers in back of my building, shouting, *"Hadebe, Hadebe!"*

The emaciated man rushed out of his shack with a slice of half-eaten white bread.

"Here's the key to my car. Oh! Roaches, terrible roaches! I'll pay you. Please get them out. Spray. Do anything. Please."

I returned to my flat to call Grice. "Where would Van der Merwe get all those roaches?"

"Easy," he said. "From the entomology department at the university."

"Surely they'd wonder why he wanted them."

"Probably," he said. "But who questions BOSS? Why not consult the U.S. Consul? They could register a complaint with the government on your behalf."

The U.S. Consul. Of course! Why didn't I think of that?

"I'd like to see the Consul," I told the receptionist.

"You have an appointment?" she asked.

"No, but the matter is urgent."

"He's fully booked this week," she said. "You can see an assistant, but you'll have to wait." A dozen people waited in the reception room.

"I'll come back after lunch."

I walked to the Indian area, intentionally named "Gray Street," a bustling commercial street with sari stores, record and spice shops, and restaurants. After a meal of chickpeas, vegetables, and rice to a background of street vendors hawking T-shirts, Indian records, and plastic buckets, I hurried back to the Consulate.

A squat man sitting in a smoke-filled office answered telephone calls while I told him about the harassment campaign. "Harassment," I repeated. "Security Branch or BOSS erased my tapes. Wiped out ninety-two reels. Disconnected my brakes. Abusive calls. So many things!"

"There's nothing we can do," he said.

"Surely you can register a complaint with the government."

"Miss Deane, this government won't listen to us."

I left in disgust. Perhaps President Ford would have said the same thing. After all, the three hundred American companies operating in South Africa earned more than they earned in all the countries of the world combined. Thanks to cheap black labor.

The time was four-thirty, almost the end of the working day. I'd left my roach-infested Toyota home, and buses would be overcrowded at that hour.

I strolled leisurely, recalling how I'd begun the Who's Who. Blacks on my Board had suggested I visit Soweto, the sprawling black township near Johannesburg to meet physician and civic leader, Harrison Motlana. "We need his blessing," they said.

Editor Kunene traveled with me to the potholed township nine miles from Johannesburg.

Motlana, a young, articulate physician, agreed that a *Who's Who of Black South Africans* was long overdue, but warned that it wouldn't be easy. "You have to be made of steel," he said. "Are you?"

Kunene told him I was the first woman to drive halfway around the world alone in a Land Rover. "Imagine, London to Kathmandu! No money. Just an accordion."

"Then she's the one to write a *Who's Who*," Motlana had agreed.

When I reached the bottom of my block of Berea Road, I craned forward toward Regency Court. I must be imagining things. An upright piano on the street? That easy chair. Same style, same color as mine. What's it doing there? And that long thing lying on the street that looks like a casket. What is that? *Oh, my God! That's my filing cabinet!*

I banged on the supervisor's door. The landlord, he said, had ordered him to clear my flat because I owed rent. I owed nothing, I told him, not one rand. He shrugged. He was just following orders.

Reassembling my life took three weeks. Mounds of paper from files in my cabinet lay scattered over my rug. Reference notes with recipes. Old telephone bills with press clippings.

I wanted to play out my rage on the piano. Stretch my fingers into wide minor ninth chords that would blast through the building. But I couldn't. Three keys were missing.

11

NEW YORK

1953-54

The odds were against me. Too old, too poor. But at twenty-five, I went back to NYU for a degree in psychology. An M.D. cost too much and took too long. Besides, I could work in a medical mission as a psychologist.

I found an apartment on East Forty-Ninth Street between Lexington and Third. A third-floor walk-up over the Bazaar Club, a prostitute bar. Sonny, the landlord, worked with the New York crime syndicate, got eighty dollars for the women's trysts, took a cut, paid the cops to look the other way, and gave the girls a portion.

Across our narrow street, a doorman kept watch in front of a red brick building. The *other* America. On the corner, the Shelton hotel. Across Lexington, the Waldorf. Strange, how reality shifts. A month earlier, I was living on Chicago's Humboldt Boulevard. Now, on Manhattan's east side. Friends I knew in New York years earlier dressed and spoke like different people. What is real, when "reality" shifts like that?

On an off-night from my nightclub job, I lounged on my sofa, legs propped on my cocktail table, sipping a shot of Jack Daniels. *Lay your feelings on the table,* I told myself. *What do you see?*

An alien who doesn't belong. Not at NYU, sitting behind kids ten years my junior. Not in nightclubs, where I'm a human mermaid filling requests for "Harvest Moon." Where men from Tennessee send business cards marked, "Room 203. Fifty bucks."

I don't belong with my folks, either. They didn't approve of my marriage because Bart was poor. They didn't approve of my divorce because that was worse. I don't belong anywhere. I feel sorry for me.

Why am I so different? Why do I seek permanence when everything has a beginning, middle and end? Why do I feel that *something* must be changeless, and I've got to find it? Why don't money, family and fame motivate me like they do others? Normal people want to *have*, and I want to *be*. But I can't figure out how to do it.

My thirteen-week contract for TV commercials required me to play accordion, sing, wear fishtails, and above all, never exceed size twelve. But rehearsals, classes, and cramming for tests left no time for meals. I survived on sugar buns, éclairs and malteds, gaining nine pounds in three weeks. My stomach bulged at the dress rehearsal, and the back zipper of my gown got stuck below my waist.

"You look like *Before* instead of *After*," the producer said. "And only two weeks to go!"

"Don't worry," I told him, "I lose weight fast."

I rang my doctor, and said I had two weeks to lose ten pounds.

"No pill will take it off that fast," he said. "But Knickerbocker Hospital runs an in-patient program for compulsive eaters. Complete rest alone in a room on a hundred calories a day. You'll lose five pounds a week."

I rang Knickerbocker. "We have a room available," a clerk said.

"The cost?"

"Two hundred dollars a week."

Where would I get two hundred bucks? What if—? An idea struck me that would load me with guilt, but it was worth it. I couldn't afford to lose the TV show.

A few months earlier, I'd played the main ballroom of the Edison Hotel during a thunderstorm. "Don't drive," the manager urged, "it's risky. I'll get you a room." Craig Sommers was his name. Nice guy. He got the room, and stayed.

With the receiver in my hand, and my finger in the dial, I paused. Did I really want to do this? I'd never done anything like it. I'd feel awful. But if I didn't do it, I'd lose the show.

I turned the dial and watched it rotate back. "Craig, you won't believe it. I'm pregnant. I can have an abortion at Knickerbocker, but it costs two-hundred bucks."

The thought of pregnancy must have stunned him because he didn't question the illegality. "Don't worry, don't worry," he said. "I'll bring the cash tonight."

I felt disgusted with myself, but it was too late to change what I did.

My room in the obesity ward was clean. Spartan. No nonsense, like the nurse.

"Sit there," she said, pointing to the bed. She opened my suitcase and sifted through clothes and cosmetics like a customs officer at LaGuardia Airport.

"What are you doing?"

"Checking."

"For booze?"

"No. They do that in the alcoholic ward. Here we check for cake, cookies, candy."

"You're joking."

"No. That's the rules. Why?"

"Well, I don't like it."

"Jackie Gleason doesn't mind."

"Gleason? The TV comedian? Here?"

"That's him." She pointed to the wall. "Next door."

I knocked.

"Enter if you're gorgeous."

"I'm not, but I'm your next door neighbor."

"Come in, come in."

There he sat. Jackie Gleason. A fat guy in a baggy blue robe with tousled black hair looking like a prize fighter.

"Holy cow! You *are* gorgeous. You're my next door neighbor? What are you here for? You look like *After*, not *Before*."

"My TV producer told me the opposite."

"TV producer? Hey, you're in the right room. What's your name?"

"Shirley Deane."

"Shirley, step inside, step inside." He gestured toward a half-eaten, dry salad. "Can I offer you a lettuce leaf? Guaranteed to please, if you got no taste buds. Sit on that chair," he said.

He pointed to the nurse outside his room. "I'd offer you a cigarette if that Dickless Tracy over there didn't pluck them out of my suitcase."

"You're as funny offstage as on."

"That's what I tell my sponsors."

Over the next few days, we shared experiences. The guests on his TV shows, frustrations of his career, the poverty of his youth, his dreams. My TV shows in Chicago and New York. Clubs I'd played, reviews I'd gotten, agents whom he knew.

"Addiction is in the genes," he told me in his Brooklyn accent. "My father was a booze addict. I do the count-down often, usually at Doctors Hospital. They got fresher lettuce leaves."

He whistled at the press clip I brought to show the doctor the fishtail gown I'd have to wear in two weeks.

I sang a few songs I'd written.

"You compose? If I hum a tune, you can write it?"

"Sure."

He hummed a song he called "Chocolate Reverie." I wrote the notes down and sang it back.

"Brilliant! I didn't think anybody could match my songwriter. Hey, you got everything. Looks. Experience. Talent. I'd like you on my show. What d'you say?"

Gleason didn't wait for an answer. He scribbled a number on the back of a Knickerbocker Rules sheet. "Call me next week."

After I ate the dry lettuce leaf in my room, I rested in bed.

What a break. America's top TV star offers me a chance to work with him.

So what?

So money and fame.

I don't want fame.

But money. Big money. Think what you could do with it. School, travel.

Big money means big commitment. Diving headlong into show

business. That's not the way I want to go. I'd have to cut classes. The more classes I cut, the further I am from the goal.

Cut, it's worth it. You won't get another chance like this. The most famous TV star in the country. Forget the goal. It's just a dream.

I can't forget it. I can't dream one way, and live another.

Out of Knickerbocker, I was nine pounds lighter. The fishtail fit. But the guilt over the two-hundred bucks wouldn't leave me.

I never called Gleason.

12

SOUTH AFRICA, MY FIRST SEVEN YEARS
1967-73

The dirt road to Inanda Seminary, a boarding high school for black girls, twenty-five kilometers northwest of Durban, ran past the sprawling township of KwaMashu. Matchbox sheds built for millions of blacks—the labor force for white enterprise. The road was straight. No turns, no bends, like all roads to townships outside South African cities. The government built them straight so the army could reach the townships fast in an uprising.

Inanda's multi-racial staff lived on the compound. Apartheid laws didn't apply because the United Church Board for World Ministries based in New York owned the land and funded the school. Americans called the headquarters on Riverside Drive, "The Protestant Vatican."

The staff lived in comfortable rooms in the Mission House. As the only non-missionary, I chose to live apart. "Home" was a wood and iron shack with a corrugated roof at the rim of the compound surrounded by eucalyptus trees and forty acres of unfarmed land. I got water from a rain-water tank outside my hut, and used an outhouse.

The school employed me to teach English, then promoted me to public relations officer to raise funds. I launched my crusade with a soccer game, insisting on multi-racial spectators, unprecedented in apartheid South Africa. I asked permission from Piet Koornhof, Deputy Minister of Bantu Administration. His secretary replied that they would grant permission provided I placed appropriate signs on all the toilets, entrances, and exits at New Kingsmead Stadium.

"Toilet facilities," the letter read, *"should be arranged as follows: one block of toilets, housing sixteen, should be assigned for European use; eight toilets in the other block, for African use; four toilets for Indian use, and four for Coloureds. Proper signs must also be posted at entrances and exit doors."*

With a stack of signs that I'd printed from peel-back, self-stick letters, I drove to the massive stadium on a sultry February morning. Carting signs, nails, and a hammer, I treaded the field's toilets, entrances and exits, nailing signs for African, Indian, Colored and White males and females.

On March fourteenth, 1971, two white soccer teams played a lazy game to a half-empty stadium. Next morning, I returned to Kingsmead to collect my signs from the entrances, exits, and thirty-two toilets.

There had to be an easier way to raise funds.

U.S. stockholders had been pressing the three-hundred American corporations in South Africa to get out. They wouldn't. Black labor was too cheap. They might, however, be willing to support a black school. We needed a recreation center and an ablution block with modern toilets. Students bathed as they'd bathed a hundred years earlier. Tin pitchers, bowls, cold water.

I compiled a list of American companies in South Africa. Mobil Oil, for one.

The managing director of Mobil Oil in Durban, a dour man with manicured nails, sat with his back to a wall-length window that opened onto a broad, grassy area.

I laid my photo kit on his desk, and told him that our century-old school had produced nurses who work at black hospitals, women who teach at leading black schools, and mothers of prominent doctors and lawyers. I reminded him that American companies owed Africans a debt. Our high school offered the chance to pay it.

"Miss Deane," he said, "I prefer to donate to the Wildlife Fund."

Driving back to Inanda, I said out loud, *Mister, you won't get away with that.*

My letter to the chairman of the U.S. Congressional Committee on Africa described contributions that our school had made to South Africa. It listed our needs, and the response of the American director of Mobil Oil in Durban. I posted it to Congressman Diggs in care of the Committee on Foreign Affairs at the U. S. Congress.

There I was. A simple fund-raiser at a mission school in South Africa. A woman with no status, waiting for the U.S. Congress to act. Waiting for the shit to hit the fan.

Inanda's students swept walkways, weeded gardens, scrubbed classrooms, stairways, dining rooms. Rehearsed songs and skits of welcome. Applied Vaseline to their hair, and pulled and stretched their curls. After all, how often do American congressmen visit an African school?

The U.S. Consul in Durban arranged a formal reception, assuring that the staff of the five-star hotel where the congressionals would stay would not mistake their distinguished guests for Africans.

They arrived. Five members of the Congressional fact-finding committee headed by Congressman Charles Diggs and Goler Butcher, a civil rights activist and staff director of the congressional committee on Africa.

Students garlanded them. They sang Zulu chants. The cook prepared a banquet. Black, white and colored teachers ushered them through buildings and grounds. The principal presented a slide show of century-old photographs. The girls sang Zulu songs in the auditorium. They presented skits on gratitude, education, service.

Before the congressionals left, Diggs drew me aside. "We're very impressed. Don't worry. You'll hear from me soon."

Two weeks later, a bulky registered envelope arrived, marked, "Congress of the United States." Diggs wrote, *"I remain imbued with the conviction that Inanda is making a significant contribution and must remain alive ... "* Goler Butcher wrote, "*We are making every effort to carry forward your cause."*

They enclosed a round trip ticket to New York. "*Your first appointment,"* Diggs wrote, "*is with Raleigh Warner, chairman of Mobil Oil. Other appointments will follow."*

The news awed the staff, students, and school Board, but not me. I knew that I was only a pawn in an international chess game.

On a stop in Germany, I met directors of an organization of German churches, conservatively dressed, middle-aged women who had not forgotten the era of Nazi oppression. They would meet to discuss our school's needs.

Next, New York.

"Mobil Oil headquarters," my note read, "is at 150 East 42nd Street. Near Grand Central Station."

All I knew about Chairman Raleigh Warner was that he went to boarding schools and to Princeton. That he was the son of a rich oil executive. And shrewd.

When the chairman's office door closed behind me, I found myself in a room as massive as the Queens rink where I roller-skated in my teens. All space. Far away at the other end of the room stood a gleaming mahogany desk. Sitting behind it, a lean man, silent and unsmiling, in a dark gray suit. Between us, a narrow plush red carpet. I'd heard of red carpets, but had never walked on one. Treading slowly, my feet sank and rose like in a dream sequence. I giggled without a sound. Me, in the office of the chairman of Mobil, the world's leading producer of gasoline. Here, where decisions were made that affected hundreds of millions of people around the world.

The Mobil mogul sat motionless. Who was I to deserve the courtesy of rising to offer a greeting, even a handshake? After all, I'd trapped him. I was the insignificant female who used congressional muscle to push her agenda.

When I reached his desk, Warner surprised me. He stood, and extended a hand. "What's on your mind, Miss Deane?"

Inanda's highest priority was an ablution block, but I knew that Mobil would boast of its gift to American stockholders, and a row of toilets wouldn't do. Instead, I laid out our plans for a recreation center. Halls, audio visual room, tuck shop, canteen, lecture room, debating room, "quiet" room. "We could call it, 'The Mobil Center,'" I said.

"That's possible," he told me. "Our Board will discuss it, and contact you."

The angular lines of his taut face softened slightly. Or was it relief that I hadn't asked for fifty million dollars?

I made the fund-raising rounds of companies that operated in South Africa. Lubrizol. Remington. Royal. Otis. Chase Manhattan. Ingersoll-Rand. IBM. To save time, I stayed at the Iriquois, a small, roach-infested hotel on the west side of Manhattan, instead of staying with my mother in Queens.

A week before I left New York, I visited her. She worked as a secretary in a downtown office where men praised her skills, she told me. Life had a purpose.

Mom and I dined at Luchow's, a German restaurant on East Fourteenth Street. She was in her mid-sixties, chic in a beaver coat, concerned about the coming presidential election. She'd vote for George McGovern because he opposed the Vietnam War, but she feared that Nixon might win. And isn't it dangerous that the Soviets keep landing unmanned spaceships on the moon?

This wasn't the mother I remembered, who sat at home watching sitcoms and smoking two packs of Camels a day. This Mom was bright, engaged in life. I imagined her at ninety. Wrinkled and arthritic, but still in control.

Students garlanded me on return. The news had preceded my arrival. German churches would fund our water supply and sewage system, and build a new ablution block. IBM would construct a secretarial school at Inanda Seminary. The first, ever, for black women in South Africa. Mobil Oil would erect a Mobil Student Centre. Not only would they fund it, but in September of that year—1972—the entire Mobil Oil Board would travel to Durban, and Chairman Raleigh Warner would lay the foundation stone. Such an event had no parallel in Mobil Oil's history.

Ditches were dug. Pipes laid. Plans drawn for entertainment, invitations, meals. Students wrote and rehearsed plays about Mobil's gift.

One month later, we received word that Mobil's planned visit to our school had upset Prime Minister Vorster. A visit by the ilk of Mobil to the only school in South Africa with a live-in multiracial staff would humiliate the South African government. It would slap the apartheid doctrine in the face.

Mobil backed out.

Inanda's staff and students raged. They threatened to wire Mobil's affront to the *New York Times*. I raged, and wired Raleigh Warner. "*Your change of plans could trigger dire repercussions.*"

Two days later, Warner wired back. Mobil Oil had revised their plans. Their entire Board would fly to South Africa *with their wives*. While the men met with government officials in Johannesburg, their wives would visit our school. Mrs. Raleigh Warner would lay the foundation stone.

What strategy! Mobil Oil had castled on the global chess game.

On "Mobil Day," Mrs. Raleigh Warner, clad in a short-sleeved brown tailored dress, her auburn hair styled in a pageboy, laid the gray-black stone marked, *"Mobil Student Centre, Inanda Seminary. This stone was dedicated by Mrs. Raleigh Warner, Jr. on behalf of Mobil Oil Corporation, 26 September, 1972."*

The Natal Mercury published a two-page article captioned, "Shirley no longer yearns to be a roving minstrel." About my Land Rover expedition halfway around the world. My show business career. My work with Tibetans in Nepal. Fund raising for Inanda. They reprinted photographs of me teaching geography to Tibetan children, and driving my Land Rover through the Persian desert with two armed guards.

After *The Daily News* published my resignation from Inanda Seminary, a stack of letters arrived in my post box. Corporation directors, church officials, the congressional black caucus, KwaZulu government ministers, teachers, and students expressed surprise and regret. As the Bureau of State Security and Security Branch probably read my mail before I did, they would have speculated about my plans, and readied their gear: agents, surveillance, telephone tapping. All their tools in place, long before I penned my first words to *Who's Who of Black South Africans.*

13

NEW YORK

1953-54

Thousands of Americans wanted a Tucker car, and I was booked to play for the man who invented it. Preston Tucker. "Friday at the Waldorf," my agent told me. "Six to nine. A hundred fifty bucks, but you gotta be original. Write a special. Tucker calls his car *The Tin Goose.*"

The Forty-Second Street library carried magazines and newspapers about the story:

> The most revolutionary car in history. First car with an engine in the rear. A helicopter engine. Take it apart and put it together in twenty minutes. Tops a hundred twenty miles an hour. The only manufacturer who cares about safety. First car with seat belts and padded dashboard. Safest on the road. Headlight in the center. Curved bumper to deflect blows. Air cooled.

The company made fifty cars, but The Big Three, Chrysler, GM and Ford, ran Tucker off the map. They organized campaigns to keep him off the market. Bribed his employees to become saboteurs. Pressured raw materials suppliers not to deal with him.

Great minor chords echoed through my mind. Chords of corruption, tyranny and crime. But I needed more than chords.

I could have written a symphony about the injustice. General Motors, Chrysler and Ford blowing trumpets to pressure government agencies. *Grill him. Harass him with investigations.* Bass fiddles bullying flutes as the Securities Exchange

Commission conducted a "secret" investigation. Horns "leaking" it to the press to ruin him. The SEC soprano singing an aria: *He defrauded his shareholders, ran a ponzi scheme, his promised "cars of tomorrow" don't exist.* Drums pounding as Tucker is subpoenaed to provide records.

Eight new shiny Tucker cars brought the records to the courthouse, proving that his cars did exist. Tucker was indicted anyway. Jurors found him not guilty, but it was too late. He'd lost everything. Now, six years later, he was working on another car.

I had three days to compose, practice, memorize. I thought about it in my psychology class and at home, and came up with a title: *The Man from Ypsilanti*, but I couldn't follow it up. With just two days to go, I resorted to a simple jingle.

On Friday, I typed the words on a file card, brought it with me to the Waldorf, and taped it to the top of my accordion.

That's all I had. A thirty-second ditty.

In the Waldorf convention room, a tall man in a dark-blue suit with a maroon bow tie and a quick step approached the bandstand. "Preston Tucker. Welcome." He held my hand in a strong grip. Not handsome, but he exuded a fiery force.

"I'm honored, Mr. Tucker."

"Preston, Preston, please. What kind of music do you play?"

"Whatever you like."

He came from Michigan so I thought he'd want a polka, but he didn't ask.

"What's that amplifier for? We got a mike here."

"I always use an amp. Not for volume but for resonance. Doesn't sound like a squeezebox with an amp."

"How interesting. Never saw an accordionist with an amp, and I'm from Michigan. We got lots of accordionists up there."

Tucker returned to his colleagues on the other side of the room, poured a drink, and chatted. I played "Tea for Two," eyeing him. He quit talking to listen. Unusual. A man tapped him on the arm, but Tucker waved him off to listen to me. The other man listened too, he had no choice. Men didn't usually listen at parties like that.

Tucker tapped his foot when I played "You Must Have Been a Beautiful Baby." Called the attention of his friends. "Look. Listen." They looked and listened.

At break time, he strode up. "That was great. Hi-fi accordion! How about that! Never heard an accordion like it. When we sit down to dinner, could you play something special? You know, like a concert."

"Guests don't usually listen when they eat. They want to talk."

"They won't talk. They won't eat. They'll listen."

I powdered my face in the restroom. Oh, God! The man wants a concert, and all I've got is a thirty-second ditty! Damn. I should have prepared a suite. Well, I can always play a semi-classic like "Dark Eyes," but that doesn't feel right.

When I returned, I strapped on the accordion with a sinking feeling. The men had seated themselves at the dinner table. "Hey, guys," Tucker called out, "I want you to be quiet. This is a treat. She's no ordinary squeezeboxer."

I had to think fast. A week earlier, I'd played an original at the Hotel Pierre. I could do it again, and link it to the jingle I wrote.

"Gentlemen, an original: "Taxi, please."

I crooned my song about a lonely woman whose lover left her. She calls a taxi. I played the taxi theme with a bellow shake, pulling the accordion in and out minimally and fast to make it sound like wheels.

At the Copacabana she hears Sinatra sing, "You Make Me Feel So Young." I sang sixteen bars. She leaves. *Taxi, please*. Again, the taxi theme. This time, she goes to the Twenty-One Club where Edith Piaf sings "Mam'selle." A third taxi brings her home.

To a soft background, I talked: "Penny sees a notice under her door: *You won a Tucker car!* Next day, men gather on her lawn with bouquets of flowers. Among them, the lover who had left her. She stands on her porch, singing:

There's a secret that I'm keeping in my garage,
It's not a Chrysler or a Ford or a Dodge,
Individual suspension with an engine in the rear,
Padded dashboard, safety glass, so you never have to fear.

The car of tomorrow, one you'll never ever borrow
But if you're good, then one day you may see,
The secret that I'm keeping, in my garage,
It's not a Chrysler or a Ford or a Dodge.
I will never let it loose; it's my beloved Tin Goose.

The men rose to applaud, and Tucker strode up. "My God, that was terrific! Tell you what I want to do. I want to start a record company featuring your hi-fi accordion. You'll be known throughout the country. *Shirley Deane* will be a household name. Come, join us for dinner."

He seated me next to himself. "Hi-fi accordion, first in America! Your future's made, honey. Write your number on this card. I'll ring you next week."

After dinner, he asked where I lived.

"Across the street," I said. "Near Third."

"How'd you get here?"

"Walked. With my luggage carrier."

He called a bellboy. "I want you to help this lady," he told him. "Carry her accordion, amplifier, and recorder to her door. Report to me as soon as you get back. I'll take care of you."

"Yes sir, yes sir."

At home, I poured a Scotch. I should have been thrilled, but depression descended on me like water over rocks. How could I tell Tucker that I didn't *want* to be a household name? I didn't *want* to make a fortune on recordings. I didn't *want* to perform from coast to coast. I couldn't tell him. It would hurt him.

A few days later, the phone rang. Tucker, probably. Let it ring. I don't know what to say. It stopped, rang again in five minutes. Then in ten. Three hours later, a wire arrived. *Call immediately,* and a telephone number.

I wired back: *Hold plans for a few days. Letter follows.*

Dear Mr. Tucker, I began. No good. *Dear Preston*. No good.

Dear Preston Tucker,

This letter is hard for me to write, maybe the hardest I've ever written. I wish I could do what you have in

> mind. It's a dream, and you can make dreams come true. But I confess I have a competing dream, a psychology degree so I can work like Dr. Schweitzer somewhere in the East. A long haul, but it's the only dream that matters.
>
> Your dynamism impressed me. I wish your aim could topple mine. But success in recordings and personal appearances from coast to coast wouldn't feed my hunger for a different kind of life. I beg your forgiveness, dear Preston. And I thank you for everything you are.

No one but the professor was in my psychology class when I woke up. I'd fallen asleep on my textbook. From his desk, Dr. Weigert peered at me above his spectacles.

"You can not do show business and go to college," he roared in his German accent. "Four hours' sleep is no good. You need eight. Everybody needs eight."

I sat there long after he'd left. He was right. I'd have to cut back on gigs. But could I do it with rent, fees, books, clothes, gas, and Chrysler bills? Maybe I could just work weekends. But agents often booked me out of town on weekends, so I missed Friday classes. When booked with a band, I had to rehearse. That cut into class time.

I'd have to face it. School didn't work with show business. No time to study. School didn't work without it. No money for fees. Show business didn't work either. Playing "Mairzy Doats and Dozee Doats" and wiggling in fishtails was living to please others. That's slavery. More than anything in the world, I wanted *freedom*.

"Money will buy freedom," my friends told me. But the rich I knew weren't free. The more they owned, the more they craved. "You can buy a penthouse with money," friends said. But a penthouse would root me to one street in one city. I didn't want an anchor. I wanted to be free, to be *me*. But I didn't know what "me" meant.

Something else troubled me. You can't press anything you love into permanence. Relationships, looks, health change constantly. If I could find something that didn't change, I'd know that *that* alone was worth living and dying for. I didn't know where to look for it. I knew only that I wouldn't find it on Broadway or in front of a TV camera.

Manhattan was cold and dismal on the February afternoon that I left NYU. I strode toward Washington Square Park clutching three texts, *Abnormal Psychology* on top, its purple jacket moist with tears. Midway through the park I stood still, like a catatonic patient in a mental ward, gazing at the dark brick building I'd walked away from, for the last time.

Old men played chess on stone tables in the park. A few wobbled drunkenly on benches. Some who sat alone scouted for an opponent. At another time I would have played. I loved chess. The focused minutes and hours stripped the hells from my life. Only chess could do that. Strategizing, scheming. If I move there, he'll retreat. If he moves here, I'll capture that. Planning, plotting, counter-plotting. But I couldn't play then. I couldn't think of anything but why my life was so different from everybody else's.

"Hey lady, siddown. Whassa matter? Wanna game?"

An icy wind chilled my back. "Checkmate," a player belted out.

That was the right word. I couldn't win the game I tried to play. I was locked in a closet. My dream was outside, and I couldn't open the door.

"Got a Park Avenue gig," my agent told me. "It's posh. Play an original."

As much as I yearned for a life with more meaning than show business, I had to pay the rent.

The library was the only place where I could compose. The cavernous reading room on the third floor, nearly empty of people, felt austere. But I worked well in austere rooms. Clutter stymied me.

Lay your feelings on the table, I told myself.

A melody played in my head. I wrote the notes down like I was taking dictation. Often I wrote words first, and put them to music, which was easier. This time, music came first. A title followed: *There's a child in me that wants to live but it has no air to breathe.* That turned the spigot on. Words flowed.

Backstage, I peered through the slit between the curtains. A full house. My psychiatrist friend, Bill Hastings, a small man who moved and talked fast, his sister from Seattle, and his partner, Reggie, sat up front.

"Ladies and Gentlemen, Shirley Deane."

I stepped out without a smile. I'd smiled enough. Tonight I'd be *me.* I'd play and sing what was in my heart, and what was in my heart was very dark. My song burlesqued and ridiculed the kind of life that is lived from the outside in. Lived to please. To accommodate. To conform.

I played for me, and the effect was electric. I eased the tension with a parody on "Mairzy Doats and Dozy Doats," and followed it with a few bars of *Toccata and Fugue in D minor*, singing, "*I'd rather play a fugue by Bach.*"

Then, my old strategy to stop minds from straying. A wide stretched-out chord, glissando to the bottom of the keyboard, and a sudden halt. I had them.

But a stray thought flitted across my brain like a mosquito on a TV screen. *My environment is as changeable as a garment.* That insight freed me like a caterpillar suddenly aware of its wings, but it threw my focus. Where was I? What was I playing? What was I singing? I was standing under bright lights, facing a silent, expectant audience, and my mind went blank. I tried to backtrack but all I could think of was the thought that awakened me and threw me off: *Why should my environment imprison me when I can step out of it at will?* Oh, God, help me!

I was looking down at my closed bellows. They opened a little, and a hiss of air escaped. "*Air!*" I voiced. "*Air! There's a child in me that wants to live, and it just found the air to breathe!*"

A rhyme formed from my stray thought:

Why should we change to suit our milieu?
Let's change our milieu to suit me and you.

Oh, what the hell! Beneath the Park Avenue glitz, this joint is no different from McNally's saloon on Third Avenue. What can I lose?

"Sing it, folks, sing it." Just like McNally's. They sang.

Why should we change to suit our milieu?
Let's change our milieu to suit me and you.

Words flowed through my mind that linked the verse to my theme.

There's a child in me that wants to live,
And it just found the air to breathe.
It's goin' to blossom, it's goin' to grow,
It's already starting to teethe.
The key is to live from the inside out,
Not to change who we are, to please,
But to nourish our child with courage and clout,
And let her unfold with ease.
No more will we change to suit our milieu,
Let's change our milieu to suit me and you.

"One last time, folks."

No more will we change to suit our milieu,
Let's change our milieu to suit me and you.

I closed with a flurry of chords. The audience cheered. I bowed.

Bill, Stephanie, and Reggie took me to the Russian Tea Room near Carnegie Hall. The maitre d' led us through the crammed bar to a reserved table in the dining room. An accordion, balalaika, and tambourine played a fast paced Russian folk song.

Bill ordered vodkas and caviar. "You were dynamite," he said. "I got goose bumps. You took us from philosophy to psychology to the gut."

"I couldn't help crying," Reggie said. "You sang about me, living in a closet."

"We're all in a closet," Stephanie said. "That's why it had such impact. There's a kid in all of us that wants to live."

"The difference between Shirley's kid and ours," Bill said, "is that her kid screams too loud to ignore."

"What's ours doing?" Reggie asked.

"Riding a rumble seat. Distracted by sights, sounds, status. Stuff that keeps us looking out instead of in."

A waltz sounded familiar. "Excuse me," I stopped a waiter. "That song. What's the name?"

"*Dosveedanya*," he said. "It means *goodbye*."

"*Dosveedanya*," I repeated. The question that floated through my mind when I got stuck on stage floated through my brain again. Why should my environment imprison me when I can step out of it at will?

"I got it, folks! When I'm me, life works! From now on, I'm not going to dream one way and live another. Know what? *Dosveedanya!* I'm going!"

"Where?" Bill asked.

"Around the world."

"C'mon, girl. You won a jackpot?"

"I don't need a jackpot. I won't stay at Hiltons. I'm going to work my way around the world on my accordion."

"And the medical mission?"

"I'll find one. And I'll work there if all I can do is sweep the floor."

At home, sipping Scotch and listening to Kostalanetz and his strings, I felt like a newborn. I would design my life myself. *Deane designed by Deane*. If freedom had a taste, it would beat chocolate. I'd tell Jackie Gleason to forget his "Chocolate Reverie." Make it the "Freedom Reverie."

For years I'd felt like a marionette dangling from strings that others pulled. I didn't know I could tear loose and walk free. Maybe we all build our prisons and spend the rest of our lives trying to get out of them. But freedom doesn't happen from the outside in. It happens from the inside out.

Now I was off for the world. I had determination and a passport. I'd start in Europe, go to Africa, the Middle, Near, and Far East. All I needed was free passage to Europe.

I rang ocean liners to introduce myself. Professional musician, classical and jazz. Entertainer with ten years' experience on TV, radio, and clubs. Reviews by Walter Winchell and Earl Wilson.

"Sorry, we don't book one way. Round trip only."

I tried cruise liners. "Sorry, we don't book entertainers. Passengers get entertained on shore. We only book bands."

"I can organize a band in a week."

"We're booked for the next three years, thank you."

Stuck.

"I know you don't like Broadway," my agent said, "but Jack Dempsey's club wants you for two weeks."

The long narrow bar with tables at the back was packed every night. Autographed pictures of the boxer adorned the walls. Bruised, smiling, accepting trophies.

On the last night of my contract, I thought, to hell with requests. I'd play for me. Men at the bar made too much noise so I pulled my ruse. A loud B-flat minor-ninth chord, the kind of screaming sound Hollywood uses to unfold a drama. Pulled the bellows wide, ran the chord straight down to a single bass note, and stopped short.

People quit talking in the middle of sentences, their glasses poised halfway to their mouths. I played a strong four-four beat that mimicked a bass and snare drum. Then the melody—Jerome Kern's "Smoke Gets In Your Eyes." They smiled. Heads nodded. Bodies swayed. I closed my eyes, leaned back, played what I felt.

On my break, three blond men in their twenties introduced themselves. They were musicians, they said, playing on a Norwegian liner docked in Manhattan for a few days. Arnulf, a large, buoyant man with a ready smile, played drums. His friends called him *Silver Rabbit,* he told me, because his hair was so light.

Knut played bass. "My English not good."

"I'm Finn, piano," said the eldest. "My English, too bad."

"This is the first time we hear jazz on accordion," Arnulf said. "Can you play a jam session with us?"

"Sure," I said. "When? Where?"

"Tonight, when you finish. On our ship, the *M/S Oslofjord*."

At midnight, the men carried my accordion and amp to my car. I felt like a taxi driver as I drove to the docks, listening to them trade excitement in Norwegian, and direct me in broken English. Their ship looked as massive as the Queen Elizabeth.

In the main ballroom, wall maps showed the *Oslofjord's* routes. The Caribbean, North Atlantic, Arctic Circle, Baltic Sea.

I pulled on my accordion and pointed a finger down. That means one flat, key of F. They knew the code. Knut whistled as I played an ad lib intro to "Dancing on the Ceiling." Arnulf's brushes rotated softly on his drum skin. Finn, the pianist, played when I took a break. He knew that piano and accordion don't mix.

Four hours, thirty tunes, six whiskeys later, we quit. They talked Norwegian.

"We want you with us," Arnulf said. "Our ship leaves in a few days for the Christmas cruise to the Caribbean."

"I don't want to go to the Caribbean," I told him. "I want to go to Europe."

"We go to Europe next year in June, for the *Midnight Sun* cruise." He pointed to a wall map. "Iceland, Norway, Sweden, Finland, Denmark, Germany, France. Then back to New York. You can join us."

"I don't want to come back to New York. I want to work my way around the world. Europe, Africa, the East."

More talk, more whiskey, and the plan emerged. I'd play the Caribbean cruise, and then the cruise to Europe in June. When the ship reached Oslo, Arnulf would get me a job. He and Knut would join me when they finished their contract with the ship.

"Sounds great," I said. "But suppose the captain doesn't want an accordionist?"

"Captain is boss of the ship," Arnulf said. "We're boss of the music. Come tomorrow. Captain will write a letter to Thomas Cook agency. Cook does the contracts."

They poured the rest of the bottle. "*Skol!*" they toasted. "To our new band!"

I put my accordion in the case.

"Leave your accordion and amp here," Arnulf said. "Very safe."

Driving back to East Forty-Ninth Street in the early morning sun, I told myself I must be mad. I left my Excelsior accordion and Gibson amp with three strange guys. Never saw them before last night. I'm out of my head. My accordion, with hand-made Italian reeds. Nothing like it in New York. What was I thinking?

At home, I slept with my clothes on. Arnulf called at 9 a.m. "The captain wants to see you. Bring passport, clippings, photos."

On my way to the pier, I mulled over the events of the previous night. I played on the bandstand at Jack Dempsey's, wondering if I'd ever get to Europe. In walk three strange men who ask me to jam on their ship. A day later, I get a job. First, to the Caribbean. Then to Europe. What a coincidence!

But for the first time in my life, I wondered: *Is there really such a thing?*

On a mild December afternoon, the *M/S Oslofjord* sailed southward from the New York harbor for a ten-day cruise to the Caribbean. Only one thought occupied my mind: in June, six months hence, I'd stand on that same deck, waving goodbye to my parents and goodbye to America. I wouldn't return until I'd seen the world—Europe, Africa, the East. The Caribbean tour would be fun, but I could hardly wait for June.

I scanned the passenger list. "*James C. Petrillo!*"

"Who's he?" Arnulf asked.

"President of the American Federation of Musicians."

I spotted Petrillo pacing the deck. A short, pudgy man with glasses who looked no different from his portrait that hung on the great wall of Local 802 in Manhattan. Respected, loved, even worshipped by our local's thirty-two thousand musicians.

"Sir, I'm from Local 802." Petrillo grimaced. Perhaps he'd booked a Norwegian liner so American musicians wouldn't trouble him.

"Just one picture with you, sir?"

Arnulf snapped it. The photograph showed him in a gray suit, double-breasted jacket, black and white tie. I wore a black jersey with a green and black sequined skirt and high-heeled shoes. I clung to his right arm, my hands clasped around his elbow. His arms stuck to his sides.

Our trio played in the dining room every evening. I'd worked with many drummers and bassists, but Arn and Knut were more than a rhythm section. They turned our bandstand into sacred ground, a floor space where you start with a consciousness keyed into earth, and end in a space you never knew existed, but it's where you belong. They heard my heart, and though we stood as three figures, we played as one. That excited me, it validated my being. But off the bandstand—that was something else.

In Caracas, Arn and Knut assumed the role of guardians. At the Tamanaco Hotel restaurant, they wouldn't allow me out of their sight. They escorted me even to ladies' rooms, waiting outside the door to shepherd me back to our table. They stayed sober in Curacao until I retired to my cabin. Then they loaded up theirs with tax-free bottles of Crème de Café, and partied all night.

By the time the ship docked in St. Thomas, I'd had enough supervision. I told Arnulf I wanted to dine alone. He didn't advise it, but if I insisted, I'd have to remember that our ship would sail for Puerto Rico at nine p.m. "Be on board by eight," he said. The next night was New Year's Eve, when we'd head back to New York.

At six, clad in a low-cut black dress, dangling earrings, and spike-heeled shoes, I ambled along cobblestoned, palm-lined streets. Muted sounds of Latin rhythms mingled with cool jazz. From a darkly curtained club called The Grotto, a piano, drums and guitar played, "Every Time We Say Goodbye." A deep throated woman sang:

Everytime we say goodbye, I die a little,
Everytime we say goodbye, I wonder why a little…

Inside, men with their women and men on their own glanced up briefly from tall barstools and tiny tables for two. I chose a table near the door, and ordered a Brandy Alexander. A slender, dark-skinned woman sang:

You go to my head, and you linger like a haunting refrain,
And I find you spinning round in my brain,
Like the bubbles in a glass of champagne…

"Another Brandy Alexander," I ordered.
"Can you sing 'Tenderly'?" I asked the vocalist.

The evening breeze caressed the trees tenderly,
The trembling trees embraced the breeze tenderly…

"One more round, please."
"Can you sing, 'All the Things You Are'?"

You are the promised kiss of springtime,
That makes the lonely winter seem long…

The bartenders eyed me curiously as I sang with her. The short hefty one could have doubled as a bouncer. She didn't smile, just mixed cocktails and counted cash.
"Another Brandy Alexander, please."
I asked the vocalist if she knew the song, "I've Got an Island."

I've got an island in the Pacific,
And everything about it is terrific…

She sang her own lyrics to the second verse:

I've got an island in the Caribbean,
And nothing about it is plebian…

"Ah! Music for musicians," I told an empty chair. "For the in-group. Palm trees, Brandy Alexanders, cool jazz."

The loud blast of a ship startled me. I checked the clock. 9 p.m.!

"Oh my God! My ship!" I leapt out of my seat, tossed a ten-dollar bill on the table, flung open the door, kicked off my spikes, stuffed them in my bag, and raced to the pier.

Too late. The ship had sailed. I blew it, blew my dreams. I wanted to hurl myself flat on my face on the wooden boards beneath my feet. I despised me. There I stood, alone, gaping at passengers on deck waving to anybody, to anything. One American musician on board, and she misses the boat. With Petrillo there! Oh, God! And tomorrow is New Year's Eve. My lifelong dream gone to hell because I'm so dumb.

The passengers faded into tiny dots that blended with the black of night. Slowly, almost blinded by profuse tears, I made my way back to the Grotto.

At 4 a.m., the Grotto floors were swept and washed, chairs piled on tables. Stapes, short for Stapleton, the bouncer's last name, and her partner Debbie served me chicken, vegetables and coffee.

"There must be a way I can get to Puerto Rico to board my ship," I said. "It won't leave for New York until night-time."

"Face it," Stapes said. "Tomorrow is New Year's Eve. Everything's booked. Planes, pilots, ships. New Year's Eve is New Year's Eve. Wire the captain, tell him you're sorry but you can't do anything. You'll meet him in New York next week. It's no big deal."

I wanted to jab her jaw with a left hook like the framed picture in Jack Dempsey's bar. "I don't care if every plane and ship and pilot in the hemisphere is booked," I said. "There's got to be a way out. Imagine! My name and photo plastered all over the ship. The president of the American Federation of Musicians on board. The only American musician, featured for New Year's Eve, and I pull a no-show. My only chance to get to Europe, and I blow it."

"We have a few friends with Cessnas," Debbie said. She was soft-spoken, in her late twenties. "Maybe somebody can fly you to Puerto Rico for a reasonable sum. At seven I'll start calling."

At seven a.m. in their small pink cottage, Stapes snored while Debbie called from their kitchen phone. "Thanks anyway," she said again and again. Hours passed.

"I hate myself," I told her. "If this were someone else's fault, I'd flatten them. But what do you do when the fault is yours? How can I be so dumb?"

"Don't be hard on yourself," Debbie urged. "It could happen to anybody. A night off, good drinks, good music."

In the bathroom mirror, I saw a street woman. Smeared mascara, messy hair, a low-cut black garment meant for midnight.

"Good news!" Debbie's voice cut through my self-abuse. "A friend of a friend will fly you to Puerto Rico for fifty bucks."

"Great! I've got travelers' checks."

Debbie threw me a shawl and hustled me into her car for a breakneck dash to the Caribe airport. I paid the pilot, and climbed into his four-seater Cessna.

I caught a taxi at the San Juan airport. The driver raced to the pier where I bolted up the gangplank to my cabin, washed, changed, and appeared on the bandstand at cocktail hour.

"Wait till you hear what happened!" I told Arnulf.

"*Feefahn!*" he cursed. "I don't want to hear it."

"What's the matter?"

"You had a good night with that guy?"

"What guy? What are you talking about?"

"The guy you slept with all night and all day."

"What?"

"Your cabin door was locked. All night, all day."

"Listen to me. I was at a club with great music. I heard the ship's blasts at nine. I raced to the docks, but it was too late."

"Hah! Good story. You were in your cabin with Petrillo."

"Petrillo? That fat old man? Don't be silly!"

"First he's a god. Now he's a fat old man."

"I can't believe that you don't believe me!"

"How did you get here if you missed the ship?"

"A pilot flew me in a Cessna."

"Hah! Good story. Private pilot on New Year's Eve."

Why didn't Arn believe me? What enraged me was not just

that he didn't believe me. It was the fact that his disbelief *mattered*. Why should I care if he or anybody didn't believe me? But I *did* care, and that stripped me of freedom. My mind was the problem, not Arnulf. Freedom was what I wanted. Freedom from *myself*.

14

DURBAN

May-September, 1976

Piercing screams and the crash of metal roused me at midnight. Two cars collided at the intersection where I'd almost hit a bus. Bodies lay on the road. Drivers fought.

I rang for an ambulance. A man asked if the bodies were black or white. (Ambulances were designated for both.) I couldn't see from the eleventh floor, but couldn't bear the thought of a "white" ambulance rejecting a black body or a black one leaving a white. "Both," I said, and hung up.

I fell into a deep sleep, dreaming that I lay in bed beneath a ceiling of square wooden tiles. Three male fingers lifted a corner tile stealthily, revealing two black eyes peering down at me. Without a sound, the long bony fingers replaced the tile. I screamed, and carted my sheets to the sofa.

Voices woke me at 2 a.m. Noise in the hallway was rare at that hour, but I heard them clearly. Men speaking Afrikaans. A commotion. Someone pulling the knob of the outside door to my apartment, trying to open it. Why? They'd never open it, not with that dead bolt in the floor. Still, I donned a robe, and locked my living room door.

The voices grew louder. I wished I understood Afrikaans. *Venster*, someone shouted. The word for "window" was the same in German. Why would they say that? The window in the narrow corridor between my living room door and the door to my apartment overlooked the back of the building. Anybody trying to get through that eleventh story window would kill themselves. But I heard the word clearly. *Venster*.

A commotion followed. High pitched voices mounting.

"*Optel—hold.*" Hold? The only way a man could get through the window would be for men outside the apartment to support him as he reached around the corner of the building, grasped the sill, broke the glass, and climbed through. But who would take that chance? He could fall eleven stories to his death.

Crash! Glass crashed on my corridor floor. *Someone was in my apartment!* Shouting in Afrikaans to men outside the door. Unlocking the dead bolt fixed to the floor. Opening the door. Afrikaner men, in my apartment! Advancing toward my living room.

I rushed to the window. Berea Road was lifeless. Stores shut, Caltex closed, nobody there. No one to scream to. I dialed the police. No answer. Nobody at the police station? I dialed again. No answer. *Why?* Police are always there. Police are police, BOSS is BOSS. Maybe some officers work for both agencies, but not all.

The men rattled the knob of my living room door. "Open, open!"

I rang Grice. No answer. Why? He kept a telephone near his bed. I dialed Percy Thomas, my Board member. He kept his phone on a night-table along with a butcher knife. No reply. Why? Oh! I get it. BOSS agents are manning the telephone relay station.

"Open! Open!" The men shook the door knob violently. I raced to the window again. Saw no one. Raced to the phone to try Thomas and Grice again. No answer. What am I doing, racing from phone to window to phone? Useless! Can't I see it?

Truth dawned. I had no choice of actions anymore. My only choice lay in *re*actions. The moment I became aware that I couldn't escape or call anyone, that all I could "do" was choose a *re*-action, a curious calm spread through my body and mind.

I eased myself into my recliner facing the living room door, legs outstretched. I wished I could write to my mother to tell her that I loved her, but it was too late. The door gave way.

Eight Afrikaner policemen stormed my living room, guns drawn. "Where's the Bantu? The Bantu?"

"No Africans here," I said. "No one here."

"Someone called police. Said a Bantu is here. A Bantu with a white woman!"

They thought they'd catch an African man in a sex act with a white woman. A contravention of the Immorality Act.

"Who called?" I asked.

"A neighbor."

I doubted it. The break-in could have been Step Ten in the *Manual of Harassment*. A ruse to shatter my sleep and life.

"Look around," I told the officer.

They searched with flashlights under my bed, the bathroom, the closets. While an officer about twenty years old poked behind and beneath my sofa, spaces barely big enough for rats, the telephone rang. I asked him to take the call.

He picked up the receiver. "Who? Not here." He hung up. "A man asked for an officer who's not here," he said.

"Probably the same one who calls every night. Curses and threatens."

"You must report that, Madame," the officer said.

"To whom?" I asked.

"To Colonel Steenkamp. Chief of Security Branch."

I packed. With a suitcase, typewriter, a ream of paper and notes, I drove to the home of Percy Thomas. One hour later, obscene, threatening phone calls began. I moved to the Royal Hotel, staying three days as the manager's guest. To the Holiday Inn for another three days as that manager's guest. To a residential hotel until I found nails in my tires. To a Catholic convent as a guest of Mother Superior.

By then, I'd become famous. Pictured on the front page of every English language newspaper. *The Star*: "Terror campaign against author…A woman has become the victim of a vicious campaign of terror and intimidation…aimed at stopping her work on a reference book dealing with outstanding Black South Africans…"

The Daily News captioned its four-column article, "Terror Campaign bid to end woman's work on book."

The Natal Mercury printed a denial. "No terror complaints for seven months…"

I deserved that. A year earlier, I'd hosted a party and invited the press, but excluded the Mercury reporter because of personal dislike. Friends had warned of repercussions.

A day after the *Mercury* denial, *The Daily News* retaliated with a four-column article captioned, "Victimised woman speaks out. Seven-Month Terror Campaign: The Facts." The article disclosed the erasure of tapes, disconnected brakes, the roaches in my car, the break-in, anonymous calls. I had become a celebrated culprit, which swelled my circle of black friends, but narrowed my circle of Indians and whites. When whites I knew shunned me on the street, I felt like a rape victim after the press exposed the rape.

What matters, I told myself, is not what others think of me. It's what I am doing. I'm writing about a dimension of South Africa's history that otherwise might be lost. A book about blacks who gave something back to their people. Everyone has something to give, in which all, thereby, are entitled to share.

Tension between students and government, demanding that Afrikaans should be the official medium of instruction, peaked in June. On the sixteenth, youth went on strike. They boycotted classes, refused to write exams, and marched in protest. They waved posters, chanting, *Amandla Awethu!* (*Freedom Now!*)

Armed police threw gas canisters, but the students marched ahead. Police opened fire, students screamed, ran, fell. By the end of the day, over five hundred lay dead. South Africa's era of quiet resistance had ended.

My Board insisted that I leave Durban. I was too well known. My green Toyota, too quickly spotted. I moved to an apartment in Pinetown, less than an hour's drive from Durban. To a new building with giant wings back-angled like a plane. No one recognized me. No one followed me. No calls woke me at night. Until the call came from Queens, New York. From the superintendent of the building where my mother lived.

"Her mind is going," he said. "Come back, fast."

I had to go. I was her only child. I packed, stored my furniture, borrowed cash for a return ticket, and left. With all my notes for the *Who's Who of Black South Africans*.

15

NEW YORK
1976-77

"Who are *you*?" Mom asked. She stood in the foyer in a brown button-down housedress. A sitcom played on TV in the living room. A mound of dust on the fake fireplace looked like golden snow in the late day sun.

I hugged her. "I'm your daughter, Mom."

"Daughter?"

Tears pressed forward as I took her hand, led her to the living room, and turned off the TV. We sat on the sofa, side by side.

When I had seen my mother four years earlier, her black hair was brushed and fluffed. Mascara, full and thick. Rouge, lipstick, a stylish suit. Yet here she was, hair gray and matted like an Indian yogi. No make-up. A housedress with torn pockets. Grasping my hand tightly, like she feared I'd drop it. Gazing at me with a child's wide eyes. That's what tore at my heart—her need for me. Our roles, reversed.

Guilt plagued me. She'd lived alone too long. Had she lived with me, her mind might not have deteriorated. But I'd make up for it. I'd care for her from then on. Bring her back to South Africa. To a safe apartment, with cooking, cleaning, and nursing help.

Memories flooded my brain as we gazed at each other. How she would lift me onto that same sofa when I was three. Lay a notebook in my lap, a pencil in my hand, and move my fingers to write "A," "B," "C." The double-story dollhouse she gave me when I read a book at four. The night she stayed up when I had chicken pox, holding my hands so I wouldn't scratch and scar my face. The fiddle she bought when I turned six because she saw "the music in me." And the squat, bushy-haired Professor Moskoffian whom she hired to teach me in our living room. A teacher who liked to stand when he played, and liked me to stand when I listened. "It shows respect," he'd said.

One day he played "My Country 'Tis of Thee" in the key of G, but played an F natural.

"It should be F sharp," I interrupted.

"You telling teacher how to play?"

He pressed harder on the strings, deliberately playing the wrong note. I got mad, and raised my bow to strike his behind because that's where Mom struck me when she was mad. I swung. My bow hit the wall and split, and sharp wooden splinters pierced his buttocks. He jumped, cursed, and probed the rip with his fingers as Mom rushed in.

"What happened?"

"She—" he pointed at me with his bow "—she struck me."

"My daughter struck you? Where?"

"Here, here," he shouted, pointing to the torn seat of his trousers.

Mom roared with laughter. The professor slammed his violin into its case and stalked out, shouting in his native Armenian with every backward glance.

When Dad came home, Mom showed him my broken bow. "See these split ends? They punctured the professor's rear end. I told you Shirley was born with a musical ear."

"Shirley was born with chutzpah," Dad said.

I cleared out Mom's apartment, and brought her to a Boston doctor of alternative medicine renowned for slowing the progress of dementia. He prescribed a vegetarian diet, Chinese herbal packs, massages, and sitz baths. If she improved, I could bring her back to South Africa, he told me. If not, a foreign land would add to her disorientation.

My mother would *have* to recover.

Our furnished two-bedroom apartment on Boston's south side faced an old oak tree. The raucous laughter from the Irish pub below us sounded to Mom's ears like the howls of woodland life. She thought we'd moved to a forest. She took no notice of the scuffed table and chairs, the worn sofa, the ants that scurried across the kitchen floor.

An aide arrived every morning to cook breakfast and clean the apartment while I worked part-time as a proofreader in a printing press. Back at noon, I cooked lunch, ate with Mom, and while she rested, worked on the *Who's Who*. I didn't need a safe deposit box for my manuscript, nor did I hide carbon copies under my mattress. But I missed South Africa. I missed the land, my friends, the men on my Board who fueled my grit.

Mom improved. At times, she recalled what she'd eaten the previous day, or a radio program she'd heard. That encouraged me. I applied more herbal packs to her stomach. Massaged her more often. Gave her more sitz baths. Set a date for our departure. I imaged us in Durban, lunching at the Royal, driving along the beachfront.

But at times, Mom seemed worse. Like when she couldn't find the bathroom, even as she passed it. Or when she called me by my father's name, "because you take care of everything." At such moments, I felt torn by the decision I might have to make—South Africa or my mother. I could not turn my back on either one.

Rising before dawn, rushing to the Chinese market for fresh herbs, hurrying back to prepare packs for the aide to apply, running to catch a bus to work, back at lunch to cook, eat, prepare and apply more packs to Mom's stomach, massage her, and then work on my book, became too much.

One afternoon, while I set up my typewriter, Mom said she wanted a haircut. I picked up her magnifier, a sturdy one with a purple handle, to scan the telephone directory for a nearby salon.

"That's *my* magnifier!" she shrieked.

That did it. I flung the magnifier at the wall. It struck with a bang, scattering shards of glass over the kitchen floor. I got up and left.

Downstairs in the Irish pub, I asked the bartender to set 'em up. "Scotch on the rocks. Three. One, two, three."

Fifteen years had passed since I'd tasted scotch, but I drank all three. Relaxed, I returned to the apartment, apologized, cleaned the mess, and called a taxi to go to the hairdresser.

Every evening, Mom reclined on the high-backed gray sofa, stretching her skinny legs across its seats. I'd cover them with a throw, and turn on my cassette recorder to re-tape the global adventures that South African security police had wiped out. Mom loved to listen. This time, no one would wave a magnet over my cassettes. And one day, after the black Who's Who was published, I would write a memoir.

The night my mother tried to chew a candle, I knew I'd lost the battle. Massages, stomach packs, and sitz baths were too little, too late. South Africa was out, her doctor told me. Even if I stayed in America, I couldn't care for her. Mom needed medical supervision twenty-four hours a day.

I chose a nursing home in south Florida. Warm weather agreed with Mom, and a nearby friend would visit her regularly.

On my last day in the States, Mom and I sat on the veranda of the nursing home, surrounded by palm trees, listening to crickets, and holding hands. She wore a yellow cotton dress and her favorite wide-brimmed straw hat. I asked her to forgive me for leaving her alone in the past, and for leaving her alone again. I wept when I kissed her goodbye, cradling her face in my hands. Mom giggled. She no longer knew who I was.

My ticket to South Africa routed me from Miami to Rio, Rio to Luanda, Angola, Luanda to Johannesburg. A mix of depression, exhilaration and anxiety pursued me. My attaché case held my finished manuscript and the tapes of my adventures. Even if security agents seized it on arrival at Jan Smuts airport, my manuscript would be published. A New York attorney kept a copy, and a copy of my personal tapes.

During my year in Boston, Steve Biko had been murdered, the thirty-one-year-old founder of the Black Consciousness movement. I'd met him when he visited Inanda Seminary. As he left the school that day, walking alone to a car, I told him to be careful.

"Don't worry," he told me. "They'll never get me."

They did. Security Police detained and interrogated him, stripped him naked, hammered his head, manacled him to a metal grille, and transported him nude in the back of a jeep, half-dead, for a twelve-hour ride to Pretoria Central Prison. He died of brain damage on the floor of his cell. Biko's death swelled black anger, polarized blacks, and triggered an intense government crackdown.

I recalled all this while the propellers slowed at the Johannesburg airport, and the plane taxied to a halt. Despite the mental images, my anxiety dissolved. I was ready.

16

DURBAN
1978

My third floor apartment in Broadwindsor Court overlooked Broad Street, a main artery that ran through central Durban. When my telephone rang, I expected to hear obscene threats, but didn't. Before I opened my car door, I checked for crawling insects on the wheel and seats, but saw nothing. No one tampered with my brakes. Nobody followed me. BOSS and Security Branch had done all they could to prevent me from completing my book, but they failed. Only one step remained: publication.

Ned Greer sat at the senior editor's desk of Oxford University Press in Capetown. A small, edgy man with a high pitched voice. He thumbed through a few pages of my manuscript. "Looks interesting," he said. "Let me take a deeper look. You can wait in the outer office."

Periodicals on a side table listed distinguished authors of Oxford's scholarly publications. Compared with them, I stood no chance.

"You can see Mr. Greer now," the receptionist said in a BBC accent.

I dragged my feet toward his office, certain that he'd say, *Thank you. It's not for us.* I had dared to approach the world's most highly respected publisher, but never thought they'd accept my manuscript. I was prepared to ask Greer which publisher he'd suggest on the list I'd brought with me.

"We'll take it," Greer said.

I was sure I misunderstood.

"We'll take it," he repeated. "It's well written, and this is the right time for an African *Who's Who*. I want to do it fast," he said. "Expect the first galleys in a month."

While I sat in a smaller office reading over the terms of the contract and signing next to Xs, I felt like I was playing a part in a film. This couldn't be happening to me. Deane? Published by Oxford? I wasn't in the same class as Oxford authors. I was just a musician. A traveler. Someone who believed that blacks needed recognition. Even though I'd written a book, I didn't see myself as a writer.

That evening, I rang Grice from my room in a small Capetown hotel. "Accepted!" I shrieked.

"Accepted?" he asked. "By whom? Where?"

I needed to be careful, sure that his telephone was tapped. "It reminds me of where you studied." Grice had gone to Cambridge.

For several seconds I heard nothing. Then a gasp. "You don't mean it!"

"I mean it!"

Next day I met with the young woman responsible for Oxford's book jackets. She made notes as I spoke. "Performed as classical & jazz accordionist on TV in NY, Chicago, Stockholm, Vienna, Milan, and through Africa. First woman to drive a Land Rover alone from England to India. Managed a Tibetan refugee camp in Nepal. As PRO of Inanda Seminary, raised half a million rand in two and a half years. Was avid chess player and student pilot..."

That was the first time in her career, she said, that she'd filled a jacket flap without padding. Her remark made up for the inadequacy I felt in that scholarly milieu.

I wanted my name to read, *Dee Shirley Deane*.

The bulky Oxford envelope with the first set of galleys arrived in February, the warmest month of the year in South Africa. I opened it at my writing desk beneath an open window. Laid a paper weight on the galleys, and another on the corresponding manuscript.

All words, numbers and commas of Sibusiso Bengu's bio-data were correct. Next, his personality portrait. First mistake: A missing sentence. *"We're mobilizing people to struggle for their freedom."* I noted in the margin, "Deletion. See original."

I read on. Another deletion: *"We first have to depose the White masters in our own minds."* Again I noted, "Deletion. See original."

Well, the galleys were a rush job. Mistakes are inevitable.

Gone was Constance Mqwebu's sentence, *"There are no African institutions for the blind."* Again I wrote, "Deletion. See original."

Gone was Virginia Gcabashe's *"Freedom has to happen here..."*

Uneasiness stirred in the pit of my stomach. Gone was Obed Kunene's experience as a black guest in an "international" hotel where he had slept in white beds, showered in their baths, used their knives and forks, and the heavens didn't fall.

I read on. "Bhengu-Nene was grateful to the government for the Natal Code of Bantu Law because it offered her protection."

What? Grateful? For protection? Nene told me that the Natal Code of Bantu Law bound women to the guardianship of their next-of-kin males even if the males were their sixteen-year old kids!

When I read the entry for Nokukanya Lutuli, wife of the Nobel Prize winner, and noted the missing, *"decision-making must belong to us all,"* I tossed the galleys on the floor, stomped on them, called Grice, and said I was flying to Oxford in Britain to report the manipulation of my manuscript.

He suggested that we fly to Capetown first. "Maybe Greer is under government pressure."

Even the heavens fumed. Rain pounded the windows of the boardroom at Oxford University Press. Lightning cut off the lights. Greer sat at the end of a long narrow table in the darkened room. Grice and I faced one another, he on Greer's left, me on his right. He had told me to keep quiet unless Greer asked me a question. I felt too livid to speak, anyway. Too livid to look at Greer. I focused on a wall painting. Table Mountain, with its uninspiring table-top.

Grice's voice was almost inaudible as he spoke of how blacks in my book needed to be heard. How vital it was for South African whites to hear what they had to say. Greer concurred, nodding, leaning toward Grice to hear him. Grice lowered his voice even more. Greer leaned further toward him, cocking his left ear. Grice was compelling him to yield. First, physically. I'd never witnessed anything like it. Had I spoken, I'd have shouted. Greer would have leaned as far back from me as he could. I'd have hurled insults, threatened to have Oxford's headquarters remove him from his pedestal. And I'd have lost.

The two men talked in Greer's office for a few minutes. Grice did not tell me what transpired. He said only that he didn't ask Greer why he altered my manuscript, or if the government had pressured him. That didn't matter. Only the outcome mattered, the restoration of my original manuscript.

During the evening launch of the *Who's Who,* the twenty-second of June, 1978 at Grice's Durban home, he addressed the press, diplomatic corps, church officials, company directors, and friends. "Ladies and gentlemen," he began, "I always thought I knew what the word *perseverance* meant until I met Shirley Deane."

Articles appeared in *The Natal Witness,* the *Financial Mail*, *Ilanga*, *Johannesburg Star*, *The Daily News.* The *Rand Daily Mail* wrote that the book reinforced belief in what the human spirit can accomplish. *The Natal Mercury* published two reviews and a full page article captioned, "Dee: a most remarkable woman…" Johannesburg's *Daily Star* captioned its long article, "Terror tactics failed to stop her book."

I read the articles like I'd read about strangers. I never thought of myself as courageous. I was merely insistent. Determined to attain whatever goal I set for myself. My dogged insistence rather than courage had brought my book to fruition.

The American Library Association wrote that I'd created "a much-needed work for developing black pride in a country split by apartheid..." I liked that. The spectacle of men ashamed of their blackness in my presence always pained me, as if my color were responsible for their shame.

Tributes from the University of South Carolina, Northwestern

University, and the *Library Journal* surprised me. I hadn't anticipated foreign interest. Best of all, the *Church Times of London* wrote that "...the variety and human quality of African achievement in the inhuman limitations of the Republic...come shining through." They'd pinpointed the single purpose for which I wrote the book.

BBC wired a request for an interview, which I accepted. I would stop in London en route to the States to visit my mother.

Before I left, a Social Science professor in Johannesburg called. A farmer he knew had deserted fourteen thousand acres, fleeing rebels in his area—the Orange Free State in central South Africa. Potatoes, wheat, corn, cattle, sheep. A few academics had formed a committee to discuss a possible multi-racial experiment on the property. He'd read about me. Would I be interested, he wanted to know.

"Of course, I'm interested!" I said. "Of course!"

A few years earlier, I'd visited Auroville, the "City of Tomorrow" in south India, founded to realize unity in diversity. UNESCO commended it as "a project of importance to the future of humanity." Why not, I thought, build a "City of Tomorrow" in South Africa?

That night, I lay in bed, painting a mental picture of a model town where blacks, whites, Indians and Coloreds could discover unity in diversity. Apartheid laws would forbid it, but United Nations backing could make the project possible.

Races and tribes whom the government had divided—Zulus, Sothos, Tswanas, Xhosas—would live together. We'd build an industrial zone like at Auroville. Men and women working in cottage industries toward self-supporting townships. Threading beads, weaving baskets, painting ceremonial masks. Farms would provide self-sustainable living. Cows for pure milk. Chickens for free-range eggs. Herbs for medicines.

We could erect a Temple to Truth that embodies the principles of all religions. In that way, we would transform not only the land, but also, our collective consciousness.

Ah! This is a project, I told myself, nodding off to sleep. After all, a book is just a book.

An Unreasonable Woman

In search of meaning around the globe

PART II

17

GOODBYE, AMERICA!

June, 1956

Mid-day on Saturday, June 30th, 1956, passengers crowded the deck of the *M/S Oslofjord* as the cruise ship's gangplank swung up and away from the Manhattan pier. I was jammed against the railing by people pressing forward to shout to family and friends below: "Don't forget to water my plants!"

I blew kisses to Mom and Dad. "Bye, folks. Bye, Manhattan!"

The cruise took just two months, but Mom didn't like the thought of her only child sailing to the Land of the Midnight Sun. Iceland, Norway, Sweden, Denmark, Finland—countries as alien as a far-away planet. She'd have felt much worse had she known that I wouldn't be on the ship when it returned.

Dad packed his pipe, struck a kitchen match, puffed hard. He tugged at the strap of the old camera slung on his left shoulder, and rocked from side to side. I loved him, but sensed that I might never hear his Irish brogue again, or see his warm Irish smile.

I was twenty-seven, but that day felt like the first day of my life. I'd lived like an alien. I didn't belong. A puppet dangling from strings pulled by agents and audiences. Conforming to the codes of show business. Fishtail gowns, seductive smiles. Working six hours a night for money to buy things I didn't want. Slotted into the market's niches.

From then on, I'd carve my own. I'd work my way from continent to continent. I'd see every bit of the globe. I'd find answers to questions that haunted me: *Does anything exist that doesn't change? Can I find anything in the world worth knocking myself out for? Why am I so different, yearning for a freedom I can't even define?*

All my life, I'd lived from the outside in. From now on, I'd live from the inside out. No guidelines. No parameters. No restrictions. I'd wear baggy pants or unsewn rags if I liked. I'd compose *Odes to Thoreau.*

"Too risky," friends had said. "That kind of life is insecure."

I must have been standing on my head, seeing the world upside down, because I felt secure with that insecurity. On the deck around me were "secure" folks. Most, over sixty, had probably worked for forty years to save the money for that cruise. Their hair was gray, their eyesight poor, their hearing weak. That kind of security did not move me. I wanted to see the world while I was young.

"Now is the Hour" played through loudspeakers, the song that topped the Hit Parade. Passengers sang and swayed.

Now is the hour that we must say goodbye.
Soon we'll be sailing, far across the sea...

Below on the pier, Mom blew a kiss and I returned it. I wished I had thanked her for making me practice scales. I wouldn't have been on that ship without a mastery of the accordion. If only I'd hugged her and said, "Thanks, Mom." But whenever I tried, my arms stuck to my sides.

She cried. Dad puffed hard on his pipe. Good thing they didn't know that I wouldn't be back until I'd seen the whole world. Good thing they didn't know that all I had was a hundred bucks.

Tugboats nudged our liner into the harbor. I loved to watch those symbols of humility—the eyes, ears, and muscles of an ocean liner but only a tenth its size. They swung us around to face the open sea. Broad, boundless, unknowable, like my life.

The midsummer sun dazzled the water like footlights on a world stage. Loud blasts signaled that we were ready. The tugs released their hold. A surge of power, as slow and irresistible as fate, launched the *M/S Oslofjord,* and my life.

18

M/S OSLOFJORD & SCANDINAVIA

June, 1956

The billboard in the port side smoking lounge listed activities for the day. Bridge tournaments, deck games, bingo, ping-pong. A talk on *Majestic Norway* by Liaison Officer, Joe Granquist. Latin dances with Marlene and Michael. A screening of *Summertime* with Katherine Hepburn and Rosanno Brazzi.

Our trio played for dinner and dancing. We jammed to my favorites—"All the Things You Are," "Tenderly," "In the Mood." I loved playing with the Norwegian musicians. They listened to my phrasing and followed my lead as though we'd played together for years.

In Reykjavik, passengers lined up at the banking office for Icelandic currency, chatting about bargains they'd find. Not me, with only a hundred bucks to my name. Money wouldn't have been a problem if I could have worked in Norway when we got there. But Thomas Cook Agency insisted I play on board until we reached Le Havre. From there, I'd head back to Norway, overland. A train to Paris. Another train to northern Germany. A hired car to the harbor. A boat to Sweden. A train to Oslo. I'd arrive penniless, like my mother's parents arrived on Ellis Island, sixty years earlier.

While passengers toured Reykjavik, I studied Norwegian and practiced for my Oslo audition—on my bed. Cabin A66 had no room for chairs.

My accordion, amp, microphones, extension cords, converters, transformers, and adapters for the ship and Europe, and portfolios of press reviews, photos, and music, lay under the bed. My Gründig recorder, tape reels, record player, records, radio, typewriter, camera equipment, maps and language books lay stacked along a wall. Along the other, suitcases with toiletries, cosmetics, winter and summer clothes, theatrical gowns, and stocks of silica gel to keep the accordion moisture-free so the keys wouldn't stick.

I'd haul my possessions around the world like a ball and chain. A donkey carting its master's house. But this was no holiday, this was life as usual. Transplanted.

At Oslo, Arnulf wheeled out my accordion for the audition. If I passed, I'd have a job when I returned to Norway. If I failed—I dared not think of it.

A customs officer pointed to the case. "Open."

"That's just my accordion. I'm auditioning for the State Booking Agency."

"Open."

I unlocked it.

"Value?"

I showed him my old receipt.

"Duty. You have to pay duty."

"It's only for two hours."

"Even for two minutes you pay duty."

"That's absurd!"

"Wait," Arnulf said. He hurried to his cabin, brought back a shoebox, and exchanged hushed words with the officer. The official turned to the right, left, behind him. He took it.

"Okay," he told me, "Go. Go now."

"Arnulf, what in the world was in that shoebox?"

"Shhh," he whispered. "Bourbon."

The audition room had a few hard chairs, a table, an upright piano, and snare drums in a corner. Three men from the State Booking Agency sat facing me, papers and pens in hand. I could have been a high school student taking an oral exam.

I pulled on my accordion in a flood of late day sunlight, played "Flight of the Bumble Bee," "A Foggy Day in London Town," with Arnulf on drums, and the piece I'd practiced for weeks: A tale that I narrated in Norwegian about mystical mountain beings while playing an accordion rendition of a Grieg folksong.

The men applauded like I'd played a concerto. I stunned them, they said. They never heard an accordion sound like that. They'd launch me on Oslo radio. Book me at Oslo's newest hotel. Book our trio when Arnulf and Knut returned to Oslo.

While they thumbed through my press clippings, I drew their eyes to my fishtail gown. "Shall I wear this?" I asked.

"No, no," the director said. "Dress simply. Don't detract from your sound."

I could have hugged him.

Now I had a job lined up in Oslo, but I'd have to play on board until the ship arrived at the last port in Europe before it sailed to the States. We docked at Stockholm, Helsinki, Copenhagen, Hamburg. Finally, Le Havre. Arnulf, Knut and Finn took an hour to haul my luggage down the gangplank and into a taxi. They stacked suitcases on the front and back seats, left a small space for me, packed the trunk, tied up the bags that stuck out, and piled the rest on the roof.

We don't possess possessions, I thought. They possess us.

I gave Arnulf a letter to give my mom when their ship arrived in New York. I wrote that I wouldn't be coming back, that I'd gotten a contract to play in Oslo. I asked them to give Arnulf some sugarless gum for me. And straws from the A&P that you put in milk to taste like chocolate.

Paris was warm and humid on the August day that I booked into the Newton hotel on the Rue de l'Arcade.

"Two dollars and fifty cents for one night," the desk clerk said.

"Hot water?" I asked.

"For baths, extra cost."

"How much?"

"Two-hundred fifty francs. About seventy-five U.S. cents."

I could afford one night, one bath, one meal.

Next day I boarded a train to Grossenbrode, Germany, a small town that looked like a page from *Hansel and Gretel*. Six porters carried my luggage to a harbor car that would take me to Heiligenhafen ("holy harbor") for a boat to Malmo in Sweden. The whole town watched the spectacle. A foreign woman with six porters and twelve bags. I focused straight ahead.

From Malmo, more porters and taxis hauled my bags to the station for a train to Oslo. When my taxi arrived at Arnulf's home on Tåsenveien Street, the door of every home was ajar. Women stood in their doorways like guards, arms folded, watching my taxi driver remove bags from the inside, the roof, the trunk.

For the first time, I missed New York City. I craved the anonymity of East Forty-Ninth Street where you never see the same person twice.

Grannies, folks my age, and kids packed Oslo's broadcasting studio. I'd never played for such a wide age range. How would they respond to my bold original—what an accordion concerto would sound like if Grieg had written it? Would they understand my blend of Bach and jazz?

I played my opening chords, edgy. But sixteen bars later, I could have been Heifitz at Carnegie Hall. Eyes were riveted on my left hand skipping around the bass, and my right hand racing up and down the keys, clicking shifts between notes to alter the tone. Had I worn overalls, it wouldn't have mattered.

The audience gave me a standing ovation. Listeners called. Could Miss Deane play the Hotel Atlantic in Stavanger? The Flower Exhibition in Fredrikstad? The new hotel in Elverum?

Next day, the *Aftenposten* printed a review with my photo. The reporter wrote that my arrangements "made great success. She showed her musical tools, and demonstrated different effects. She was fantastic."

"*Americans like to look,*" I wrote Mom, "*but Norwegians like to listen.*" I felt like a debutante at a coming-out party.

Arnulf and Knut returned to Oslo with bottles of Scotch, cans of meat, A&P straws, and a note from my parents asking me to return.

On our first hotel performance as a trio, the rotating swish of Arnulf's drum brushes, and Knut's steady moving bass beat summoned feelings in me that I couldn't tap alone. Playing solo was like growing up an only child. You had to inspire yourself. Playing with bass and drums was like seeing my own reflection through multiple mirrors.

After our opening show, we partied in a friend's walk-up flat. Golden haired Britt wore no makeup, and sang like Peggy Lee. Her bald-headed pianist husband, twenty years her senior, played piano. I sat on a couch between them drinking aquavit, an innocent looking potato whiskey. Musicians drank, joked, and crooned. A few on chairs, some on the floor. Arnulf drummed on the rug with two soup ladles.

Peer's father stepped out of his bedroom in pajamas to go to the bathroom.

"He doesn't mind the noise?" I asked Britt.

"He's used to it. This flat is his. Couples wait years to get a flat of their own."

Britt's oval face shone like a clear mirror through which I saw myself. I saw my intolerance, the distinctive mark of an American. I was living at the home of Arnulf's parents, already cold, though this was summer. Arn's joke about having central heating because the wood stove was in the center of his house did not amuse me.

His mother toiled for hours in her kitchen, preparing herring, cod, salmon, trout, lutefisk, and stockfish. She poached, grilled, baked, fried, marinated and pickled, but I seldom smiled. I disliked fish, and couldn't tell her. They had no meat.

Norway's transportation vexed me even more than its food. I waited half an hour on a trolley queue to go to an *apotheque* for toothpaste. On another queue to go to a *parfumerie* for skin cream. On a third to buy candy at a *chocolado* shop. Two hours to buy three things that Americans get in five minutes at Whelan's drug store. I'd fume on my rough trolley seat. Deane, wasting half a day on public transport! And while I fumed, the jovial Nordic goddesses seated around me delighted in their good fortune. A ride to where they wanted to go. Good company. A seat.

I longed to change, but it was too late. Too late for a woman born and bred in New York City. I saw it clearly. The less people have, the more tolerant they are. The more spoiled, the less they put up with. It works like a seesaw.

More English than Danish echoed through the crowded Foreigners' Bar in Copenhagen. Cockney accents, Brooklynites, Australian English. Women with their men, women with women, men with men. Swedes, Brits, Germans sharing jokes. Drinking Brandy Alexanders, Manhattans, beer, wine.

Only I sat alone, at the end of the bar. Nobody to talk to. Why didn't somebody ask my name? Where I came from, what I was doing there. I'd have told them I was in show business on a two-week holiday. I'd played Norway, and I'd play Sweden after my break. But nobody cared. Why should they? I chose this lonely path. I had friends in New York, but gave them up for the world. I wasn't sorry. I just wished somebody would talk to me.

A thirtyish woman in jeans, freckled and fragile, pushed through the crowd to my end of the bar. "Manhattan," she called to the bartender. "Strong."

"Make it two," I added.

Three Manhattans later, we were friends. Patti Shore worked in Nuremberg as principal of a school for dependents of U.S. military personnel. In her spare time, she played pool with GIs, and healed wounds caused by white military families who resented blacks hiring German domestic help. She got engaged to a Dane—Henri Pelletier. But a month before the wedding, he confessed that he preferred men, and returned to Copenhagen.

Patti invited me to a party at his penthouse. Henri had an accordion, she said.

Henri's living room was bare. Just an oriental rug, oversized cushions around the walls, exotic plants beneath tall windows. Bottles of wine and champagne, and plates of Danish cheese and biscuits were spread on a table in an adjoining corridor.

Patti and I were the only women among twenty artists and actors.

She poured drinks while they danced with one another. When the music stopped, she sang German beer songs. "In Germany I have to act respectable," she said. "Here, I let my hair down."

Henri brought his accordion. "Mademoiselle, music, please."

For an hour, I played pops and the American sing-alongs I'd always abhorred. I wondered how Danes knew the words to songs like "Let Me Call You Sweetheart," "Alexander's Ragtime Band," and "I've Been Workin' on the Railroad."

Patti told me I'd be a hit at military bases in Germany. "I'll start you off," she said.

That night in bed, I replayed the evening. I walk into a strange bar in a strange city and country. An American woman invites me to a party where the host has an accordion. I play, and she offers to start me off in Germany. *What a coincidence!*

Like my last night at Jack Dempsey's on Broadway. I felt depressed, with no way to get to Europe. In walk three musicians who ask me to jam on their ship. Next day, I'm offered free passage across the Atlantic. Can that be coincidence? If not, what is it? God? Can we know God? Or are we stuck forever with blind faith?

The following morning, a Sunday, I strolled through Copenhagen's gardens and squares, along tree-lined avenues and down crooked streets. Boys on bicycles rode by and winked. I passed red brick buildings that housed government ministries, and a pink home where a woman sat on the porch and hooted with a cigar in her mouth.

An old Catholic church sparked my curiosity. Its weathered mahogany door was unlocked. I stepped inside and liked the feel of it. The musty air, the dim light that showed faded paintings on the wall.

I moved down the aisle, facing a bigger-than-life-sized crucifix. My thoughts ceased. I lost awareness of my surroundings, my body and identity. Twenty minutes passed like that, transfixed and immobile.

When normal consciousness returned, I thought about the day in a Piper Cub. I was about to crash into power poles, but a force intervened to save me. Did that same force root my feet to the ground, and stop my thoughts? If so, why?

I wanted answers, but all I got were more questions.

19

SWEDEN TO GERMANY

1957

I leaned back as far as my seat would allow on the overnight train from Stockholm to the port of Malmo. I kept my hands in my lap lest they touch Alvar by mistake. He sat next to me, snoring, his mouth wide open.

The three months that passed since I left Copenhagen ran through my mind like a film. Sweden's leading entertainment agency, *Konsertbolaget*, had booked me on TV in Stockholm and as a solo act at the Bacchi Vapen, a club owned by the fiancé of actress Sonja Henie. It was at the club where I met Alvar.

"I read about you in the press," he said. A small-boned man with pale lips, and eyes that drooped like a bloodhound's. "I'm Alvar Olsson, mechanical engineer."

His handshake felt limp. We were jammed together at the packed bar by patrons toasting cocktails and belting orders to the bartender. I told Alvar that my drummer and bassist would arrive from Oslo the following week. We were booked in northern Sweden.

I was sipping a martini, biting into the olive, when he said, "Train connections to the north are poor. I have two cars. I'll lend you one if you have an international license."

I felt a push to say what I'd say in New York. "*Tell me another one.*" But next day, I got an international license. And I got Alvar's car.

For three months, drummer Arnulf, bassist Ivar and I played luxury hotels in towns throughout Sweden. Between engagements, the Norwegians rode with me while Alvar drove ahead with our luggage. He hauled our instruments into hotels where there weren't enough porters. Brought us to his parents' home on Lake Karlstad for lunch. Translated for us. Took us to dinner. Answered our questions, but seldom asked any.

When our contracts ended, we convoyed back to the Stockholm Railway Station, Alvar ahead, with our luggage. "That guy is too good to be true," Arnulf remarked.

The Norwegians and I waited on the platform, hugging as their train to Oslo pulled in. They'd played a key role in my life. They stopped for a drink at Jack Dempsey's on Broadway at the right time. Arranged my cruise to Europe at the right time. But our link was over. We were brought together like atoms that bump into one another and move on. Like all relationships, short or long, but always temporary.

I was off to Nuremberg where I would stay with Patti Shore on her Army base. Alvar offered to help with my luggage to Nuremberg. Then he'd fly to Spain for a holiday. I preferred to travel alone, but dreaded hauling my twelve cases, scouting for porters, checking that nothing was missing.

"Okay," I told him, "but I want to make it clear. We won't share hotel rooms."

We got the overnight train from Stockholm to Malmo where we boarded a boat to Copenhagen. There, a Scandinavian Airlines clerk informed us that Nuremberg had no airport. We'd have to fly to Frankfurt and take a train from there.

"Can I bring my twelve suitcases?" I asked.

"Oh, no," she said. "Two only. Send the rest by rail."

I turned to Alvar. "I can't cope with my luggage, Alvar. I'm beat."

"Don't worry," he said, "I'll do it."

He loaded my suitcases, accordion and amp with great care into a taxi and climbed into the front, placing two small bags in his lap, and one under his feet. "Train station," he told the cabbie.

Alvar was such a good man. The dullest I'd ever met, but who couldn't trust him? Besides, I'd met his parents.

Patti picked us up at the Nuremberg train station and dropped Alvar off at the Kaiserhof Hotel. He'd wait there until my luggage arrived, he said, since the shipping documents were in his name.

"When your stuff comes," he told me, "I'll get it and call you. You'll pick it up, and I'll go on to Spain."

"You're lucky to have a friend like that," Patti said, as we drove off.

I'd never been on a military base. Snack bars with hotdogs, hamburgers and coke. A theatre screening American films. Bowling alleys, poolrooms, a hospital, a library with the *New York Times* and *Chicago Tribune*. No wonder Americans rarely left base.

Four days later, Alvar called. "Meet me at the Reichhof Hotel," he said.

"The Reichhof? But you were staying at the Kaiserhof."

He hung up. His voice sounded eerie, like an echo. Patti was working so I taxied to the Reichhof. Climbed to the second floor, and knocked. Alvar opened the door a crack. His hair was disheveled, his lips, white.

"What are you doing here?" I asked. "Why didn't you stay at the Kaiserhof?"

He stood mute. I checked his room. "Where's my luggage?"

A police officer raced up the steps. "*Politzei*," he roared. "Come!"

"Me?" I asked.

"Both!"

We followed him to a police car, and sat in back. "What's going on?" I asked.

The cop didn't reply, and Alvar sat like a waxed display. At the prison, two officers hauled him to a cell. Another led me to a room, and locked it from the outside. The room was bare but for two chairs and a table with a pitcher of water and cups. A door at the back led to a toilet.

I banged on the outside door. "What's going on? Somebody, call the American Consulate. Please!"

A cop unlocked the door. Two GIs stormed in.

"Wow!" the corporal said. His eyebrows snaked like a caterpillar. "A Yankee chick in the klink! Whatcha doin' here?"

"I don't know. Can you get me out?"

"Whaddya do?" the private asked, scanning my skirt and legs.

"Play accordion."

"Accordion? I love accordion. You play polkas?"

"For God's sake! I'm locked in the klink, and you're asking about polkas!"

"Got your accordion here?"

"Forget my accordion! Can you call the Consulate?"

"Ain't none here. That's why the cops called the base. They figured you work for the army."

"Then get me an interpreter. A German who speaks English."

Alone, I plopped myself on the wooden chair. What am I doing here? Why did Alvar look so weird? Where's my baggage?

A middle-aged man in plain clothes entered. "I am Herr Schrader, criminal police interpreter." He spoke slowly, distinctly. "Tell me why you are here."

"I have no idea, sir."

"Then wait, please."

He left and returned ten minutes later. "Are you Mrs. Olsson?"

"No! I'm Shirley Deane."

"Mr. Olsson said you are Mrs. Olsson."

"I don't care what he said. I'm not anybody's wife. I'm Shirley Deane."

"Mr. Olsson was staying at the Kaiserhof Hotel."

"I know."

"He made long distance calls to Sweden, Spain, and the U.S. Ran up a bill of three-hundred dollars. The hotel manager demanded money. He wouldn't pay. He slipped out the back door, and booked into the Reichhof Hotel, signing in as Mr. and Mrs. Olsson. His wife would join him shortly, he told the desk manager. When the police found him and demanded money, Olsson said he had no money, but he had twelve cases at the train station that came from Copenhagen. They were worth ten thousand dollars."

"What? Those aren't his! They're mine!"

Schrader left again. On return, he said that the Nuremberg train station did not have my luggage.

"Then it's still in Copenhagen," I said. "Ask Olsson for the receipt. And please get me out."

"Madame, I am not a policeman. I am only an interpreter for

the criminal police." Moments later, he told me that Olsson had no receipt. "He gave your luggage to Porter Number Four at the Copenhagen station."

"For God's sakes, call Porter Number Four. And ask someone to get me out."

I paced the room until Schrader returned. His face had paled.

"Miss Deane, Porter Number Four does not work there anymore."

Porter Number Four does not work there anymore. That can't be. My stuff. My accordion, amp, gowns, brochures, recordings. They're the legs I walk on. Can legs vanish? I can't work without them. I can't earn, can't travel. I must be dreaming.

An officer entered the room. The men spoke in German.

"The police uncovered Olsson's criminal records," Schrader said. "He's been jailed before. A Swedish psychiatrist diagnosed him as a psychopath."

Psychopath! After Nick in Chicago, I thought I would never again be hooked by a psychopath. I knew the symptoms, but Alvar had none.

"We notified Interpol," Schrader said. "They'll hunt for your baggage."

Like a zombie, I ambled along the narrow winding streets at dusk, resting on the stone steps of Santa Clara's church. My eyes trailed couples strolling arm in arm on their evening *spaziergang*. Words battered my brain. My Excelsior accordion, gone. The Gibson amp, gone. Handmade gowns, gone. Recordings, press reviews, photos, gone. Without my tools, I can do nothing. So I *am* nothing. Can a human being be nothing? How far did I sit from the court that tried Nazi criminals? What about their victims, those they didn't gas outright? Men and women stripped of clothes, medicine, food, water, sleep. Yet some found meaning in their suffering. My torment is trivial compared with theirs. Could I find meaning without possessions? With no way to earn a living?

I don't know how long I sat on those stone steps, but something happened there. A load was lifted from my heart. A burden gone.

I felt free, light, unencumbered. How I would live and work, I didn't know, but that didn't matter. Freedom mattered, and I had that.

The U.S. Army Hotel provided an interpreter for a dollar an hour while I taxied to and from the police station, civil court, criminal court, customs house, and railway station. Interpol found my luggage in a Copenhagen baggage storeroom, and sent it to Nuremberg, but I had no retrieval documents. The highly valued accordion and amplifier troubled the customs officials more than my suitcases.

"You will have to prove that the accordion is yours," an official said.

"Easy, sir." This was Bavaria, the home of bockwurst, beer, and polkas. For the first time, I didn't mind playing "The Beer Barrel Polka." A short four-bar intro in the key of C, and I was off.

Two officers hopped across the narrow baggage platform, quick-stepped, stamped their feet, and polkaed down the hall. Two more joined them. I raised the key from C to D and picked up speed. Now, eight customs officers hopped, stamped, galloped, leapt. I raised the key to E, then F, then G. The men panted. I played a finale like I'd close a concerto.

Round-trip tickets to Spain were cheap, and I needed a holiday. From Barcelona, I posted a card to Alvar Olsson at the Nuremberg jail: "*Hasta La Vista, amigo!*"

20

MUNICH
1957-58

Military clubs in Frankfurt, Ramstein, Landstuhl, Kaiserslautern, Stuttgart, and Munich booked me six nights a week, four weeks a month, every month. One morning, at the Bachelor Officers Quarters on a Munich army base, I asked myself a question: *What am I doing? Working to live or living to work?*

Nobody but the bartender was at the Officers Club at five p.m. I sat at the end of the bar, nursing a Manhattan, the crimson cocktail coating my throat like liquid velvet. A silver-haired colonel shuffled in, and laid his cane on a bar stool. "Aren't you the accordionist?"

"I am."

"Want a drink?"

"Thanks, yes."

"You look glum. Why?"

"I abhor what I'm doing. Might as well be back in the States in show business."

"What would you like to do?"

"What Schweitzer did. Somewhere in the East."

"You want an MD?"

"Always did."

"Look into the University of Munich," he said. "They have a good medical school. It's cheaper here than in the States."

A dozen stone steps led to the door of the University of Munich medical school on Pettenkoffer Strasse. I climbed up, stepped in, and knocked on the admissions office door.

"I'd like to enroll," I told the secretary.

She scanned my NYU transcripts. "You speak German?"

"A little. But I learn languages fast."

"Only the Rector decides if your German is good enough," she said. "To enroll this semester, you must see him in three weeks."

Three weeks to master German! Could I do it? Maybe, with a good teacher, and full immersion.

In the office of an elementary school near the train station, I asked a secretary if I could meet with an English teacher. Any English teacher.

Frau Behrens entered. Fiftyish, stocky with dark brown hair tied in a bun at the back. A bearing like a sergeant.

"Frau Behrens, you'll think I have nerve, but I must ask. In three weeks I'll take an oral admission test in German with the Rector of the University of Munich. The only way I can pass it is to live with a German teacher. Full immersion, Americans call it. I'll pay you whatever you want for three weeks. The principal of an American school in Nuremberg would be pleased to give you a character reference."

We agreed on a hundred dollars for three weeks plus housework. I'd pay for my food.

I moved in. Every wall of Behrens' two-bedroom apartment was lined with oak shelves, each crammed with Bavarian beer mugs, cuckoo clocks, religious icons, music boxes, gnomes, and Hummel figurines. English labels beneath the figurines described them: "Girl feeding ducks." "Boy playing flute." "Female with deer." "Boy herding sheep." "Chinese girl with parrot." "Lady in a petticoat."

I prayed that Behrens would not ask me to dust the shelves.

"You will prepare dinner every day," she instructed. "We'll dine together." She typed a menu for the week: Fried sausages, goulash, herring in sour cream, grilled bratwurst with sauerkraut, smoked pork chops, wiener schnitzel, Spanferkel. I could have bawled. I'd never cooked any of it. I hadn't even eaten goulash, pork chops, or bratwurst. In fact, I didn't cook, but I couldn't afford to lose my chance. After all, Frau Behrens came from Berlin and spoke "high German." Not the Bavarian of Munich.

On our first session, my accent stunned her. "Superb," she commented.

"It's the same in all languages," I told her. "I have a musical ear so I sound like a native. But I'm always short on vocabulary."

She insisted that I learn thirty new words a day.

On my fifth evening, after a catastrophic goulash, Behrens assigned me to the vacuum. And the shelves.

Every day when she came home, she would run her ring finger along the edge of the shelves and on the "girl feeding ducks," the "boy playing flute," and the rest. If dusty, she would tell me in German to go to a housewifery school instead of a university.

After dinner, Behrens would sit at her kitchen table, listing questions that the Rector might ask me, and the answers, which I memorized.

Why do you want to study medicine? Why not study in the US? Where is your family? How will you pay for your studies?

The Rector, regal with graying temples and a mischievous smile, scanned my NYU records. He asked me in German why I wanted to study medicine.

I answered in German. Fast. "To work like Dr. Schweitzer."

"How old are you?"

"Twenty-nine."

"Why didn't you finish studies in the United States?"

"I tried, but I had to work nights. Couldn't get enough sleep."

"Where are your parents?"

"New York."

"How will you pay for your fees?"

"I'll work weekends, playing accordion at American military bases."

"Where do you live?"

"In a school teacher's home."

"Where did you learn German?"

I'd planned to say "in high school," but changed my mind. "From my mother," I told him. Well, that wasn't too far off. Mom spoke Yiddish.

The Rector grinned. "You talk like a Berliner. *Hoch Deutsch. Gut!*"

He sent me to an office that handed me a list of my assigned courses, printed in English and German.

Systematic Anatomy (Herr Professor Lanz)

General Zoology (Herr Professor Frisch)

Inorganic Experimental Chemistry (Herr Professor Wiberg)

Experimental Physics for Medicine and Pharmaceuticals (Herr Professor Faessler)

Introduction to the Preparation of Experimental Procedures for Medical Pharmaceuticals (Herr Professor Lanz)

I read the last one three times. I couldn't even picture it.

At home with Frau Behrens, I shared the news. "I'm a student!" She was cutting cabbage near the kitchen sink. "Look at my courses, Frau Behrens!" She rinsed and dried her hands, and checked my list. I hoped she'd let me stay. "Can you help with vocabulary?" I asked.

"No," she said. "I don't know the vocabulary for Zoology or Chemistry or Physics. They're not my fields. Besides, I want my house back. I want my life back. You must find another place to live."

I moved into a small residential hotel a block from the university.

In Systematic Anatomy I sat at the back, hiding behind a student. God forbid, Herr Professor Lanz should call on me. He drew a diagram on the board that looked like an elbow. Maybe it was a knee. I'd find out later. I copied it in my notebook but before I finished, Herr Professor erased it and drew another.

At the close of the session, I asked a Turkish student if the diagram I'd copied was an elbow. "Elbow?" He cocked an eyebrow. "That's part of the lab equipment we'll use to prepare slides. Don't you understand German?"

"I do, yes. I just wasn't listening. By the way, where can we leave books we don't need? Or must we carry them around?"

"Didn't you hear what Herr Professor said? We must look for

an empty locker. When we find one, we put our own lock on it. If anything is in it, it's ours. Departing students must clear lockers. If they don't, the university takes no responsibility."

He turned away.

Margrit from Austria, a dyed blond with a shrill voice, said she'd found a human skeleton in a locker. "A prize find."

I searched the rooms for a locker, found an empty one, and pulled it open. The cavernous eye sockets of a human skull glared down at me from the upper shelf. I grabbed it and showed it to Margrit.

"Oh, a prize find! A female. I'll buy it."

"No. It's mine."

Why did I want a skull? I wouldn't need it, but it was a prize find so I'd keep it. It appeared fragile, like the nasal bones might chip if handled roughly. I named it Frau Hildegaard, and swathed it in a cashmere sweater.

Herr Professor Lanz assigned me to a six-person team dissecting a human arm. Though foreign, the students spoke fluent German, and presumed I was German because I had no accent. But my lack of vocabulary betrayed me. I found excuses to leave. A stomach problem. An urgent call. Gnawing hunger.

In Herr Professor Faessler's first test in Experimental Physics for Medicine and Pharmaceuticals, I understood only two of his ten questions. What was I doing here? I wouldn't pass a single test with my limited German. The effort was a waste of money and time.

At the top of my paper, I wrote in English: *Forgive me, Herr Professor Faessler. My German is not good enough to understand your questions.*

I left the University of Munich like the day I left NYU. Tears wetting my texts. I wouldn't go back.

21

VIENNA & NUREMBERG

1957

The TV show in Vienna paid three-thousand Austrian schillings plus hotel, meals, and a round-trip ticket from Nuremberg.

My hotel room overlooked the Danube, which didn't look blue. It was muddy brown like the Mississippi. I could see St. Stephen, the Gothic cathedral built in the twelfth century. A home where Haydn had lived. A palace where Mozart performed. I loved the city. The music—Viennese waltzes I was taught as a child. The chocolate cake and Viennese coffee. Half caffeine, half whipped cream.

My TV show was scheduled for eight p.m. At six, the hotel desk clerk called a taxi, but a gogomobile showed up. A small three-wheeler driven by a bearded man with a colossal wife seated next to him. I sat in the back, held the accordion on my lap, and the amp beneath my feet.

En route to the TV station, something snapped and the gogomobile quit. The driver and his wife turned to me, shouting in German with such thick Austrian accents that I couldn't understand them. Pedestrians gathered. I glanced nervously at my watch.

"What happened?" I asked a young man through the window.

"Spring broke," he said. "Driver wants to sue you. Says your boxes are too heavy for gogomobile."

"Tell him that his wife is three times the weight of my boxes."

A taxi passed. "Stop, stop," I waved to the driver. I threw open the gogo door, hopped out, grabbed my accordion and amp, shoved them into the taxi, and slid in.

"TV studio. Stadt Theater, Skodagasse," I shouted, while the couple shrieked obscenities.

I'd have to buy a car.

The 1952 Mercedes 180, parked outside the U.S. Army Hotel in Nuremberg, belonged to the wife of a major who shipped her home when he caught her in bed with a private. Four doors and a roof rack for two hundred bucks. I bought it.

Patti Shore arranged the transfer while I got a German driver's license. Printed on gray linen paper, it was valid for life. At the Automobile Agency, I filled out a six-page form for a German plate. A clerk checked it. "You work for the U.S. Government," he said in English. "We can not give you a German license plate."

"I perform for the military," I told him, "but I'm a civilian."

He consulted a clerk at the back, whispering in German that I probably worked in Intelligence for the U.S. and wanted a German plate for a cover-up. The man returned to the counter. "You must get military license plates."

"I can't. I'm not military."

"Show me your I.D."

I gave him my passport.

"Not passport. Military I.D."

"I have none."

"You perform for the military. How do you get on base?"

"I get a temporary pass when I play on base."

"See? You are military. Not civilian."

I phoned Patti. "That's typical," she said. "For Germans, everything is either black or white. No grays. To hell with them. I'll finagle a military plate."

"Isn't that illegal?"

"Sure!" she said. "But look at the advantages. No crap. No tax. Cheap gas."

My license plate read, *U.S. Forces in Germany.* Patti gave me an official I.D. "Show this wherever you get gas," she said.

"But it says *Rose Shapiro*. Who's she?"

"That's you! For God's sakes, don't sign *Shirley Deane* or we've both had it!"

The U.S. Army Hotel in Nuremberg was a favorite for military personnel on leave. Dick Holbrook managed it, a flamboyant captain with a crew cut and the pink cheeks of a Bavarian farm boy. I sat in his office, mentally closing the open drawers of his file cabinets while he thumbed through my brochures.

"We can give you a steady job in our cocktail lounge," he said. "Six nights a week, six to nine. Good pay, room and board. We need jazz, pops, standards, blues, semi-classics, Latin, and show tunes. Can you do it?"

"I do it all the time," I told him.

He wrote out a contract for an indefinite period with two weeks' notice, and assigned me to a room on the second floor.

The job was easy, but bored me until the night I met a chubby, blonde-haired guy dining alone at a front table. Applauding every song I played. At break-time, he followed me to the lobby. "Best accordion I ever heard," he said.

"Thanks. You look familiar. What's your name?"

"Gary. I look like lots of guys. What time do you quit?"

"Nine."

"Care for a late dinner?"

"Sure."

When he left, Holbrook drew me aside. "Know who that is?"

"No."

"Gary Crosby."

"Oh! No wonder he looked familiar."

"Don't tell anyone. He's on leave. Wants to be anonymous."

"I won't. Won't even tell *him* that I know."

The Ritz had the best food and ambience in Nuremberg. Dim lights, velvet drapes, leathered booths. We sat in a corner, drinking Scotch with our wiener schnitzels.

"Never heard an accordion sound like an orchestra," he said. "How'd you learn to play like that?"

"My teacher made me practice from piano books instead of oom-pah-pahs."

"I like how you sang 'All of Me.' Sing it softly, would you?"

Gary harmonized with me. "That's great, Gary. Harmonizing off the cuff like that. You're a pro."

"I'm nothing. My father told me that. Called me a fat ass who can't do anything right."

He couldn't be talking about Bing Crosby, my mother's idol, the embodiment of decency. "What father would talk to his son like that?"

"Mine. Used to beat my behind till it bled. Beat my younger brothers, too."

He motioned to the waitress. "One more."

"Wow, Gary. You downed that fast."

"I got a limitless bottom."

"You're not the only one who got it on the behind. My dad used to whip my bottom with the buckle of his belt. Mom did, too. What's your mom like? She took your side when you got the whip?"

Gary choked up, and I grew tired of pretending. "Now I know who you look like. Gary Crosby! That's you?"

"You got it. You don't know how I hate being the son of Mr. Great. Nobody gives a shit for what I am. They only care that I'm the son of the Great One."

"But you've got so much on the ball. Good looks, sweet voice, smart."

He downed a third drink. "I'm a klutz, but I can beat the shit out of any fucker. Forgive my language. I'm like a truck driver when I booze. Like Mom."

"She was an actress in the thirties, wasn't she?"

"Yeah. Dixie Lee. She died five years ago."

"Oh, I'm sorry, Gary. I didn't know. She must have been a comfort when your dad was rough."

"She would have been if she weren't stoned all the time."

"She was an alcoholic?"

He nodded. "The bastard's fault."

"You mean—women?"

"Women. God knows how many."

Bing played around? My mind could only image him crooning "White Christmas" around his Christmas tree. His blond wife adoring him, the boys unwrapping gifts.

Gary downed a fourth Scotch. He didn't relish his booze. Didn't even taste it. He poured it down his gullet like he was putting out a fire. Maybe it *was* a fire, a blaze of hurt and self-hate. I wished I could convince him that he was okay. That he didn't need to buy his father's scorn and sell it to himself.

"I never talk to strangers like this, Shirl. For some reason I wanted to tell you everything. I'm fed up with myself. I'm nothing. Nothing but the son of Mr. Great."

"I like you for what you are, Gary, not because you're Bing's son. Tell you the truth, I never cared for your dad's voice. I'm a Sinatra fan."

He lit up. The families were close when he was a kid, he said, and got along great. He adored Nancy, Sinatra's first wife. She was like a second mom when his mother died.

Gary got quiet. "Shirl, you'll stay with me tonight?"

"I can't, Gary."

"You don't like me."

"I like you, but the sex thing is different."

"I don't attract you. I'm a fat ass."

"You're not, but you're younger than me. Almost five years."

"Shit. What does age matter? I like older women."

"It matters to me. Besides, I don't jump into bed with every guy I meet."

"You're like an old friend. I told you stuff I don't tell people I know for years. Shirl, I got ten more days in Nuremberg. You'll spend them with me?"

"Sure."

"Maybe we can cut some records when you get back to the States."

"No thanks! I loathe show business. I couldn't bear going back to it when I return to the States. I'm in it now because it's my ticket to the world."

Gary and I dated until he left. He gave me his APO address, a telephone number, and a California address. "You helped me," he said.

"How?"

"By seeing value in me that I can't see in myself."

Not long after we met, an article about Bing Crosby appeared in the military press. He'd remarried. His second wife was younger than Gary.

The front page of the Nuremberg *8 Uhr Blatt* captioned my photo, *Nürnberg gefällt ihr so gut.* "She likes Nuremberg very much."

I could spend the rest of my life like this, I thought. Performing, amassing publicity, dating, learning native words, eating indigenous foods. Forgetting why I left America.

I left to find something of lasting value worth knocking myself out for. But I hadn't found it. The universal drama repeats itself everywhere. Things come into being, and vanish. People, objects, buildings, governments, and relationships occupy a moment in time. Then they're gone. Yet everywhere, in Europe as in America, people plan for the next day, the next year, the next fifty years, and they could be gone in ten minutes. We go on dreaming, living under an illusion that tomorrow, all will be well. Better than today. What's the point of that fairy tale? I had to keep going until I found out.

22

PARIS & ROME
1958

E*urope on $5.00 a Day* suggested the Left Bank for the atypical visitor to Paris. That was me. Seekers of Truth pervaded it, anti-capitalist voices that brought back memories of my social clique at a corner table in the NYU cafeteria. Here, longhaired intellects dawdled for hours over a single aperitif at outdoor cafés. Jazz cellar clubs like the Village Vanguard in Manhattan blasted relaxed jazz.

I hunted a cheap, clean hotel to rest for a week. After that, I'd scout for work. The DuMontBlanc looked good. In the Arab Quarters on a narrow street called Rue du Huchette. Twenty minutes of hot water for a dime.

Arabic music floated up to my second floor window from the *Al Chazar* nightclub across the street. I longed to see the musicians, but the Left Bank wasn't New York. A woman alone was taken for a prostitute.

My first morning, I walked out of my room at the same time as the man next door. A pot-bellied guy with curly black hair and a Jewish nose. "You're new here?" he asked.

"Came last night."

"You sound American."

"I am," I said. "A New Yorker. You sound like one, too."

"I am. I'm correspondent for *Variety* magazine. Gene Moskowitz is the name."

"*Variety* correspondent? Next door? I don't believe it!"

"You're a tourist?"

"No. Professional musician. Working my way around the world."

"My neighbor? A New York musician?"

We stood wordless. I felt like I was playing a role in a film that somebody else wrote. Some genius I hadn't yet met.

For two weeks, Gene escorted me to fine restaurants. To first nighters at posh clubs with VIP attention. To private parties in penthouse suites hosted by French film stars. He read my reviews, and brought Jimmy English to the hotel to meet me, the man who booked the entertainment for all U.S. Forces in France.

Gene took Jimmy and me to the Mars Club one night, a jazz venue on the Champs Élysées. I sat in and played, "How High the Moon" with tenor sax, vibes, guitar, bass and drums. Jimmy had never heard jazz on an accordion. A week later, I was booked at every U.S. base in France: Orly, Orleans, Dreux, Fontainebleu,Verdun, Etain. I felt like I was viewing myself in a film, moved from scene to scene like the wind moves leaves. I wondered—could I go through life like this? Exerting no effort, just letting things happen? Could anyone?

Gene and I relaxed in a velvet padded booth at a private club for journalists from around the world. Patrons rang a bell to get in, and presented membership cards. The club was dimly lit, but Gene recognized the man who had just entered. He waved.

"Frank, come on over. Shirl, you gotta meet this guy. He's from South Africa."

"Shirley is a professional accordionist from New York," Gene told him. "Frank Collins," he said, "is a reporter with the *Rand Daily Mail* in Johannesburg."

Collins was a slender man with delicate features and the quick, nervous movements of many journalists I'd met.

Gene ordered drinks and toasted "to whatever the gods had in mind when they got us three together." He asked the house accordionist if I could play.

"*C'est mon plaisir,*" the musician said.

I played a medley of French songs in classical and jazz modes.

"I could listen to you all night," Frank said at the table. "I was just thinking. A friend of mine owns a club in Johannesburg. He booked Zsa Zsa Gabor for December, but nobody's lined up to follow her. Would you like to play Joburg?"

"Johannesburg? Would I!" *Africa!* I'd always wanted to see it. I'd start at the bottom. Johannesburg. Then north to Rhodesia. North again through the jungles of the Congo. Then—Dr. Schweitzer! "Oh, I *must* go! I *must!*"

Back at the DuMontBlanc Hotel, Frank took some of my photos and publicity. "I'll get back to you," he said. "Might take a few months."

The clock struck midnight. I sat up, couldn't breathe, and reached for my inhaler. It didn't help. I wondered if I'd recover from this asthmatic attack. I felt panic, slipped on a coat, rushed down to the desk. "Taxi, quick."

"Hospital, hurry," I told the driver.

In the emergency room of the Notre Dame hospital, I wheezed on a wooden bench. My lungs locked up. No air came in, no air went out. I got on all fours and crawled to a desk. "Help me, quick!"

A young intern came in. "Passport number, please."

"Never mind passport. I'm dying!"

"Must have passport number."

I couldn't breathe. I pounded the floor, I wanted to kill him. "Help me. Cortisone, quick!"

I felt like I was succumbing when a senior doctor walked in, took one look at me, ran out, rushed back with a syringe, got on his knees and injected my arm. He lifted me gently to a bench and sat me down. "Rest here." He patted my shoulders.

For three hours I sat on that bench, my body quaking from the cortisone jolt. I was so close to death. I wondered if I'd have bouts like that for the rest of my life.

Etain air base, three-hundred sixty kilometers east of Paris, was twenty kilometers from the famous battleground of Verdun. I'd left the narrow streets, pungent odors, and Arabic rhythms of the Left Bank in Paris for a sunny room at the Bachelor Officers Quarters surrounded by cows, trenches, and mines.

The officers were a great audience. Jet pilots, sports car fans, jazz addicts who never asked for a polka. They wanted, "There Will Never Be Another You." "A Foggy Day in London Town." "Lullaby of Birdland." I could have played for them all night, every night.

One rainy morning, I bought a pup tent for fifty cents at Etain's Army Surplus Store. Outside, I spotted a square-set colonel studying my license plate.

"Aren't you the entertainer?" he asked.

"I am."

"Where did you get the military license plate?"

My mouth went dry. My tongue wouldn't budge. It never occurred to me that driving in a small military town was a risk.

"Well?"

"It's a temporary arrangement, Colonel. The Germans wouldn't give me a license plate since I work for U.S. Forces. I had to do something."

"You'll have to explain that to the legal department," he said, and took off.

They could impound my car. I couldn't risk it. I wrote to the legal office, lying that my father was ill, that I had to return to America. I'd contact them on return.

At Dreux airbase, I took no chances; I garaged my car. During dinner with a Major, I asked for a lift to town.

"Where's your car?"

"Garaged," I said. "Needs work."

"What's wrong with it? We got ace mechanics on base."

After two Manhattan cocktails, I couldn't think of a thing to say but the truth. He burst out laughing.

"What puzzles me," I said, "is why Etain's legal department hasn't chased me."

"Your offense isn't worth their time," he said. "They have far higher priorities than a New York musician with a U.S. Forces plate. You'd be shocked if you knew."

Frank Collins' letter arrived from South Africa. I held it for some minutes, sitting on the edge of my bed at Drew Bachelor Officers

Quarters. Then I slit the envelope with a silver letter opener.

> Dear Shirley, The Colony wants to feature you in December to follow Zsa Zsa Gabor. Hugo Keleti, an international agent in Johannesburg, will draw up your contract. All travel expenses will be paid.

I'd board a Trek Airlines flight in Zurich. The trip to Johannesburg would take four days because Trek wouldn't fly at night. We would stop at luxury hotels in Malta, Cairo, and Entebbe, Uganda.

Africa! Real. Rousing. Raw. For years, I'd longed to see it. Now my dream would come true in December. This was October, enough time for Italy and Spain.

Rome was a haphazard maze of main and side streets with fountains that looked regal, and pushcart quarters that looked like Delancey Street in Manhattan.

At American Express, I picked up mail and checked the Visitors' Registry. Foreigners listed their names, home state, occupation, what they wanted to do in Italy, and a contact number. Jerry Pitman's entry caught my eyes: "Seattle. Dancer and comedian on vacation. I want to work in Europe."

Performing with a dancer would be more fun than playing alone.

Jerry, in his early thirties, towered over me. He would have been handsome if it weren't for his pimples, which he tried to conceal with Revlon. We worked out a comedy routine about an old Mississippi couple taking dancing lessons at Arthur Murray's. Jerry seldom smiled. His straight face made his punch lines so riotous that I'd roar with laughter on stage. To close our act, we impersonated Louis Armstrong and Ella Fitzgerald.

Army, navy and air force clubs booked us, and we got a week at the *Grand Hotel de Londres* in Naples. One steaming day, we strolled the bay and the crowded streets with their crumbling walkways where people cooked and ate and washed clothes.

"This is real Italy, Jerry. Like ancient times."

"The place depresses me. Those shacks," he pointed, "are pigsties."

"But the music! Opera from every window."

"And gangsters. Deported from Chicago."

Jerry was like two people. A sensation on stage. Off stage, he didn't have a good word to say about anything.

We drove north through Italy and west along the French Riviera. Jerry had worked out an infallible method of winning in roulette, he said. He wanted to try it.

We parked at a small casino. I didn't play since I couldn't afford to lose. Jerry sat at the round roulette table, confident, his back straight. I stood near, noting his facial transformation when he won a hundred dollars.

"My system works!" he whispered. That was the first time I saw him smile. "I'll be a billionaire!" But the casino closed, and we left.

When we crossed into Spain, passing Moorish architecture, I felt like I'd come home. "I love the music and the palm trees. What a change from the drab of northern Europe!"

"I don't like it a bit," Jerry said. "I don't feel safe here."

Late day sun shone bright as we drove into the U.S. Officers club in Zaragosa. An MP escorted us into the dining room, a large, square room with a low ceiling and white lace curtains on the windows. Captain DeWitt worked at a table, adding columns of figures on a balance sheet. He invited us to sit with him, and ordered coffee.

I told DeWitt that we were a professional duo. I played accordion and sang. Jerry did comedy and dance. We were a hit in Italy, I said, and wanted to play Spain.

DeWitt thumbed through my brochures, and read our reference letters. "Impressive," he said. "We can book you for two weeks starting next week."

He drew up a contract. "By the way, we're all excited," he told us. "Tyrone Power and his wife are coming tonight. They're guests of the base commander. You're welcome to come if you like. We can seat you at the back."

"*Tyrone Power?* Of course we'll come," I said. "Of course! What's he doing here?"

"They're shooting a film with Gina Lollobrigida and George Sands about an hour from here. *Solomon and Sheba.*"

"Oh, save us seats! Please!"

"Jerry," I said in the car, "I'm so excited! Twelve years ago I saw Power in *The Razor's Edge* at the Roxy in New York. I can't forget it. He played Larry, an American dropout who embarks on a quest for meaning. The guy lands in India where a sage wakes him up to his spiritual identity. I sat in that dark theater, a weird sensation creeping up my spine, like I was watching my future. I forgot all about it till now, but I never forgot Power's handsome face. I've been in love with him since."

"You plan to go to India?"

"I want to see the whole world, but I don't plan details. Life does that."

"You're planning to come to the club tonight. Isn't that a detail?"

"That's different. Tonight, I'm going to see the man I love. *In the flesh.*"

23

ZARAGOSA & TANGIERS

1958

MPs patrolled the officers' club parking area, asked for our IDs, and ushered us to the door. We slipped in. A row of officers stood in front of us. The room was packed, tables crammed together. No one glanced at us. All eyes were glued to the dance floor. There he was—Tyrone Power dancing with the wing commander's blubbery wife. Just the two of them on the floor. Around and around they waltzed to the *Blue Danube*. I couldn't take my eyes off him. This was the time to do it.

"Let's get on the dance floor," I whispered.

"Oh no, no," Jerry said. "It's for the VIPs."

Brazen, I knew. But I'd never get another chance to be in Tyrone's arms. I didn't care about the consequences.

"We've got to do it, "I whispered. "It's my only chance. We'll dance toward them, you'll cut in. You'll ask the commander's wife to dance."

"No, no!" Jerry paled, and turned toward the door. I jerked him back, gripping his hand. We stared at the couple. *Sure, it's a social crime,* I told myself. *MPs could arrest us. We could lose our contract. The military press could ruin us. But then, the other side. Me, in Tyrone's arms! I'll never get another chance. Never.*

"We got to do it, Jerry. Come on."

I didn't look at his face. I didn't look at anyone's face. I dragged Jerry to the floor.

We were there. The only dancers besides Tyrone and the commander's wife. Jerry was white. His hand shook in mine. I whispered. "I have to get into his arms." I edged Jerry toward them.

From the corner of my eyes I saw faces glare. I felt the heat, the daggers. When we got near the couple, I shoved him. "Cut in, now. Now!"

Jerry's voice was a mere whisper. "May I have this dance?" The woman grimaced and dropped Power's hand. Power turned and put his arms around me.

I was in the arms of Tyrone Power! Tyrone, stunning with his shining black hair, the gentle nose, the sensuous lips. His arms were around *me*, this man who had filled my mind and heart for a decade. He squeezed my hand. "You saved my day," he whispered. "Who are you, besides a gorgeous woman?"

"An accordionist. Working my way around the world."

"That's your man?"

"No. My showbiz partner. Dancer and comedian."

"You're beautiful."

"I've had a crush on you since I saw you in *The Razor's Edge*."

"Ah, my favorite role. We're doing *Solomon and —*"

The music stopped. Tyrone still held me. Would he ask me to visit the set? He squeezed my hand, let it go, and turned to the commander's wife. Jerry slunk off the dance floor. I floated after him.

Red-faced Captain DeWitt stood near the door. He jabbed an index finger in my face. "Bastards! Out! Both of you, out! Your contract's canceled. Damned rascals! If I ever see your faces around here, I'll…" He jerked open the door. "*Out!*"

Jerry ran outside. I followed him, looking back. Tyrone smiled and moved his lips. Did he mean to blow a kiss?

We were on the street. Thrown out. Jerry was livid. "You made a fool of me. That woman is livid! The captain is livid. We lost the fuckin' contract! You fuckin' shithead!"

Jerry's fury was like a gale outside a winter cabin, howling but leaving me untouched. I still felt Power's warmth, the thrill of his nearness, his chest on mine, his cheek near mine. "It doesn't matter," I said. "Nothing matters. *I danced with Tyrone Power!*"

"You're impossible! You embarrassed the officers. You upset the whole fuckin' place. The commander. His wife. The captain. Me. You don't give a shit for anyone but yourself!"

"And Tyrone."

Jerry was quiet next morning as we drove to the club in Madrid. He worried that our reputation would precede us. It didn't. We got a week's contract, and all that week I thought about the night in Zaragosa. Yes, it was outrageous. Yes, people got mad, but not Tyrone. And what a memory I carried away!

Driving south, we passed old castles, Arab ruins, peasants riding donkeys.

"Ah! Jerry. *This* is Spain. I love it!"

"I feel safer in Germany," he said. "But since we're here, let's find a casino."

A tourist office clerk told us about a famous casino in Tangiers. Jerry clapped his hands. "Morocco! Let's go!"

"I thought you didn't like that culture. You called it weird."

"It's weird all right. But they're so dumb down there, they'll never fathom my system. I'll skin their hides in no time."

We garaged my car in Algeciras, caught a boat to Gibraltar, and another to Tangiers. On the boat, Jerry said he'd get a hair transplant with his winnings. "Or maybe a new Buick. Or a home in Frisco."

At the bottom of the gangplank in Morocco, a bubbly young Arab greeted us. "Welcome to Tangiers. I'm your guide. I am Ahmed Ben Said." Ahmed carried our suitcases to a taxi and called out the name of a hotel.

"How much will it cost?" I asked him.

"What you can pay?"

"See what I mean?" Jerry said. "You can't trust anybody here."

"We have very little money," I said. "Five dollars a night. No more."

"Why'd you tell him that?" nudged Jerry. "We can probably get rooms for two bucks."

Ahmed directed the taxi driver to a different hotel. We checked into two small rooms on the first floor. Jerry fiddled with the lock on his door. "Unsafe," he said.

The concierge gave him a room on the second floor, which

was too close to the toilet and smelled. "Let's play tonight," Jerry said, "and get the hell out of here tomorrow with the loot."

"Fine. But, hey, tomorrow is my birthday."

Ahmed, who wouldn't leave us alone for a minute, said, "Ah, we celebrate your birthday tomorrow. We have party."

"Where?"

"The Casbah."

That night, the casino was jam-packed, the air thick with smoke. Jerry pointed to an empty seat. "Sit there while I change a twenty-dollar traveler's check."

Men and women at the table chatted in French, German, Italian, English, and languages I couldn't identify. They didn't face one another or smile. Some studied figures in tiny notebooks, acting like their life depended on where the wheel stopped.

Jerry came back with red, white and blue chips. I stood behind him and watched. He put two small notebooks on the table. One was filled with figures that looked like multiplication tables and configurations I couldn't make out.

"Hey," he covered the pages. "Quit it."

"I was just trying to see how you use a system to gamble."

"Shh. I'll tell you when we get out." He cracked a smile and whispered, "When I've cleaned out the house."

Jerry put a few chips on two numbers. The croupier said, *"Messieurs, Mesdames, les jeoux sont faits. Rien ne va plus,"* and spun the roulette wheel. When it stopped, Jerry winced, checked his notebook, wrote a few figures, put the rest of his chips on another number. Again, the croupier closed the betting and spun the wheel. Jerry winced again.

"Take my seat. I'll change a few more checks. The clean-up may take more time than I thought."

Jerry went through the same routine. Checked his system notebook, came up with two numbers, and divided his chips between them. The croupier spun the wheel. When it stopped, Jerry's expression soured. "Fuck it," he said under his breath. "They got a system of their own. I'll show 'em."

He got up, changed more checks, played more chips, lost, did it again, lost again, and picked at his nails.

"Don't change all your money, Jerry. You'll have nothing."

"Listen," he whispered. "It's gotta work. My system's foolproof. It's taking time, that's all. The dumb assholes got their own system. I'll show 'em, you'll see. When I win, it's gonna be big. I'm telling you. Big."

Jerry changed four hundred eighty dollars and lost it all. He had twenty dollars left. "Twenty bucks to my name. Oh, God!"

"I'll lend you the loot for the hotel. And you still have your ticket to the States."

"Something went wrong. It worked in France. I knew you couldn't trust 'em here. I knew it. Bastards!"

Next day was my thirtieth birthday. Jerry still fumed and swore. "I want to get out of here. The place, the atmosphere, shakes me up. I want to get out."

"We can leave later today, but let me have my birthday celebration."

Ahmed took us to the Casbah, an oriental bazaar with colorful shops and kiosks selling fabrics, carpets, tobacco, spices, sweets, coffee, incense, Arabic medicine. I loved the feel of it. The narrow winding streets, the shops with colorful rugs on the walls, the bargaining. Most of all, the music.

We climbed the wide stone steps. Ahmed told us about each store, what it sold and who owned it. The owner was always a brother, a cousin, or uncle.

We stopped at a cousin's fabric shop. Deep red and blue carpets with intricate designs covered floors and walls. Men sat shoeless and cross-legged on the floor. They talked, joked, and smoked the hookah. Sweet incense and Arabic music filled the air.

"Oh, birthday lady! Yes, we have party."

The owner, covered from the waist down in a sloppy white sarong, sent someone out to buy something, then spoke to Ahmed in Arabic. Jerry sulked, silent. The men eyed him standing behind me. Ahmed told them what had happened the night before.

Delicious sweets arrived. I ate one after another. The more I ate, the more I wanted. Jerry, still sullen, refused to eat.

"What is this marvelous sweet?" I asked the owner.

"Marzipan."

"I love marzipan! I'll have more."

A palm reader joined us. "Show your hand," he said. I showed him my palms. His head shook. "Oh, oh, oh!"

"What's wrong? Tell me."

"You, every time moving. Moving. I never see such hand."

When it was time to leave I tried to stand but couldn't. Jerry leaned on the door. "C'mon, let's go. I wanna go."

"I can't walk."

The men laughed. I laughed too, but I felt dizzy, and I was starving. Jerry kept waving me on. "C'mon, c'mon." I tried to walk but my legs wouldn't work. I held onto a pillar. "Where's Ahmed?"

"Ahmed go," the owner laughed. "Lit-tle lit-tle opium in marzipan. Lit-tle lit-tle."

"Opium!" shouted Jerry. "Oh, God. I told you so. You can't trust these shits. Now what?"

"I'm starving. I must eat."

"Restaurant, down that way," the owner pointed. "But closed. This not lunch time. Knock on door."

"We'll go back to the hotel," Jerry said.

"No, I'm starving. I've got to eat."

I'd gotten out of the shop but couldn't walk down the Casbah steps. I was too dizzy. I sat on a step, placed my feet on the one below, palms behind me. Slowly I pressed my hands down, lowered my feet, moved my buttocks down a step and sat. I shuffled down the Casbah steps on all fours.

Jerry knocked on the door to a restaurant in the heart of the bazaar. A sleepy, portly man opened it, wearing only a white sarong spotted with grease.

"She is hungry," Jerry said.

"Not meal time."

"I am starving," I shouted.

We sat in the empty restaurant, its shades drawn. A pile of dirt and chicken bones had been swept into a corner. The owner brought a menu. He said in English that he could only cook chicken and almonds. I wondered why he'd brought the menu.

"You'll pay for it," Jerry said. "I'm not spending my last twenty bucks."

I burst into hysterics. He looked so funny when he was mad, and he scowled as I ate. I was so hungry that I finished fast. "I'm still starving. Another plate," I called out.

"What! You know what this costs?" Jerry said.

"I don't care, I'm starving."

I gulped down the second plate, but was still ravenous. "One more plate," I called.

"This is ridiculous!" Jerry howled. I burst out laughing. He was mad because I was hungry. That was so funny. After the third dinner, the owner brought the bill. Six dollars. I couldn't find my change purse with local money.

"Pay," the owner told Jerry. "Or go to jail."

Jerry's expression triggered an uncontrollable fit of laughter. The day before, he didn't know whether to get a hair transplant, a new Buick or a home in Frisco. Now, six bucks were killing him.

"I'll pay you back at the hotel," I told him.

Jerry flew back to the States from Madrid. I headed for Nuremberg, eager to see if the Africa contract had come through. Eager to get on with my journey around the world.

Lourdes was jammed. A hundred years earlier, the Virgin Mary had appeared there to fourteen-year-old Bernadette. From the balcony, I could see the grotto. Men, women and children in wheel chairs. Some praying, some pleading with open arms.

"It moves me to see their faith," I told a priest near me.

"You're Catholic?" Father Kelly had a Brooklyn accent.

"My Mom's Jewish, and Dad's an Irish Jew, but I don't observe any religion."

I told him about my experience in a Catholic church in Copenhagen.

"Mother of God! You got the gift of faith in Christ! Did you pay Him back?"

"How?"

"By going to church."

"I went to Mass once," I said, "but I didn't understand it. People sit, stand, kneel, murmur, touch their lips, cross their chest. Makes no sense to me."

"Every gesture has a meaning. Study the catechism. Get baptized."

"Me?"

"You." He pointed at me. "You. A young woman, alone. You need His Hand."

"I can take His Hand without getting baptized."

"You can't. The Catholic Church is the only way to Jesus."

"Only Catholics have the key?"

"Yes. The Catholic Church is the Body of God. The only True Apostolic Church."

"Makes no sense, Father. What about Muslims and Jews?"

"They don't stand a chance till they convert."

"And people who lived before Christ?"

"They're waiting for Him in another realm."

"I have to go, Father. Gotta drive to Nuremberg."

"When you get to London, go to Bayswater Convent. The Sisters are Jewish converts. They'll teach you everything."

Depression engulfed me on the drive back to Germany. Money had dwindled, so hotels were out. I filled my tank at night, pulled to the side, and slept in my car.

At the U.S. Army Hotel in Nuremberg, Captain Holbrook assigned me a room, and gave me a new contract.

Among my letters were three from Mom. "When are you coming home?" she wrote, loading me with guilt. I should have told her I wouldn't return to America until I'd seen the whole world. But that would have upset her.

The fat envelope from Johannesburg enclosed a letter from the agent, a round-trip ticket on Trek Airlines, and my contract. I would open at the Colony in the posh Hyde Park Hotel in Johannesburg on December fifteenth, play a month, then play the Marine Hotel in Port Elizabeth on the Indian Ocean. I'd need smallpox and yellow fever vaccinations, concertina additions for my passport, and visas.

I'm going to Africa! The greater my thrill, the greater the guilt I felt toward Mom. She wanted me back, and I was going farther away.

Two suitcases, my accordion and amplifier were all I'd bring to Africa. The Army Hotel would store the rest of my baggage.

The night before my departure, I parked my car outside the Ritz where Patti Shore would pick it up next day. That night, I was booked to perform for five visiting generals. Just before the performance, my phone rang.

"This is the Provost Marshall's office," a curt male voice said. "We've been lookin' for your Mercedes for a long time. MPs found it, and we got your illegal license plate. Better get down here now."

"I can't," I said. "I'm playing for five generals tonight."

"Then get down here at eight in the morning."

"I can't. I'm leaving for Africa at five a.m."

He hung up. I rang Patti to say that I feared an arrest before I left.

"They won't arrest you," she said. "Don't worry. I'll take care of it."

By four a.m. I was packed. A sergeant drove me to the entrance of the *Bahnhof* to catch the five a.m. train to Zurich. At Zurich airport, I bought a postcard. I dreaded telling my parents because they'd worry. But saying nothing was worse.

I'm off to Africa, folks. I'll stay in touch. Love, Shirl.

24

JOHANNESBURG
1958-59

I preferred the window seat but Kirsten Privet got there first. The Swiss blonde journalist would cover Trek's maiden flight on the Zurich-Johannesburg route. "Should be a ball," she said. "Small-time airline doing big-time stuff. The captain owns most of the stock."

The thirty-six seats were filled. Propellers spun, the plane rumbled down the runway, edged upward, and turned southeast toward Malta, our first overnight stop. By the time we reached our hotel, I was too tired to do anything but sleep.

In Cairo, our second layover, a van dropped us off at the Semiramus overlooking the Nile, a fifty-year-old hotel that had hosted Winston Churchill and the Aga Khan. We dined on the roof garden under a dome of brilliant stars. Gorged ourselves on spicy kofta and hibiscus tea. Danced to the Arabic rhythms of a ten-piece orchestra. I promised myself I'd return to Egypt.

The air in Entebbe, Uganda was hot and still. Carrying our overnight bags to the terminal, we passed a young worker doing the hula hoop, giggling and spinning like an old toy top, but the hoop never fell.

After lunch at our air-conditioned hotel, a bus took us on tour along Lake Victoria, past modern European homes, coffee estates, Indian townships, round thatched huts, and half-naked natives working barefoot in banana groves.

Next day, as we were about to land at the Johannesburg airport, Kirsten pointed out the window. "Oh, look. Photographers and reporters. Must be somebody famous on this flight."

At the bottom step, Frank Collins waved. "That's her, Shirley Deane."

Photographers snapped my picture, and reporters rushed up. "Hey," said Kirsten, "*You're* it. Why didn't you say so?"

"I didn't know."

Johannesburg looked no more African than Pittsburgh. It bustled with shoppers, heavy traffic and modern buildings. At six thousand feet, it didn't feel like Africa, either. December was the peak of the summer season, but South Africans wore sweaters.

At the posh Hyde Park Hotel, a uniformed African doorman stood beneath the canopy near the *Whites Only* sign printed in English and Afrikaans. A bevy of African footmen huddled in a corner, awaiting orders. In the lobby, my feet sank into a beige carpet, and more photographers snapped my picture.

Next morning, December first, 1958, my photo appeared on the front page of the *Rand Daily Mail*.

> STAR IN OUR EYES
>
> SHIRLEY HEADS A GLAMOUR TEAM… Glamorous Shirley Deane, first of a crop of visiting celebrities of stage and cinema, arrived at Jan Smuts airport yesterday evening. She will be the Christmas season attraction at a Craighall, Johannesburg hotel…

I didn't know why the reporter wrote "first of a crop of visiting celebrities" when I followed Zsa Zsa Gabor.

On opening night, I played an original medley about my travels. When I crooned the words, *I'm a native of New York,* everybody laughed. I paused. Why did they laugh? After the show, I asked Frank Collins what I said that was funny.

"In South Africa, the word 'native' means *kaffirs*."

"What's *kaffirs*?"

"Africans."

"But I don't get it. What's funny?"

"Americans wouldn't understand," he said. "By the time you leave, you'll get it."

I began to get it at my boss's home, a mansion as long as a Manhattan block. His British wife showed me around, moving with swan-like grace on Persian carpets, past original paintings and imbuia sideboards. Two lounges (living rooms), one for her husband, the other for her. "I entertain my guests while he entertains his," she said.

Nancy breast-fed her newborn baby on a massive bed framed by hand-carved bedposts and a thick mosquito net. "It must take you an hour to make this bed," I said.

"Good heavens, we don't make our beds. Servants do. You make your own bed?"

"I don't know an American who doesn't."

An African woman in a uniform knocked, asked something in a tribal language, then closed the door gently.

"Our maid," Nancy said. "She asked how many guests we expect for dinner."

"She lives on the property?"

"All our servants do."

"How many do you have?"

"Six. A cook, cleaner, laundry person, gardener, driver, and the maid you saw who tells the servants what to do."

For the first time, I understood what real wealth means. It doesn't mean owning cars, homes, TV's. It means having space and time.

"Where do your servants live?"

She pointed to the shacks behind her tennis court.

On my night off, Frank Collins drove me around Johannesburg. Along the rim of the city we passed a road strewn with huge drainpipes. "What are those black things sticking out?" I asked.

"I'm ashamed to tell you. Legs. African kids' legs. That's their shelter."

"African kids sleep in drainpipes while whites live in mansions?"

"Tell you the truth, whites here are desensitized," Frank said. "Like the Germans got desensitized during the Nazi regime."

"Blacks enslaved by whites. Whites enslaved by greed. How long can that last?"

"Won't change in my lifetime," he said.

The image of spindly black legs sticking out of drainpipes lingered in my mind, and swelled like a festering sore.

South Africa's bantamweight champion, Willie Toweel, a slight man with delicate features and a pointed chin, didn't drink or smoke, but he sat at the Colony every night to hear me play. He told me about a Seer, an African woman called a *Sangoma*, who threw the bones. Real animal bones that tell you things about your life. I wanted to meet her.

One morning, Willie drove me to the African rural area northeast of Johannesburg where she lived. A black area barred to whites, but Willie had a pass. The *Sangoma* did not speak English, he said, but he knew her tribal language.

We parked near a row of round mud huts with thatched roofs. The Seer stood outside her hut, her tall, firm body wrapped in a red, black and white halter and a long skirt.

I stared at her headdress of ostrich feathers that hung to her shoulders. As she turned her head toward us, a long pendant swung from the back of her wig. Willie whispered that it was the gallbladder of a goat, sacrificed during the *Sangoma's* training. He said it was worn like radar to call her ancestors.

A string of horns hung around her neck, along with rows of multi-colored beads that criss-crossed part of her breast, upper arms, wrists and ankles.

We took off our shoes. Holding a cow tail's whisk, she pulled aside a woven curtain that covered the opening to her hut. A candle on a corner shrine lit the small room. Thick, hand-woven, multi-patterned cloths covered the walls. A scent of cedar incense filled the air.

The Seer gestured for us to sit on a straw mat. I knelt. Willie sat cross-legged on my right. A large impala skin covered the floor between us and the *Sangoma*. Square wooden boxes stood on it.

She squatted and looked into my face. Her wild eyes danced. She clapped her hands hard, picked up a box, and closed her eyes.

She chanted a strange sequence of sounds. Then she shook the box like you shake dice, and threw the bones. Some were large, some small. She studied the patterns in which they fell, and spoke.

Willie translated.

"You are not happy with normal life. What satisfies others does not satisfy you. You ask questions. Why are things like they are? What do things mean? What is the purpose?"

"That's incredible," I told Willie. "She's right. Ask her if I'll find the answers."

She threw the bones again. He translated. "You will."

"Ask her when."

She threw. "After many more lands."

"Oh, that must be wrong. I've already seen many lands."

She threw again, studied the pattern, shook her head vigorously. "After *many* more lands."

The experience shook me to the core, watching this African mystic divine my deepest thoughts through a tumble of animal bones. She had never seen me before, she couldn't speak my language. How could this wild, black-eyed woman with a goat's gallbladder dangling from her wig understand me, when I couldn't understand myself?

I sat in silence as Willy drove out of her area. I would never forget that woman.

At Kruger National Park, Willie and I rented a bungalow with two bedrooms. In the breakfast bar next morning, a sign in English and Afrikaans read: *Stay in your car. Don't drive over forty kilometers an hour. Remember: Elephants have the right of way.*

"That's a joke, Willie. No?"

"No."

I felt like a kid about to see her first movie.

We rode in first gear. A few antelopes raced in front of our car followed by a baboon. "They were running away from him," Willie said. The baboon peered at us, searched the landscape for the antelopes, then turned back. A few buffalos, giraffes, and zebras followed.

"Willie, look. Lions, under that acacia tree." We watched them tear into the gut of a deer. They didn't even glance at us. "It's gory, Willie."

"That's bush life," he said. "Sometimes, it's ring life."

We lunched at the Kukuza Rest Camp on vegetable soup, pickled curry fish, stewed steak, mashed potatoes, corned beef tongue, and a jam tart with custard.

After the meal, I headed for the ladies' restroom. Above the toilet was an unscreened open window. As I sat, I heard a thud and a splash. I jumped up.

A huge, hairy green tarantula struggled to get out of the bowl. He had climbed through the window, tumbled, and barely missed my behind. He tried in vain to rescue himself, grasping the enamel and sliding back into the water.

I should save him. After all, this is Kruger. Like all creatures here, he has a right to live. But I was scared. I didn't have the heart to flush him, and I didn't have the guts to save him. I walked out, a coward.

A giant poster outside the Marine Hotel in Port Elizabeth read: *Opening tonight! Shirley Deane from New York City!* I arrived at the hotel on the southern coast of South Africa in blazing noon heat, unpacked in my suite overlooking the Indian Ocean, ate lunch, and walked along the beachfront. For Whites only.

After tea, I lingered outside the hotel beneath the awning, listening to a peculiar drone that grew louder, and shut out street sounds. I turned to the doorman to ask what it was, and spotted it. A round black creature the size of a small handball suspended at eye level in front of me. It descended to the ground abruptly, rose straight up like a helicopter, buzzed and hovered before my eyes. My limbs stiffened. I couldn't budge.

"Cockroach!" the doorman's voice boomed. He rushed toward the creature waving a folded newspaper. It winged off.

"*Oh, my God!* A roach that size? That flies?"

"That's the way they grow around here," he said.

I recalled a psychiatrist friend in New York urging me to

conquer my roach phobia by becoming familiar with them. "Carry them in a test-tube," he told me. He couldn't have meant South African roaches. I'd die of a heart attack, just looking.

I wrote a song about the roach and played it on my opening night: "I Can't Expunge That Roach from My Mind." The song won more applause than my whole act.

The time had come to leave South Africa and tour the rest of the continent—Rhodesia, the Congo, Lambaréné to visit Dr. Schweitzer, the Sudan and Ethiopia. The U.S. Army would transfer Patti Shore from Nuremberg to Addis Ababa, the capitol of Ethiopia, where I'd visit her. She'd sent a form for me to sign granting her permission to sell my Mercedes.

In the Johannesburg library, I scanned telephone books for hotels and nightclubs in Rhodesia and the Congo, and posted letters to managers with my photos and reviews. All I needed were a few contracts to pay my way though Africa.

At Trek Airways office in Johannesburg, a clerk told me I would have to return to Europe as I came: Uganda, Egypt, Malta, Zurich. I said I *had* to see Rhodesia, the Congo, Sudan, and Ethiopia.

"You can't," he told me. "Your return ticket routes you as you came."

"Then I'll sell it," I said.

The six-foot, skin-and-bone clerk leaned across the glass-topped counter, pointing his long nose at my head as though to breathe sense into it. "It's only worth ninety pounds, Madam."

"How far will that get me?"

He calculated. "To the Sudan. Then you'll be stuck."

"I won't be stuck. I'll think of something."

"Africa isn't America," he said. "It's a jungle continent."

"Precisely why I want to see it."

"It's unsafe for a woman to travel through Africa alone. I urge you to go back the way you came."

"I'll take the ninety pounds, sir."

I wrote out my itinerary: One weekend in Mozambique, the Portuguese colony east of South Africa. Back to Johannesburg to pick up my luggage. North to Rhodesia. North again to the Congo. Lambaréné for Dr. Schweitzer. The Sudan.

"After that, Madam?" he asked.

"Ethiopia and Egypt."

"How, Madam? Your ticket will only take you to the Sudan."

"No idea, sir."

"You're making a mistake, Madam."

A man with the broadest shoulders I'd ever seen and manicured nails sat on my right on the flight to Mozambique. He said his country would enchant me. "Portuguese East Africa isn't like South Africa," he told me. "We have a saying: 'Wherever the British go, they leave a mess.' The British never got to Mozambique."

He handed me his card: *Eduardo Vaz, Director, Estoril Exports.* "How about dinner?" he asked when the plane taxied to a halt in Lorenzo Marques.

"I'd like that. I'd like to see the town."

Eduardo drove me to an airport hotel. "Portuguese dine late," he said. "I'll pick you up at eight."

I showered, changed, and strolled through the lobby past gift shops, florists, and boutiques. A silk dress in a window attracted me. It had a straight skirt and a short bolero. "That dress," I asked the saleslady. "Have you got it in another color? I don't like red."

"Sorry. Just red."

The dress looked chic when I tried it on, but it was costly, and red. *You can't afford it,* I told my reflection. *You need the money to travel.*

But I want to wear a new dress tonight. And the style shows my narrow waistline. It's just the red I don't like.

"I don't know what to do," I told the clerk.

"Take it. You look stunning."

I wore it to dinner with Eduardo, but felt uneasy in red. Next morning, a maid pressed it. I folded it neatly, put it back in the box that it came in, and went back to the boutique. "I'm so sorry. I couldn't wear this. Red is not my color."

"Quite all right, Madam." She returned my thirty dollars.

En route to the airport in a taxi, a voice in my head spoke loudly. *Stop, go back. Return the thirty bucks.*

No. Why should I?

It's stealing. Like you stole the two hundred bucks in New York. Remember?

I remember the fake abortion story so I could go to Knickerbocker Hospital to lose weight. But that was long ago and far away.

This was today. Return the thirty bucks.

I don't want to. I need it.

See that beggar on the curb with the burned face and distorted lips? Give him the thirty bucks. He needs it.

Why should I? I need it, too.

Then give him fifteen.

No. I deserve the thirty. I outsmarted the shop.

Give him ten.

The taxi driver pulled to a stop at the airport. "South African Airways, Madam."

I rushed inside before the voice in my head spoke again.

25

RHODESIA, THE CONGO, SUDAN

1958-59

Salisbury was the largest city in Southern Rhodesia, and Meikles was its finest hotel: A two story building that took up a city block. Men and women drank tea on the terrace and chatted in polished British accents.

A porter led me to the manager's office. "Foreign lady to see you, sir."

A man with a paunch and a monocle pushed his chair back from a teakwood desk. "Welcome," he said, and asked the porter to bring tea.

I told him that I was an American entertainer, working my way through Africa. I'd be in Rhodesia for two weeks, and wanted to perform at Meikles.

He thumbed through my portfolio. "What luck! To bring you here from the States would cost us a mint," he said.

We agreed on a fee for two weeks, to be paid in dollars. While his secretary typed the contract, he spoke of Africa. "This continent is like a colossal pot of water on heat. Part of the water is warm. Parts like ours are on the boil. Ready to burst. Our ghettos seethe with hate. Africans can't wait to burn our homes, smash our shops, attack our women.

"My neighbor asked his servant if he'd ever attack him. The boy had worked for him for ten years. The servant said he wouldn't attack him because he loved his master. But if his chief called for it, he'd ask a servant down the road to do it."

"How can you live here with such hatred and fear?" I asked.

He turned a framed photo toward me. "My wife and daughters. They're already home. I'm retiring at the end of this year, but didn't want them to wait. I'll be off soon," he grinned. "Back to the azaleas of Sussex."

The Congo had beckoned me since I was a kid. Now, I had two contracts for the country. Elizabethville in the southeast, and Stanleyville in the northwest.

Le Relais, a French cabaret in Elizabethville, had contracted me for a month. But after two weeks, I couldn't stomach another chorus of "C'est si bon," nor one more Cointreau. I was ready for the jungle.

On route to the forests of the north, my plane landed in Bucavu, the summer home of affluent Belgians who termed it "The Switzerland of Africa," a cool resort at three thousand feet up, with luxury villas surrounded by tea estates.

A small Sabena plane picked me up for the short hop north to Goma where Sabena Airlines had arranged for a Belgian guide to meet me. I spotted him as we touched down. Africa's famous safari leader, a thirty-five-year-old blond with a crew cut, clad in beige safaris, a matching shirt and knee-length socks. Two African aides stood behind him.

"You're Chris Pollet?" I asked.

"That's me," he beamed. "My Sabena telegram says, *Deane is a celebrity. Take her to lunch, then plan.*"

"That's funny. I'm no celebrity. But lunch sounds good."

His aides packed my luggage into their jeep and followed ours. We stopped at a Belgian eatery, but the aides drove on.

"Hey! They're off with my stuff!"

"Don't worry," Chris said. "It's safer with them than on Times Square. They went for an African meal."

A painting of the King of Belgium hung above our table. Waiters and guests were Belgian, and the menu was printed in French. This wasn't the Africa I longed to see.

Over spiced chicken, Chris told me that Sabena Airlines had informed him that I wanted to safari through the jungle, perform in Stanleyville, and take a side trip to Lambaréné to meet Dr. Schweitzer. Then back to Stanleyville for the flight to the Sudan.

"You know how life is," Chris said. "You never get everything you want."

He unfolded a map of the Congo. "Here we are in Goma, the northern tip of Lake Kivu. That dot," he pointed, "about three hundred miles northwest of here is Stanleyville. Doesn't sound much to an American, but I want to tell you, this is no turnpike. It could take three, five, ten days. Depends on weather, roads, who and what you meet en route.

"We'll convoy in two jeeps. Your luggage in the front one with the older driver. The younger driver and us in back. We'll go through the Ituri forest along the Ruwenzori mountain range. The Mountains of the Moon."

"*Mountains of the Moon*," I echoed. "Music to my ears."

I told Chris that I had an open-dated contract to play accordion at the Stanley Hotel for two weeks from whenever I arrived.

"Best hotel in the Congo," he said. "The only one with air conditioning. Now, about Dr. Schweitzer. To visit him, you'd have to fly to Leopoldville, rent a car to the port, and get a cargo ship to Lambaréné. I don't advise it."

"Why?"

"Unsafe." Chris lowered his voice. "Natives are waking up. We've robbed them for fifty years. Took out their rubber, uranium, copper, wood, tin. Paid them pittance in return. Two months ago, riots broke out in Leopoldville. Street fights, cars overturned, shop windows smashed. They sang *Vive l'Independence.* Chanted *Down with Belgium*. Blood ran all over the place.

"A primitive tribe cut out parts of a white man on the street. That's their culture. They eat the heart of their enemies for courage. The brain for smarts. Genitals for power."

"Oh, stop! I can't bear it." I covered my face with a napkin to blot out the image.

"A lone white woman could be caught and sold. Looking at you, I'd say you'd go for eighty head of cattle. A chief might buy you and resell you for a hundred. It's not just savage customs, it's that politics are hot. You heard of Lumumba? Patrice Lumumba, educated man. Leads a freedom movement. Stirs up natives."

"Then how will I see Dr. Schweitzer?"

"If you have oodles of cash, a pilot can fly you there and back in a private plane."

"I don't."

"Then you'll have to forget it."

I'd thought about Dr. Schweitzer since my teens. Now, so close, I found it tough to accept that I couldn't see him.

Chris booked me into a small hotel. "Rest," he said. "I'll pick you up for dinner. We'll start early tomorrow morning."

That evening, over beef and string beans, he talked about the turmoil. "Belgians aren't just selfish," he said, "we're stupid. Look at France. The French brought Africans to France, put them through college, turned them into doctors, professors, engineers. Like you sculpt from clay, they sculpted Africa's leaders. Those guys don't need to riot.

"We fools did the reverse. Turned schools into baby-sitters. One teacher for a hundred kids so they wouldn't learn much. If a dozen Congolese have college degrees, I'd be surprised. Not just that. Belgians did what Afrikaners did in South Africa. Turned tribes against each other. Now, only God can solve our inter-tribal hate. Wait and see. More blood will be shed here than in any war anywhere."

Next morning, I sat in the back of the jeep. Chris sat in front with the driver, half turned toward me. The Ruwenzori Mountains, "Mountains of the Moon," lay to the right of the dusty road from Goma to Stanleyville, their jagged peaks shrouded in mist.

Chris chatted about rainforests and mountain gorillas. I wished he'd keep quiet so I could capture the feel of the jungle. The thick canopy, the slivers of sunlight that passed through gaps to reach the forest floor, palms stretching outward like giant arms.

I saw my first palm tree in Palm Beach at nineteen, a sight that filled me with ecstasy, until the whole street came into view—palm trees planted the same distance from one another, like a stage set. In the Congo, nobody tailored nature. The whole jungle was singing a song of freedom. It was singing my song—"The Freedom to Be."

Monkeys shrieked and jumped from branches to the forest floor to snatch fallen fruit, then scampered back up the trees through endless tangles of green. Herds of buffalo and elephants headed toward water. We drove past doll-like huts that pygmies had made from huge leaves. How can they live with such little protection?

Native women clad in multi-colored skirts with basket-loads on their heads and babies strapped to their backs glided blithely by and smiled, toothless. Naked children ran toward us, ecstatic at the sight of foreigners. A six-foot Watussi watched us from outside his mud rondovel with his old mother, her naked breasts sagging to her waist.

"He's a chief," Chris said.

"He looks gentle."

"Sometimes he is."

Chris sat straight. "Oh, God! See those claw marks in the mud? That's the leopard man. He walks on all fours."

"He's a human being?"

"Right. A cannibal."

"We'll see him?"

Chris slunk down. "I hope not."

Before dark we stopped at a rest camp. My cabin was near the road. Chris and the two drivers took cabins at the far end. Other rooms were empty except for a custodian.

"Now don't get scared," Chris said. "Lots of creatures come out only at night. But you're safe indoors."

The jungle was so loud that I couldn't sleep. Buzzing, squealing, shrieking. Bats in trees outside my window sounded like they had built-in amplifiers.

At dawn, I opened my door a crack. Hundreds of pygmies with bows and arrows squatted on the forest floor. When they saw my door open, they sprinted toward me. I tried to scream but no sound came out. My heart pounded. I slammed the door and leaned against it.

Chris knocked. "They only want to sell you their bows and arrows."

I bought a dozen, and gave them all back except one.

We drove past rice fields and cotton plantations to the air-conditioned Hotel Stanley in Stanleyville where I signed a two-week contract. One hour of music at dinner for guests—Belgian men on business visits. The easiest job I ever had.

On departure day, Chris drove me to the airport, assuring me that we'd meet again. I knew we wouldn't, and wondered why so many people feel compelled to say that.

Sabena Airlines' manager checked my ticket to Khartoum, the last portion of my Africa ticket. "Sir," I said, "South African Airways' manager in Johannesburg told me I don't need a visa for the Sudan. He said permission to stay two days in Khartoum is granted at the airport. Is that correct?"

"Correct, Madame."

Only a few passengers disembarked in Khartoum. The rest continued to Europe. While I waited for my baggage at the pick-up area, a large man with a thick mustache and an Arabic name on his lapel tag approached me. "Passport."

The concertina additions of my passport fanned out when I opened it.

"Show me Sudan visa."

"No visa. Sabena Airlines said I don't need a visa. I'm only staying two days."

"You can not stay two hours without a visa. You must leave on the next flight."

"Where to?"

"Athens."

"I'm not going to Athens. I'm going to a hotel for a few days. Then by train to Ethiopia. I want my baggage."

"You will not go to hotel. You will go where we tell you to go."

"I will *not* go where you tell me to go."

"You can not stay here without visa. That is illegal."

"It's not my fault. Sabena said I don't need one."

"Sabena is not Sudanese government. We do not take orders from Sabena."

"I want my luggage. I will go to a hotel and stay two days."

"I *told* you. You can not stay even two hours without visa. We get you out on deportation order."

"Give me my luggage. I want to go to the nearest hotel."

"We will not give luggage. We put it on the next flight in one hour."

"I will report you to the American government."

"Report. We do not work for the American government."

This heavy-set man towered over me. He wore a pendant with a symbol of Mecca. Officers watching and listening were also Muslim. Would they dare to force me?

"I have to go to the toilet."

"There," he pointed.

One thing about Muslim men—they'd never enter a ladies' toilet, and I saw no women employees. If I stayed in the toilet until the next plane left, I wouldn't be on it. They couldn't put my luggage on it if I didn't check in. I had to take the chance.

I walked inside the smelly restroom and locked myself in a toilet. A plane landed. Men pounded on the outside door. "Come out! Come out!"

My heart raced. Even if they dared to open that door, they would never open a woman's toilet door.

The plane took off, the voices died down. I walked out.

Eight men fumed. "You know what is jail? We put you in jail. Understand?"

"Sorry." I rubbed my stomach. "Stomach problem."

Three policemen arrived. "Your passport."

"I need it," I said.

"*We* need it," the senior officer said.

Their police car followed my rickshaw to the Acropole Hotel, where a room cost two dollars and fifty cents. The policeman who held my passport spoke with the hotel manager as I signed in, and turned to me. "We keep your passport. We return it in forty-eight hours. Then you leave. Understand?"

Khartoum was the poorest city I'd seen. No vegetables, no fruit, no soap, no toilet paper. Electric power was off most of the day. When on, the lights were too dim to read by. Ceiling fans barely rotated. Only tepid water came out of the taps.

From my second floor window, I watched bony Sudanese in shabby clothes saunter along the hot, dusty streets. The sight of them pained me. I, too, had no money. Yet I was educated and confident. I could make my way anywhere in the world. These people had no education, no confidence, no options.

Two days later, I sat on a wooden seat in a literina, a two-car diesel train headed east. I thought of what my friend, Bill, had asked before I left New York. "What will you do if you run out of money in a place like Ethiopia?"

I told him I didn't know. I didn't know then, either, as the literina chugged its way slowly toward the Ethiopian border.

26

ASMARA, ADDIS ABABA, DJIBUTI

1959

Island in the sky, they call Asmara. Eight thousand feet above sea level. I wondered if anyone spoke English. I wanted to find a small hotel, and rest. The Sudanese train to the Ethiopian border, the long wait at Customs, the longer wait at the airport for a flight to Asmara had sapped me. A good sleep, a meal. Then I'd think about what next.

Two porters carried my luggage through the airport to the glass doors. It was two p.m., a sunny day in April, but the air felt like October in New York.

"Madame want taxi?" a porter asked.

"Please." He whistled to a taxi driver.

I thought I was seeing things. That couldn't be an American jeep parked in front. Four sergeants glared. I glared back. American sergeants in Ethiopia?

"Christ! Who's that?" one said.

"Excuse me, guys. What in the world is an American jeep doing here?"

"Picking somebody up."

One guy stood. "Hey wait a minute. She's American."

"I mean, what are you guys doing in Ethiopia?"

"We're stationed at Kagnew Air Base."

"An American base? Here?"

"What's a gorgeous American dame doing in this hole?" the driver asked.

"I'm an entertainer. Working my way around the world."

He turned around. "Guys, ya hear that? American entertainer! Hey, lady, if all you can do is stand on your head, you're booked!"

Two sergeants got out to bring their guest back in a taxi. I rode in the jeep with the other two. Ross, shaped like a triangle. Monroe with a high pitched voice. "We'll get promoted for bringing you back," Ross said.

Signs along the wide Asmara streets were in Italian: *Trattoria, Lasagna, Pensione.* "How come?" I asked Monroe.

"In the thirties, Mussolini wanted this part of the country, Eritrea, to become the Rome of Africa. He colonized it, and dethroned Haile Selassie. It didn't last. The Brits got the emperor back on his throne in 1941. But Asmara remains "little Italy."

"But what's a US base doing here?"

"It's classified," Monroe said. "We can't say much. All we can tell you is that it's a communications base." I figured that at eight thousand feet, they probably decoded and recoded messages from all over the world.

Along an open field to our right, an old man squatted with his pants down, scraping two rocks together. "What in the world is he doing?" I asked.

"Tell her," Ross said.

"Nah, you tell her," Monroe said.

"He's trying to make as much noise as he can. In Ethiopia, the sound of a fart is an evil omen."

I burst out laughing. "You mean one's own?"

"Anybody's."

I hoped Ethiopians were wrong. I'd heard lots of farts in my time.

The American flag flew on the left side of the Kagnew gate, the Ethiopian flag on the right. The men drove me around the base. A total community, though no larger than a half-mile square. One-family homes, apartments, barracks, a mess hall, clubs, a hospital, pool, gym, golf course, movie theater, boxing ring, tennis courts, bowling alley, schools, a chapel, offices, PX, repair units, Bachelor Officers' Quarters.

"You can't stay there," Ross pointed. "No non-military personnel allowed."

Within an hour I was booked for a month at clubs for enlisted men, NCOs and officers, with an in-house band to back me up.

And on the base TV. The editor of *The Kagnew Gazelle* had interviewed me for a full-page article.

I checked into a small hotel owned by a family from Sorrento, ate a plate of pasta, and relaxed on a rocking chair on the balcony overlooking a busy street. With a clipboard and paper on my lap, I penned a note to my New York friend, Bill.

Remember when you asked what I'd do if I got stuck in Ethiopia? Well, I got stuck. Here's what happened . . .

One morning on base, everyone was outside cleaning walkways, sweeping grounds, whitewashing buildings, waxing cars. Officers stood at attention at the gates as limousines pulled in.

"What's going on?" I asked an MP.

"See that limo? The Emperor is inside."

"What's the Emperor doing here?"

"Going to the dentist to pull a tooth."

"All this tumult for an emperor's tooth?"

"Well," the MP said, "Haile Selassie isn't just a head of state. He's also a direct descendent of the Queen of Sheba."

Even so, I thought. A tooth is just a tooth.

When my contract ended, the Officers Club captain asked what parting gift I'd like. "A fake ID," I told him. "So I can get into any PX to buy Kleenex and Noxzema."

My card read, *Rose Anderson, wife of Sergeant Stephen Anderson.* I hoped I'd remember the name. In Nuremberg, I was Rose Shapiro.

Patti Shore waved when I got off the plane in Addis Ababa, the capital of Ethiopia. Situated in the foothills of the Entoto Mountains, it, too, rises almost eight thousand feet above sea level. Patti lived in a flat on the fifth floor of a high-rise in the American compound, half the size of her flat in Germany. We lounged on the rug, drank wine, and ate deer meat with boiled potatoes and canned American asparagus.

My laughing fit rattled glasses as Patti described how she sold my Mercedes. Only she and her accomplice, a Major, knew that the name, Rose Shapiro, was fictitious. They rigged files to show that Shirley Deane, then in South Africa, signed the release of a Mercedes which she'd bought in Germany from Rose Shapiro whose military files had mysteriously vanished. A bottle of bourbon clinched the hundred-dollar sale.

I told Patti I planned to go to Cairo for a month. "Then Beirut, Damascus, Jerusalem, and Haifa."

"We have no military bases in those areas. How will you work?"

"Where's the nearest base?"

"Turkey. Enough bases to keep you busy for a year. Get a ship from Haifa."

The cheapest way to get to Cairo, she told me, would be a train to Dire Dawa, a small town east of Addis. Another train to Djibuti, a free port in French Somaliland. She pointed to a dot on the map at the southern tip of the Red Sea where it joins the Gulf of Aden. "Here."

"From Djibouti, hop a ship on the Red Sea to Alexandria," she said. "Then take a bus to Cairo. Thing is, since the Suez crisis, it costs as much to go through the Canal as it costs to cross the Atlantic. Get a job on a ship like you did in New York."

My mood darkened as Patti drove me to the train station. I'd lose her friendship, a bond that mattered to me in Copenhagen where we met, in Nuremberg, and there, in Addis. Now I wouldn't have it.

Bear it, I told myself. *Connecting and disconnecting is what life is about.*

But that rational voice didn't ease the emptiness that gnawed at my gut in her jeep. The same gnawing I felt in Stockholm when the Norwegian musicians boarded their train back to Oslo. At the hotel in Paris when Gene Moskowitz told me how much he'd miss me and my music. At the Johannesburg airport with Frank Collins. At the Congo airport where Chris Pollet hugged me, and said, like many before him, "We'll meet again." I knew they were wrong, just as I knew I'd never see Patti again.

My one-car diesel train crept past mud-walled shacks and terraced hills. Past hardworking, dark-skinned hands that glistened in the sun as they tended coffee plants. From Dire Dawa in eastern

Ethiopia, I rode another literina that descended the hills northeast toward the sea, halting at the port of Djibuti in French Somaliland.

The whole country was hardly bigger than the port. Maybe that's why it was the only French territory in Africa to decline France's offer of autonomy. France didn't care. Djibouti had a profitable rail line to the interior.

Le Monocle Hotel was a ten-minute walk from the port. Rooms had ceiling fans, the concierge assured me. "But electric power not always work." This was the end of May, and the temperature had soared to a hundred and three degrees.

The street to the port was dusty and sun-baked. My skin and mouth felt parched. At the docks I stood motionless. Throngs of stevedores and longshoremen shouted orders in French. Huge cranes spun, trucks pulled in and backed up to freighters. Laborers loaded and unloaded crates, barrels, sacks. Tons of timber and sugar and grain rolled into covered warehouses. Noise. Crowds. Dust.

A docked cargo ship flew an American flag. I wondered how I could find the captain. *Go, kid. Just go.*

"*Non, non,*" a longshoreman waved me off in French. Two men passed me, chatting. One spoke with a Brooklyn accent.

"Sir, where can I find the captain of that ship?"

"You're lookin' at him," he said. A mean-looking man. "What do you want?"

"I'm American."

"So what? So am I."

"I need to get to Egypt, sir. I can't afford a commercial liner. If you're going up the Red Sea, could I work on board? I play accordion."

"Listen, lady. I got enough troubles without a squeezebox player. That's the last thing I need." He took off. Both of us New Yorkers in this hell-hole, and he didn't give a hoot. If Americans don't give a hoot, who would?

Back to my hotel. The temperature had climbed to a hundred and eight. I showered in cold water, dried myself and stood under the ceiling fan. The blades rotated slowly, then quit. Sweat poured down my body. I felt sorry for myself.

Again I walked to the port, past souvenir shops and a noisy bar at the end of the street. A drink would help, but alcohol is bad for health in the heat. Still, I needed it.

The place was noisy and dark, and stank of beer and fish. Men stood three deep at the bar. Cut-out pinups of nude women were pasted on a mirror that covered the wall in back. Men stared. I was the only woman there. Maybe I was the only woman who'd ever been there. I moved to a square table near the window and slipped into a torn seat. With a tissue, I wiped up a blob of ketchup along the edge of the table.

A waiter came. "Madame?"

"Red wine."

The wine tasted like Manischewitz. I'd need six of them to feel better. Before I finished, the waiter returned. "That man," he pointed, "he wants buy Madame drink."

"*Merci*. I'll take it."

A chunky man with a boyish smile extended a hand. A rough-skinned hand with short, fat fingers. He looked like a hard-drinking seaman.

"Can I sit with you?" His accent was German.

"*Bitte*," I nodded.

"*Sprechen sie Deutsch?*"

"*Yah*. But I haven't spoken in a while."

"You live here?"

"No. I came to get a ship to Egypt, but I can't afford the Suez fare."

"Ahh. Few can. You are alone?"

"Alone."

"Please excuse me, but why is a beautiful woman alone? In Djibouti?"

Over two more wines I told Hans that I had hungered to see the world, worked my way through Europe, enrolled at the University of Munich, and played my way from Johannesburg to Asmara. "But my money won't last if I spend it on the Canal."

He grinned like he didn't believe a word I'd said. "What do you do, sir?" I asked.

"I'm captain of a cargo ship."

"What ship?"

He pointed out the window to a ship with a German flag unloading huge crates.

"Where do you go from here?"

He sipped his beer and grinned. "Alexandria."

"Alexandria? Could you take me? I play German songs." He shook his head. "We don't need music."

"I can type, I can clean."

"No," he said. "We hire our help in Germany."

He could be my only chance, but he doubted me. "Look, can you wait here? I want to get something, I'll be right back."

I hurried up the inclined street to my hotel in steaming heat, picked up my brochures, and raced back. Hans was cradling a beer at the bar.

We sat at the same table. "Here, sir. Have a look here." I opened my brochure to pages on Germany. "This is from the *Nürnberg 8-uhr Blatt*. Here's one from Frankfurt."

Hans read every word of every article, including reviews from New York and Johannesburg. "*Ach, Du liebes Bisschen!* I didn't believe a word you said. I thought you were, you know—" He nodded toward the mirror pinups. "One of those. I told my friends your story was what Americans call cock and bull."

I hoped Hans would say that he'd take me. He didn't.

"That Frankfurt article says you play chess. True?"

"True."

"Let's play. Tell you what. If you win, I take you to Egypt."

"Oh, my! *Danke, danke!*"

"Don't thank me yet. You must first win."

The barman looked through a games box. Cards, dominoes, dice, checkers. A dirty old chess set. Hans set up the board. Bar noise subsided. Men strode over to watch. Eight moves into the game, it was clear that Hans could outplay me blindfolded. My queen was at risk, but he didn't take it. I took his instead.

"*Schach Mat!*" I yelled.

"Oooph! You won!"

Two days later, I knelt on the bed of a cabin on Hans' ship, peering through portholes at a surreal scene. The ends of hundreds of ships stuck up through the surface of the Red Sea like the limbs of corpses in a mass grave.

A German magazine on my night table told the story.

The Suez Canal was the commercial lifeline between the Middle East and the rest of the world. When Egypt, with its close ties to the Soviets, nationalized the Canal, Britain and France panicked. They thought Middle East oil would be cut off, so they collaborated with Israel to attack. One week later, ten thousand people were dead, injured or missing. But the oil flowed.

Ironic that something so valuable to so many should provoke such carnage. Maybe that's typical of human nature. The greater the worth, the more selfish the desire.

I stared at the massive rusted hulks that reached out of the Red Sea. Where do the bones of the dead rest, I wondered.

FROM THE SHIRLEY DEANE SCRAPBOOK

New York City, 1947

Walter Winchell
In New York

Bravorchids: Bud Taylor's organ wizardry at the Sheraton Lounge..."Land of the Lost" via ABC Satdees...Stan Kenton's "Theme to the West" record. Enter-tune-ment...Jean Sablon's Victorecord, "A Tune for Humming"...The Rainbow platter of "Movie Parade"...Nype and Cote at the Maisonette...Shirley Deane's accordeane-solos at the Dixie Terrace Room...Orchids (by the corsage-loads) to the Revere Camera people of Chicago. This sponsor is the only one our ears ever met who appears to know why radio was invented: Mainly to make listeners happy with a boy

Walter Winchell's newspaper column was syndicated in over 2,000 newspapers worldwide from the 1920s until the early 1960s. Here, he wrote in his trademark clipped-style column, which he began *"Bravorchids*....Shirley Deane's accordeane solos at the Dixie Terrace Room."

DAY, JUNE 2, 1950, ATLANTIC CITY, N. J.

ATLANTIC CITY PRESS

ACCORDIONIST

Publicity photo while appearing at the Sun and Star Roof atop the Senator Hotel in Atlantic City, June, 1950.

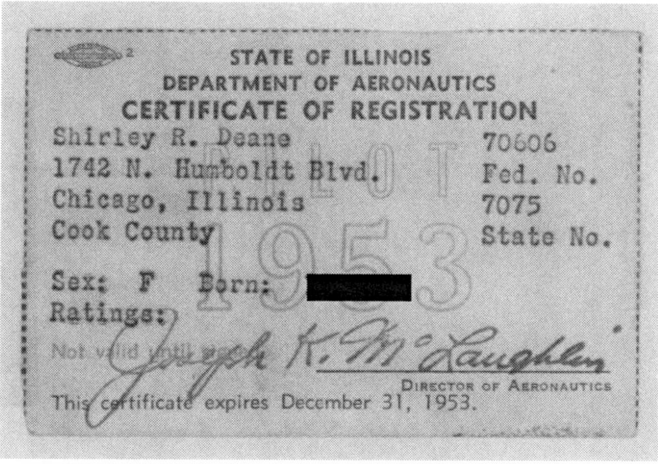

STATE OF ILLINOIS

DEPARTMENT OF AERONAUTICS

CERTIFICATE OF REGISTRATION

Shirley R. Deane — 70606
1742 N. Humboldt Blvd. — Fed. No.
Chicago, Illinois — 7075
Cook County — State No.

PILOT 1953

Sex: F Born:

Ratings:

Not valid until

Joseph K. McLaughlin

DIRECTOR OF AERONAUTICS

This certificate expires December 31, 1953.

My student pilot's license issued by the State of Illinois, 1953.

With James Petrillo on the M/S Oslofjord's Christmas cruise to the Caribbean, 1955.

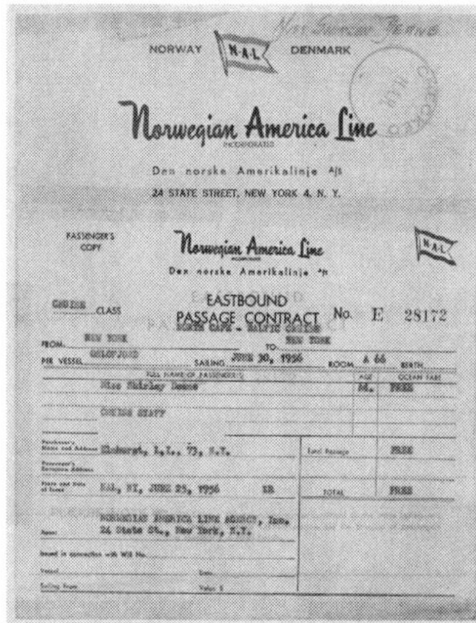

NORWAY N.A.L. DENMARK

Norwegian America Line

Den norske Amerikalinje A/S

24 STATE STREET, NEW YORK 4, N. Y.

PASSENGER'S COPY

Norwegian America Line

Den norske Amerikalinje A/S

EASTBOUND PASSAGE CONTRACT No. E 28172

CLASS

FROM NEW YORK TO NEW YORK

PER VESSEL OSLOFJORD SAILING JUNE 30, 1956 ROOM A 66 BERTH

FULL NAME OF PASSENGER(S) AGE OCEAN FARE

TOTAL

My contract for the Midnight Sun Cruise from New York City to Iceland, Norway, Sweden, Finland and Denmark—June 30, 1956

NORTH CAPE DIPLOMA

It is hereby certified that

M

passenger on

cruising in the Land of the Midnight Sun,

has to-day visited

NORTH CAPE

the Northernmost point of Europe.

NORDKAPP

9-7-56

N.LAT. 71°10'21"

NORDKAPS VEL A/S

My diploma for having reached the northernmost point in Europe.

Bra „Show i Store Studio"

The Norwegian *Aftenposten* newspaper, Monday, October 8, 1956: As guest musician on a popular Norwegian radio show.

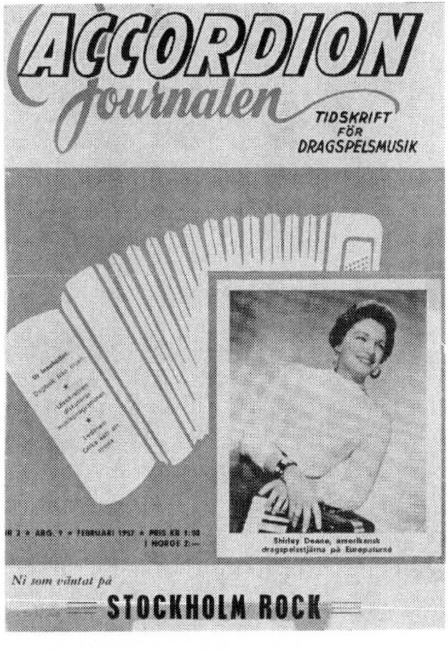

ACCORDION Journalen TIDSKRIFT FÖR DRAGSPELSMUSIK

FEBRUARI 1957

Shirley Deane, amerikansk dragspelsstjärna på Europaturné

Ni som väntat på STOCKHOLM ROCK

"Shirley Deane, American accordionist in Europe."

Redaktør: KARL OTTO HOFF

Jazz og moderne dansemusikk

Arnulf Neste i Sverige tre måneder

Trioen Arnulf Neste, Shirley Deane og Knut Ljungh ombord i Oslofjord.

Engasjement i Shirley Deane's trio i sommer

en tid. Hadde en del utenbys en- gasjementer og spilte bl. a. på blomsterutstillingen i Fredrikstad.

Siste halve året har hun jobbet i Sverige med fine kritikker over- alt.

Norwegian press reports that my trio consisting of Arnulf Neste on drums, myself on accordion, and Knut Ljungh on bass would perform in Sweden for three months.

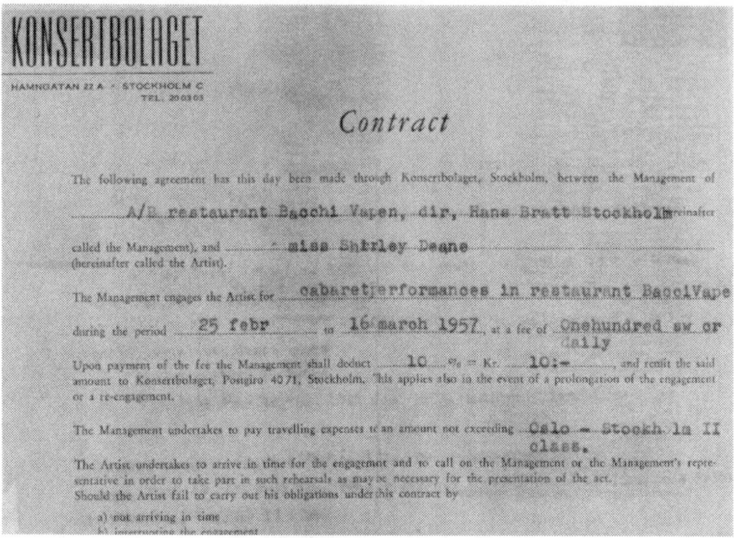

KONSERTBOLAGET

HAMNGATAN 22 A · STOCKHOLM C
TEL. 200303

Contract

The following agreement has this day been made through Konsertbolaget, Stockholm, between the Management of A/B restaurant Bacchi Vapen, dir, Hans Bratt Stockholm (hereinafter called the Management), and miss Shirley Deane (hereinafter called the Artist).

The Management engages the Artist for cabaret performances in restaurant BacciVape during the period 25 febr to 16 march 1957, at a fee of Onehundred sw cr daily

Upon payment of the fee the Management shall deduct 10 % = Kr. 10:-, and remit the said amount to Konsertbolaget, Postgiro 4071, Stockholm. This applies also in the event of a prolongation of the engagement or a re-engagement.

The Management undertakes to pay travelling expenses to an amount not exceeding Oslo - Stockh la II class.

The Artist undertakes to arrive in time for the engagement and to call on the Management or the Management's representative in order to take part in such rehearsals as may be necessary for the presentation of the act. Should the Artist fail to carry out his obligations under this contract by

a) not arriving in time

My contract to perform at the Stockholm nightclub, Bacchi Vapen, owned by the fiancé of actress Sonja Henie (February 12, 1957).

Dragspelsstjärna från USA till CH

CH-VALERESK SOM ALLTID överlämnade Pelle Lundgren en ros till Centralhotellets nya attraktion, dragspelsartisten Shirley Deane from USA.

On radio in Sweden. (March 18, 1957)
Heading: “Accordion Artist from USA”

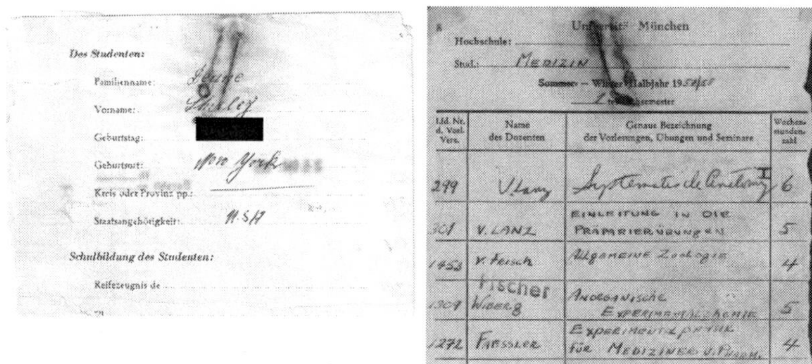

Des Studenten:

Familienname:

Vorname: Shirley

Geburtstag:

Geburtsort: New York

Kreis oder Provinz pp.:

Staatsangehörigkeit: U.S.A.

Schulbildung des Studenten:

Reifezeugnis de

Universität München

Hochschule:

Stud.: MEDIZIN

Sommer- — Winter-Halbjahr 1957/58

Lfd. Nr. d. Vorl. Verz.	Name des Dozenten	Genaue Bezeichnung der Vorlesungen, Übungen und Seminare	Wochenstundenzahl
299	V. Lanz	Systematische Anatomie I	6
301	V. LANZ	EINLEITUNG IN DIE PRÄPARIERÜBUNGEN	5
1453	v. Frisch	Allgemeine Zoologie	4
1304	Fischer Wiberg	ANORGANISCHE EXPERIMENTALCHEMIE	5
1272	FAESSLER	EXPERIMENTALPHYSIK FÜR MEDIZINER	4

(Left) Registration certificate for University of Munich Medical School, Winter 1957/8. (Right) My schedule of courses at University of Munich Medical School.

8 Uhr-Blatt

Montag, 16. Dezember 1957

Nürnberg gefällt ihr so gut . . .

Shirley Deane, amerikanischer Fernsehstar, ist in Nürnberg eingetroffen, um im Rahmen der US-Truppenbetreuung mit ihrem Akkordeon zu brillieren. Auf ihrer Reise durch die ganze Welt, die sie u. a. durch Venezuela, Puerto Rico, Curacao, England, Norwegen, Schweden, Island, Finnland, Dänemark, Spanien und Österreich führte, ist Miß Deane von Nürnberg so stark beeindruckt, daß sie noch einige Wochen hier bleiben will. Foto: Pawlos

The Nuremburg Review: "Nuremberg delights her."

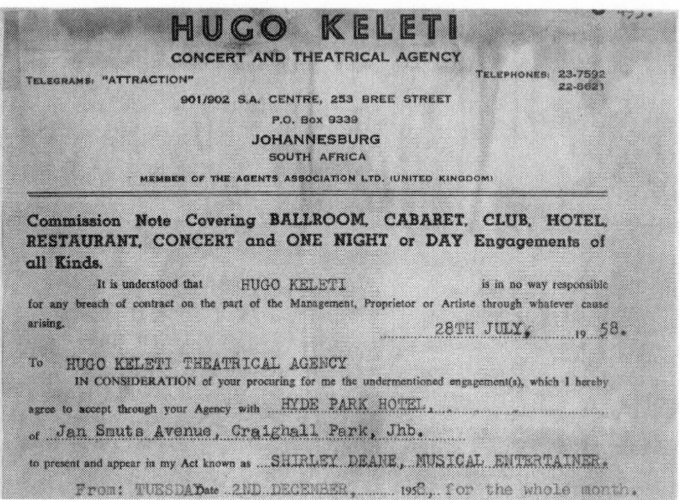

HUGO KELETI
CONCERT AND THEATRICAL AGENCY

TELEGRAMS: "ATTRACTION" — TELEPHONES: 23-7592, 22-8621

901/902 S.A. CENTRE, 253 BREE STREET
P.O. Box 9339
JOHANNESBURG
SOUTH AFRICA

MEMBER OF THE AGENTS ASSOCIATION LTD. (UNITED KINGDOM)

Commission Note Covering BALLROOM, CABARET, CLUB, HOTEL, RESTAURANT, CONCERT and ONE NIGHT or DAY Engagements of all Kinds.

It is understood that HUGO KELETI is in no way responsible for any breach of contract on the part of the Management, Proprietor or Artiste through whatever cause arising.

28TH JULY, 19 58.

To HUGO KELETI THEATRICAL AGENCY

IN CONSIDERATION of your procuring for me the undermentioned engagement(s), which I hereby agree to accept through your Agency with HYDE PARK HOTEL,

of Jan Smuts Avenue, Craighall Park, Jhb.

to present and appear in my Act known as SHIRLEY DEANE, MUSICAL ENTERTAINER.

From: TUESDAY Date 2ND DECEMBER, 1958, for the whole month.

My contract for the Hyde Park Hotel, Johannesburg, from December 2 to 31, 1958 (following Zsa Zsa Gabor).

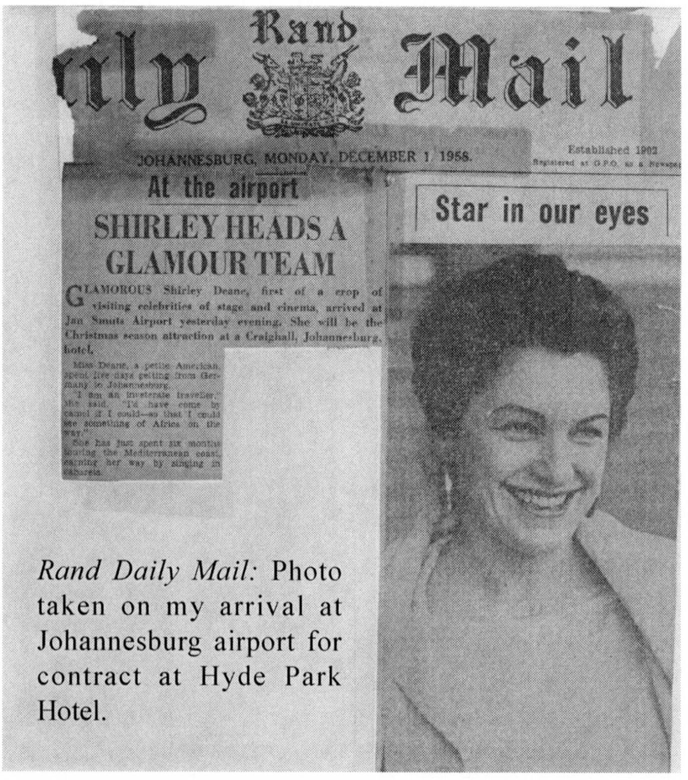

Rand Daily Mail

JOHANNESBURG, MONDAY, DECEMBER 1, 1958.

Established 1902

At the airport

SHIRLEY HEADS A GLAMOUR TEAM

GLAMOROUS Shirley Deane, first of a crop of visiting celebrities of stage and cinema, arrived at Jan Smuts Airport yesterday evening. She will be the Christmas season attraction at a Craighall, Johannesburg, hotel.

Miss Deane, a petite American, spent five days getting from Germany to Johannesburg.

"I am an inveterate traveller," she said. "I'd have come by camel if I could—so that I could see something of Africa on the way."

She has just spent six months touring the Mediterranean coast, earning her way by singing in cabarets.

Star in our eyes

Rand Daily Mail: Photo taken on my arrival at Johannesburg airport for contract at Hyde Park Hotel.

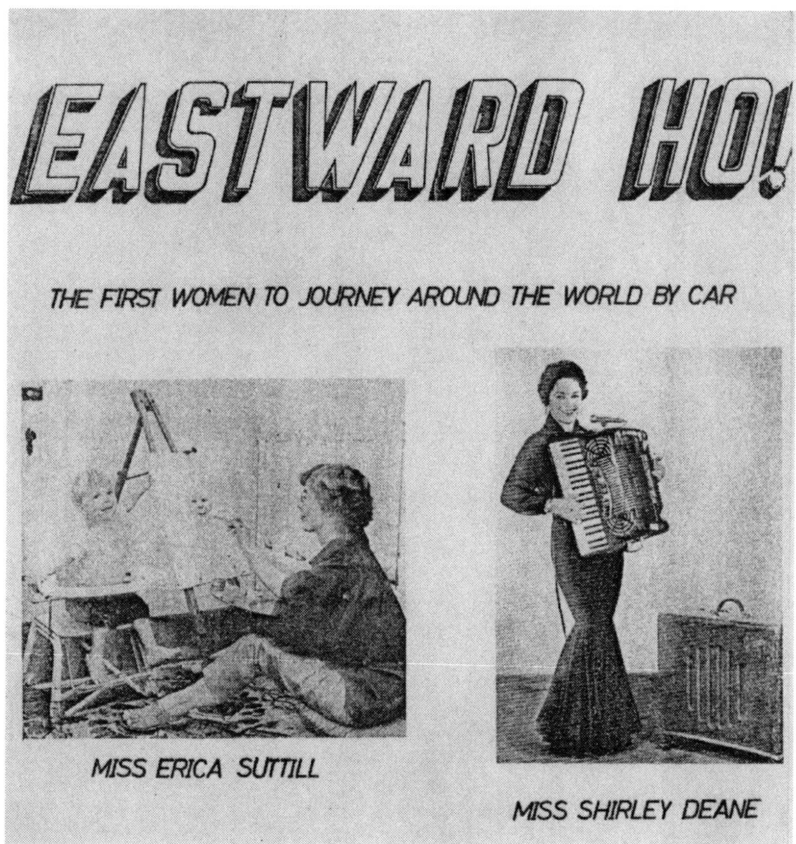

Cover of brochure that artist Erica Suttill and I prepared prior to our overland journey by Land Rover from London to Malaya (now Malaysia).

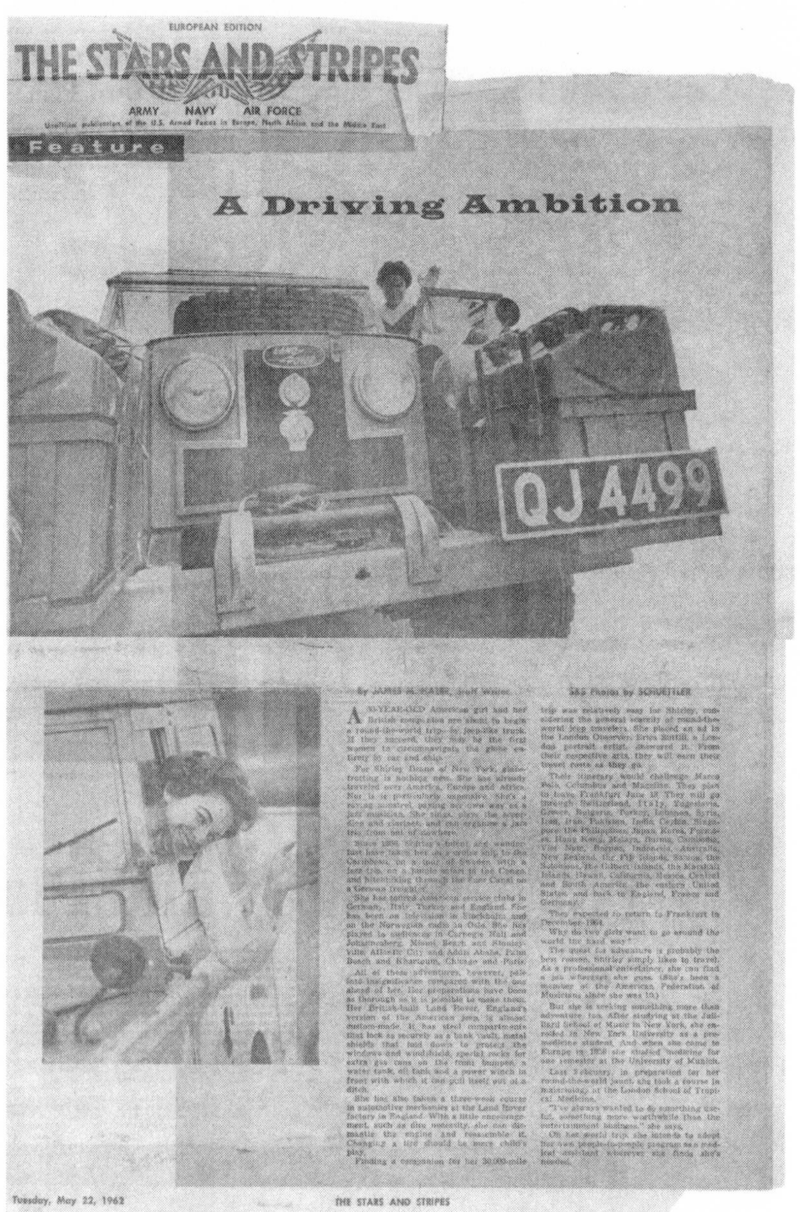

EUROPEAN EDITION

THE STARS AND STRIPES

ARMY NAVY AIR FORCE

Unofficial publication of the U.S. Armed Forces in Europe, North Africa and the Middle East

Feature

A Driving Ambition

Tuesday, May 22, 1962 THE STARS AND STRIPES

The Stars and Stripes (May 22, 1962)

Frankfurter Rundschau

Dienstag, 24. April 1962 · Jahrg. 1[illegible]

Weltreise mit zehn Gängen

Eine ungewöhnliche Frau in einem ungewöhnlichen Fahrzeug

Ein ungewöhnliches Fahrzeug kann man seit einigen Tagen auf den Frankfurter Straßen beobachten. Es ist ein hochbeiniger englischer Geländewagen mit Allradantrieb, acht Vorwärts- und zwei Rückwärtsgängen und einer Seilwinde über der vorderen Stoßstange. Am Steuer dieses dumpf brummenden Monstrums sitzt eine Frau. Und diese Frau kann den Wagen nicht nur fahren, sondern auch in wenigen Stunden zerlegen und wieder zusammenbauen, wenn es sein muß. Das ist keine Uebertreibung: sie hat einen sechsmonatigen Lehrgang im Herstellerwerk des Wagens hinter sich.

Miß Shirley Deane will schließlich mit diesem Wagen in den nächsten zweieinhalb Jahren eine Weltreise unternehmen — und Reparaturen im Mittleren Osten oder in Asien können sehr kostspielig werden. Start zu dieser nicht ganz alltäglichen Expedition ist Frankfurt. Hier trifft Miß Deane zur Zeit ihre letzten Vorbereitungen. Die elegante, lebhafte Dame, die vor nicht allzu langer Zeit ihren dreißigsten Geburtstag gefeiert hat, verfügt über beträchtliche Erfahrungen im Weltenbummeln.

Seit die gebürtige New Yorkerin vor nunmehr sechs Jahren ihre Heimatstadt verließ, befindet sie sich auf einer permanenten Weltreise. Nicht daß sie von den Zinsen eines Millionenvermögens zehren könnte: Mit ihrem Akkordeon und als Schlagersängerin verdient sie jeden Pfennig selbst. Wenn sie von ihren Erlebnissen erzählt, kann man sie beneiden. 1957 fuhr sie mit einem Schiff vom Karibischen Meer nach Oslo. Die Passage verdiente sie sich, indem sie die Mannschaft mit ihrem Instrument unterhielt. In Oslo trat sie in einem Nachtklub auf, und kurze Zeit später landete sie auch beim Rundfunk. Ein einflußreicher Schwede, der ihre Sendung gehört hatte, holte sie nach Stockholm. Sie trat im Fernsehen auf und gründete dann ein Jazztrio, mit dem sie durch ganz Schweden reiste.

Manchmal klappte es nicht mit der Musik: Als sie über das Rote Meer nach Aegypten reisen wollte, hatte sie statt 200 Dollar nur 55 — zuwenig für die Passage. Der Kapitän eines deutschen Frachters machte sich nichts aus Musik, er war schachbesessen. Als er merkte, daß er eine erstklassige Schachspielerin vor sich hatte, streckte er die Waffen: „Wir spielten von morgens bis in die Nacht Schach", erinnerte sich Miß Deane.

Sie hätte genauso gut dem Schiffsarzt bei einer Operation helfen können, denn irgendwie hat sie es im Laufe der Jahre fertiggebracht, auch einige Semester Medizin zu studieren — zwei davon in München. Nach Deutschland kommt sie häufig und gern: „Die Deutschen haben mehr mit den Amerikanern gemeinsam als alle anderen Völker, die ich kenne", sagt Miß Deane.

Diese Reise ist übrigens die erste, die sie nicht allein unternimmt. Eine englische Malerin, die über genausoviel Temperament und Energie verfügen muß wie Miß Deane, wird sie begleiten. Anfang Mai kommt Miß Erica Suttill aus London nach Frankfurt. Dann werden die Koffer in den Geländewagen verstaut, und ab geht die Fahrt. Die Reiseroute liest sich wie das Inhaltsverzeichnis eines Weltatlasses: Italien, Griechenland, Türkei, den ganzen Nahen Osten, Indien, Burma, Japan, Australien, die Inseln im Pazifik, Hawaii, dann in die Vereinigten Staaten, Südamerika und wieder zurück nach Frankfurt. o-k

Weltreisende Shirley Deane
(FR-Bild: Bohnacker)

The Frankfurt Daily News: World Trip with Ten Gears (April 24, 1962)
Photo taken of me in my Land Rover, typing on a Royal portable typewriter on my glove-compartment pull-out desk.

Hürriyet

GÜNLÜK MÜSTAKİL SİYASİ GAZETE

BİR cipte yola çıkan Amerika'lı kadın gazeteci Shirley Deane, daima Doğu'ya gitmek suretiyle 2,5 senede memleketine varacak. Yukarıdaki resimde, şimdi Ankara'da bulunan ve Türklerin misafirperverliğinden çok memnun olan Bayan Deane'e bir köylü, yol gösterirken görülüyor. (Foto: H. - T. Tuğcu)

Hep Doğu'ya giderek Amerika'ya ulaşacak

(Above) Driving alone in Ankara, Turkey. Asking for directions, 1962.
(Below) Beirut, Lebanon. October 5, 1962.

The Daily Star

ذي دايلي ستار يومية سياسية تصدر عن دار الحياة

BEIRUT LEBANON TEL: 221840-41-42 P.O.B. 887

FRIDAY, OCTOBER 5, 1962

THE DAILY STAR BEIRUT LEBANON

WORLD TRIP: Miss Shirley Deane stands beside her Land Rover at Beirut yesterday as she prepared for her journey eastward. Miss Deane leaves Beirut today.

... داخل سيارة
ال « لاندروفر » التي
ابتاعتها
في لندن ،
بعد أن
خطف الحب رفيقتها .

Beirut, Lebanon, October, 1962.

شيرلي دين ،
المغامرة
الاميركية الكبيرة ، في
حلقة من
حلقات الجنس
الخشن التي
لا تفتأ تحيط بها .

— كنت لاعبة « اكورديون » على شاشة
التلفزيون الاميركية ... وكان لي برنامجي
الخاص اقدم فيه فرقتي وبرامج موسيقية
منوعة ... وكنت احب عملي حبا عظيما .

● هوايتي ... والحب الكبير

جدا ، والا لما كان وقف في وجهه شيء...
ولي وجه الصعوبات والعراقيل رأيت ان ابتعد
بحياتي عن ذلك الحب بالرغم من الالم
الكبير وانا واثقة من ان حبي للسفر
سيشفيني من ذلك الالم .. !

● بين بلدان العالم

وتقول « شيرلي » انها أعجبت كثيرا
بالبلدان الشرقية وخاصة بلدان البحر
الابيض المتوسط . فالناس في هذه المناطق
لطيفو المعشر ، مضيافون ، يشعرونها

Lebanese press reporter interviewing me along with three young Bristish men traveling by Jeep (Beruit, Lebanon, October 1962).

KAYHAN
INTERNATIONAL EDITION

(Vol. IV) No. 896 TEHRAN, MONDAY, OCTOBER 15, 1962 (MEHR 23, 1341) PRICE: 5 Rials

ENTERTAINER TURNS TO GLOBE TROTTING

A young American woman, equipped with a Land Rover, a course in mechanics, canned food, a make-shift kitchen, an accordian and an ability to sing is presently passing through Iran in a bid to make a tour of the world. Hav- ways her home. She sleeps in it, cooks in it; employs a water-purifier to get her drinking water; makes milk out of the powdered product; and lives, when on the road, on canned food.

When faced with mechanical trouble, she repairs the automobile herself, having been pre-armed with a mechanics course she took

Teheran, Iran, October 1962.

Driving east, away from the setting sun, across the Iranian desert.

Aiming a rifle in the Iranian desert with my two armed escorts, 1962.

This photo was taken in 1962 in the Persian desert near Zahedan where I met four Australians traveling west to the U.K. in a jeep. At the end of the line, are my two escorts.

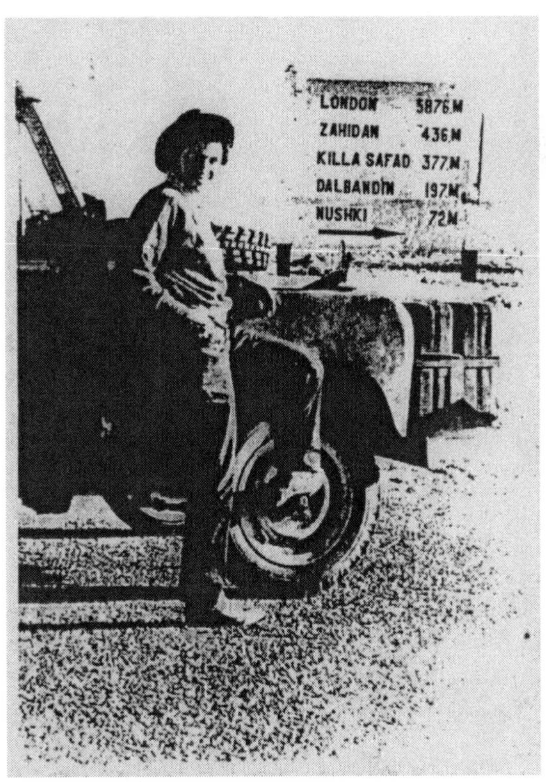

Driving east, alone, in Pakistan, 1962.

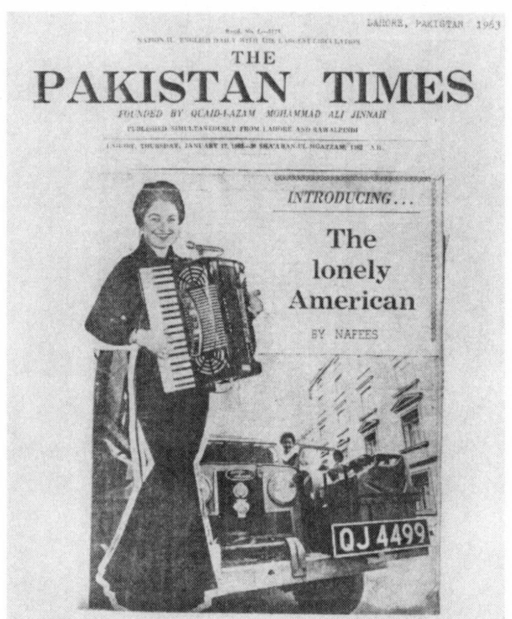

LAHORE, PAKISTAN 1963

THE
PAKISTAN TIMES

FOUNDED BY QUAID-I-AZAM MOHAMMAD ALI JINNAH

PUBLISHED SIMULTANEOUSLY FROM LAHORE AND RAWALPINDI

INTRODUCING...

The lonely American

BY NAFEES

The Pakistan Times, the largest English daily newspaper, Lahore, Pakistan, Thursday, January 17, 1963.

Shirley Deane and her Land Rover in Delhi.

ROUND THE WORLD ON A MUSICAL RIDE

A Young American Mixes Jazz With Mechanics

MOTOR MECHANIC

It was in Somaliland that Shir[illegible] Deane decided to do the rest of the globe by [illegible]. She returned to Germany and [illegible] together yet another Shirley Deane jazz trio. Money was soon raised [illegible] engine and reassemble it, [illegible] says. Flat tyres simply do no[t] bother her.

On her eastward thrust, Mi[ss] Deane has passed through Switzer[-]land, Italy, Yugoslavia, Greec[e], Bulgaria, Turkey, Lebanon, Syri[a]

The Times of India, New Dehli, June 1963. The article claims that I drove through Switzerland, Yugoslavia, and Bulgaria, which was untrue.

BROOKLYN SECTION

SUNDAY NEWS

NEW YORK'S PICTURE NEWSPAPER

LARGEST CIRCULATION ON LONG ISLAND

New York 17, N.Y., Sunday, July 21, 1963

It Adds Up—World Trip. Stick a pin in the globe to mark the spot where Shirley Deane of Elmhurst, Queens, is resting on her car, and the spot will be in Pakistan. Shirley's ambition is to be the first female New Yorker to drive round the world. She's heading for Malay Peninsula, then Thailand. —*Story p. 32*

This photo was taken in London in 1961 when I had just purchased my Land Rover. It shows my first license plate, issued for domestic use only. When I left the U.K., I was given an overseas license number of QJ 4499.

A New York News reporter interviewed me in New Delhi in June, 1963. His article and this photograph were printed in the New York Sunday News on July 21.

*"**Eastward Ho!**"* on a Nepali road from Kathmandu to Trisuli.

The Trisuli refugee camp for Tibetans in Nepal. Here, I am teaching an outdoor geography class to the children of Tibetan refugees, holding a map to show them Tibet where they came from, Nepal where they were, and India where they would join the Dalai Lama. I started a clinic, raised funds, and carted food and medicine regularly from Kathmandu along a narrow, treacherous road. After a year, the last of the Tibetans had crossed the Himalayan range into India. Eight years later, on December 6, 1972, this photo of me and my Tibetan students appeared in the *Natal Mercury*, a newspaper in Durban, South Africa.

In October of this year, construction will begin on a new student union building – a gift from an American firm, and towards the end of the year Inanda will embark on its most important project of its second century of operation – the expansion of its facilities to accommodate more students.

Time marches on and Inanda is marching right along with it!

Shirley Deane

Shirley Deane (Public Relations).

Public Relations officer and Fund Raiser for Inanda Seminary, mission high school for African girls near Durban, South Africa, 1972

The Staff—1968.

Inanda Seminary staff photo. One of only two high schools during the apartheid regime to have a miltiracial staff. I am seated front row, fourth from right.

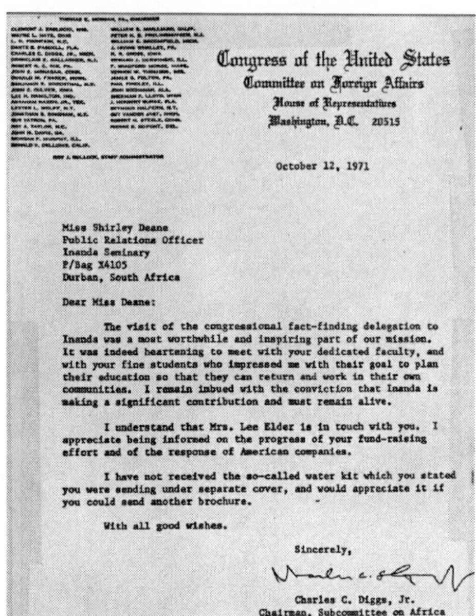

Congress of the United States
Committee on Foreign Affairs
House of Representatives
Washington, D.C. 20515

October 12, 1971

Miss Shirley Deane
Public Relations Officer
Inanda Seminary
P/Bag X4105
Durban, South Africa

Dear Miss Deane:

The visit of the congressional fact-finding delegation to Inanda was a most worthwhile and inspiring part of our mission. It was indeed heartening to meet with your dedicated faculty, and with your fine students who impressed me with their goal to plan their education so that they can return and work in their own communities. I remain imbued with the conviction that Inanda is making a significant contribution and must remain alive.

I understand that Mrs. Lee Elder is in touch with you. I appreciate being informed on the progress of your fund-raising effort and of the response of American companies.

I have not received the so-called water kit which you stated you were sending under separate cover, and would appreciate it if you could send another brochure.

With all good wishes.

Sincerely,

Charles C. Diggs, Jr.
Chairman, Subcommittee on Africa

Letter to me from Congressman Charles Diggs, Jr. of Michigan, Chairman of the Subcommittee on Africa after the congressional visit to Inanda Seminary.

Mrs. Raleigh Warner, wife of Mobil Oil Chairman Raleigh Warner, Jr., laying the foundation stone for Inanda Seminary's Mobil Student Centre. To her left is Chief Mangosuthu Gatsha Buthelezi, and to her right, Inanda Seminary accountant, Mr. D. McDonald. (September, 1972)

Writing my first book, *Black South Africans: A Who's Who* (Oxford University Press, 1978), during which time I was harrassed by the apartheid government's security police.

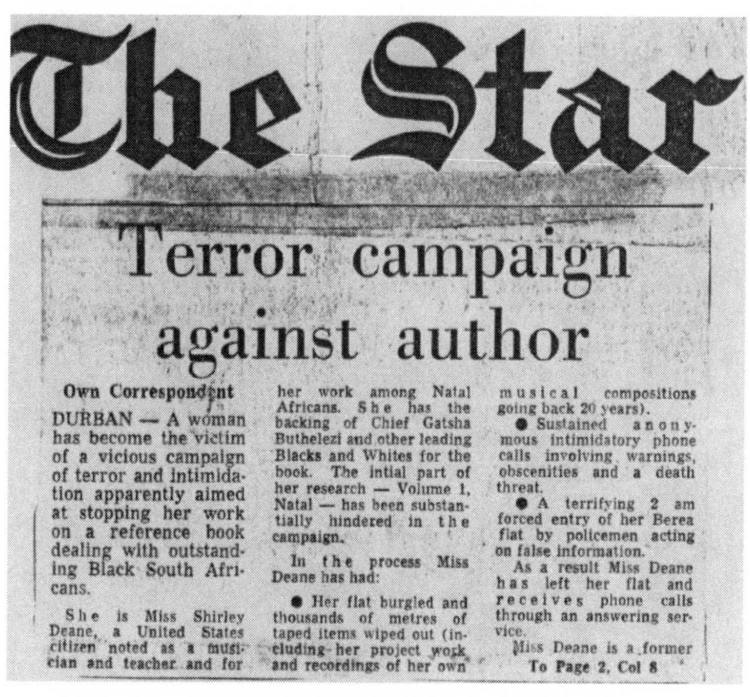

The Star

Terror campaign against author

Own Correspondent

DURBAN — A woman has become the victim of a vicious campaign of terror and intimidation apparently aimed at stopping her work on a reference book dealing with outstanding Black South Africans.

She is Miss Shirley Deane, a United States citizen noted as a musician and teacher and for her work among Natal Africans. She has the backing of Chief Gatsha Buthelezi and other leading Blacks and Whites for the book. The intial part of her research — Volume 1, Natal — has been substantially hindered in the campaign.

In the process Miss Deane has had:

- Her flat burgled and thousands of metres of taped items wiped out (including her project work and recordings of her own musical compositions going back 20 years).
- Sustained anonymous intimidatory phone calls involving warnings, obscenities and a death threat.
- A terrifying 2 am forced entry of her Berea flat by policemen acting on false information.

As a result Miss Deane has left her flat and receives phone calls through an answering service.

Miss Deane is a former

To Page 2, Col 8

From *The Star*, Johannesburg's newspaper, Friday, May 14, 1976

The Daily News

Established 1878 · DURBAN, FRIDAY, MAY 14, 1976

'Terror campaign' bid to end woman's work on book

Daily News Reporter

A DURBAN woman has become the victim of a campaign of terror and intimidation apparently aimed at stopping her work on an important reference book dealing with outstanding Black South Africans.

Steenkamp, head of the Security Branch in Natal.

At the interview Colonel Steenkamp was visibly perturbed and said he would ask the Durban C.I.D. to investigate. This the C.I.D. did but during the police investigation the frightening harassment was stepped up.

Intimidation started when Miss Deane began work on the project last October. She undertook the task virtually singlehanded, although the selection of candidates for the reference book was done by five leading Black members of a trustee committee.

The other members of the committee are Mr Grice; the former director of the Natal Chamber of Industries, Mr Percy Thomas, and Dr Conrad Strauss, who is a senior banking executive.

After much of the work had been done, and during . visit to Cape Town, Miss

NOISES

Twenty cassettes containing details of her interviews were also wiped. It was soon after this that the phone calls began in earnest. Many were from a man with a Slavonic accent. .. senior police officer raised the possibility that it could be the work of the U.S. Central Intelligence Agency.

Then a strange incident occured. At 2am one night there was a loud knocking on her door which she was afraid to answer. Then a uniformed policeman burst in through a window and let several others into her flat.

They told her someone claiming to be a neighbour had reported seeing a "Bantu male" going into her flat and hearing loud noises. They had burst in because they thought she might be being attacked. Like Colonel Steenkamp, these police (who found only Miss Deane in the flat) were courteous and

From *The Daily News*, Durban, May 14, 1976

Dee Shirley Deane, author of South Africa's first Who's Who of black people tells SUE GARBETT the story behind the story of her book.

Terror tactics failed to stop her book

DEE SHIRLEY DEANE — "almost as if black people hadn't made a contribution to this country."

Someone should write a book about Dee Shirley Deane. It would be a tale of great courage, much adventure and a love of people.

The fact is she has written a book.

It's the first of its kind in this country, a Who's Who of leading blacks, called "Black South Africans."

There's a tale behind her telling of the lives of 57 of Natal's leading blacks.

And it nearly wasn't told because someone tried to kill her before she could write the book.

Not long after she began work, she became the victim of a vicious campaign of terror and intimidation apparently aimed at stopping her project.

Her Durban flat was burgled and thousands of metres of taped items wiped out (including her project work and recordings of her own musical compositions going back 20 years).

She received anonymous intimidating telephone calls involving warnings, obscenities and a death threat.

No brakes

"I got into my car one day and found myself hurtling down the steep street unable to stop because the brakes had been tampered with. Luckily I managed to stop the car against a curb," said Miss Deane in her controlled, quiet manner.

"I moved nine times in six months in an effort to get away from my intimidators."

As suddenly as it had started, the terror campaign against her stopped. Maybe someone somewhere finally realised she is an apolitical person who was writing an apolitical book.

"The selection of candidates for the reference book was done by five black members of a trustee committee. Initially it was going to cover the whole country but we couldn't raise enough money and decided to limit it to Natal."

It features 47 men and 10 women in fields ranging from art to banking, music, agriculture, medicine and religion.

"The criteria the black committee laid down for inclusion differed from that which we whites would use. We put educational and vocational achievements at the top of our list and they put willingness to sacrifice self in the interests of others at the top of theirs."

I could sense the approval of the latter choice in Miss Deane's voice.

She confirmed it.

"I come from New York city which is strictly an individually orientated society. In South Africa the black people are so community orientated, it's something we really miss out on."

No blacks

Miss Deane had been living in South Africa for

Europe, the Middle, Near and Far East, and the Americas.

She was the first woman to drive a Land-Rover from England to India, paying her way through music and travel articles.

Among other things she has studied and practised Vedanta, Yoga and Eastern music at an ashram (monastery) in India. In addition:

● She has managed a Tibetan refugee camp in

The Star, Johannesburg, September, 1978.

After a four-year campaign of harassment waged against me by white South African security police in a bid to stop my book, I am shown here, with members of my board, signing the first published copy of *Black South Africans: A Who's Who, 57 Profiles of Natal's Leading Blacks*.

My Board of Directors.

BLACK
SOUTH
AFRICANS

A WHO'S WHO
57 Profiles of Natal's Leading Blacks

Dee Shirley Deane

OXFORD UNIVERSITY PRESS

27

CAIRO

1959

The party in the houseboat on the Nile was in full swing. The American diplomat who'd invited me whispered, "See the big, brawny guy with the fierce black mustache? Ex-ambassador to Sweden. Careful. He's Nasser's right-hand man."

I kept an eye on Mostafa Lotfy as he towered over a chatty British woman, now and then shifting his gaze to me.

The American introduced us at the buffet table. What did I want to do here, Mostafa asked. See the Pyramids, ride a camel, listen to Egyptian music, I said. He'd be honored to oblige. He had the time, and a chauffeured Mercedes.

On our first date, a camel ride, Mostafa helped me to mount the beast as the camel sat back. "As soon as he feels your weight," he said, "he'll raise his back to stand. Hold the hump tight."

I screamed when the camel raised his rump, sure that I'd fall over his head. I tried to grip the massive hump. "This is no handle!" I shouted.

"It's your only handle now!" Mostafa shouted back.

When the camel began to trot, all I could think of was that I'd have to go through the same procedure when we stopped.

During the next three weeks, Mostafa walked me through the Khan-el-Khalil smoky bazaar that sold everything from Nescafé to oriental carpets. We listened to street musicians drumming Arabic rhythms surrounded by squatters with hokey water pipes. We dined and danced on the Semiramus rooftop where I'd stayed on my way to Africa. Under a starry sky he taught me an Arabic song.

Ya Mostafa, ya Mostafa, Ana bahebak, Ya Mostafa.

"It means, *I love you, Mostafa,*" he said.

One day, sitting in the back of his Mercedes, we rode through a residential area. As we turned onto Kasr-el-Nil Street, Mostafa told the chauffeur to stop, and pointed to a three-story red brick apartment house with open terraces. "Like that building?" he asked.

"I do. Why?"

"A friend owns it. Flats are furnished, and they have daily cleaning service. I could get you one. It's cheaper than your hotel, and you can rent it by the month."

I hesitated. A few months were too long to stay in any country, since I still had so much of the world to see. On the other hand, I could learn a lot in Egypt.

I unpacked my bags at Thirty-three Kasr-el-Nil. My flat was bright and cool, with a shaded balcony. Simple furniture, linens, bedding, dishes, silverware, even light bulbs. Ahmed, the teenage building cleaner, came daily.

One morning after he left, I noticed that a five-dollar bill was missing from my top dresser drawer. It hadn't occurred to me to hide money. When Mostafa picked me up for lunch, I settled in the back of the car, and mentioned it casually. "I was surprised," I told him. "Ahmed seemed like a good guy."

Mostafa said nothing. For several days Ahmed didn't show up. One morning I spotted him in the garden at the back. When he saw my face, he started to cry and held up his arm. His right hand had been chopped off.

"Ahmed! What happened?"

He cried and turned away. Another servant told me.

When Mostafa knocked on my door, I flung it open. "*Bastard!* How dare you report the theft to the police? It cost Ahmed his hand. How dare you?"

"Take it easy. That's how we deal with thieves."

"I didn't tell you so you could tell the police! I didn't give a damn about the five bucks. How dare you report it when you knew the police would chop off his hand?"

"Take it easy."

"Damned primitives!"

"Don't call us primitives! A pickpocket stole my wallet in Times Square, and a cop laughed. That's why Americans have so much crime. *You're* the primitive ones!"

"I hate you! I hate you for reporting it when you knew they'd chop off his hand. I hate *me* for telling you. Get out! I can't stand the sight of you!"

I cried all night.

Next morning I changed two hundred-dollar travelers' checks for Ahmed, but he had left. For three days, his friends searched for him, but no one knew where he'd gone. Disgusted with myself and disgusted with Egypt, I packed and boarded a bus to Port Said. From there, I got a boat to Beirut.

While the ship sailed northeast along the Mediterranean coast, I sat on deck, depressed. Every blemish that I tried to conceal from myself had surfaced. The two hundred bucks I took from a friend in New York, lying that he'd made me pregnant. The red silk dress that I wore in Mozambique, pressed, returned, and got my money back. Worst of all—Ahmed's hand. I wished I could toss my dirt into the sea, but it clung.

Beirut was the Paris of the East, but I was in no mood to stay long. I checked into a hotel on Burj Square, and stopped for lunch at a restaurant on Parliament Street. "Americans like mezzeh," the waiter said. "Forty hors d'oeuvres with cheese and fish and raw meat."

Ahmed would have to eat it with his left hand. How would he cut the meat? To erase the thought I ordered a glass of arrack.

I strolled the main streets, surprised to see Dior dresses and Purdah, loaded donkeys and Lincolns, crosses and Mecca symbols. The American University. Ford. First National City Bank. Chase Manhattan. Pan Am. No American would be lonely there.

A shared taxi took me to the Syrian border. On the other side, another shared taxi drove me fifty miles southeast, past thousands of acres of cotton crops. I stopped for a night in Damascus, the oldest inhabited city on earth, a melting pot of Arabs, Kurds,

Armenians and Turks. I ambled through bazaars that sold handwoven silk with patterns visible on both sides. At every stall the owner told me his name. It was always *Ahmed.*

If only I could have made up for it. Found him, brought him to New York, supported him for the rest of my life. But I tried to find him, and failed.

Shared taxis took me to Jordan and onward toward Jerusalem. We passed villages of mud huts, caravans of weighted donkeys carrying nomads, endless camps of Palestinian refugees. The sight of kids in tattered clothes, snatching food scraps from trash bins, darkened my mood.

In Jerusalem I walked down the dim passages of the Church of the Holy Sepulcher where Greek, Armenian, Ethiopian, Coptic and Syrian Christians held services. I wished the sacred shrines would wipe out the images in my head. Skinny black legs sticking out of drainpipes. Tiny Palestinian hands clutching crusts from smelly bins. Ahmed's handless arm. But the shrines had no effect. I needed a mental broom.

The concierge in my Jerusalem hotel told me that a German tour group was going for a swim in the Dead Sea the next morning. I should join them.

"I can't swim."

"Madame," he said, "everyone can swim in the Dead Sea."

I was moody on the bus amidst the noisy chatter of German tourists. When we arrived, I changed into my bathing suit, stepped into the sea and stood still. I never liked water, never trusted it. No matter how hard YWCA teachers in New York tried, they couldn't teach me to swim.

"Float," a German man urged. I lay down in the shallows, but my ankles, calves, thighs and arms were covered with so many mosquito bites, some scratched until they'd bled, that the salty water made me feel like I was lying in fire. I spent the day brooding on shore, thinking of how apt it was to sit on the shores of the Dead Sea when I felt so dead inside.

I had an exit visa from the Jordanian Authority, and an entry visa for Israel. Jordanian police scanned my papers, and let me through the Mandelbaum Gate that sunlit morning, a curious name since there was no gate in view. Just a narrow walkway with a military police post on each side. Two Arab porters followed me, carrying my luggage. I walked the long narrow strip of pavement called "No Man's Land" bounded by concrete walls and barbed wire coils. An eerie sensation like walking on an un-named planet.

Two Israeli porters waited for me halfway across. I turned around. The Arab porters had put my luggage down, and were going back to their side. I felt like I was playing a neutral role in a silent film set in the Land of Nowhere. The Israeli porters picked up my bags and led me to a military guard at the Israeli post.

"Shalom!" the guard grinned. The word means peace.

At the Haifa port, I climbed up a gangplank to a Turkish ship, and presented my ticket to Turkey.

"Down those stairs, Madame."

I descended the stairs, and presented my ticket again.

"Down those stairs, Madame."

One more flight.

"Down those stairs."

Steerage Class, D-deck. A dormitory packed with peasants and caged chickens. Even the Chicago stockyards didn't stink like that.

Two days and two nights to go. *It's okay, kid,* I told myself. *You can do it.*

28

ANKARA

1959

Ankara, the arid capital of Turkey, dates back to 1000 BC. The city is old and new and hot and dry. Women in Dior dresses strolled alongside peasants in baggy pants and tunics. But no one was veiled. Turks are Turks first, and Muslims after that.

The U.S. air base was "classified." A special pass admitted me, but I couldn't stay on base, unlike Incirlik in southeast Turkey, where I stayed on that base, got hair cuts at the base salon, shopped at the Post Exchange, enjoyed films at the theater. All this despite the fact that Incirlik was so critical an airbase that Kruschev wanted it dismantled. U.S. jet fighter bombers remained stationed near the long runway twenty-four hours a day. Giant radar installations would warn the U.S. government of Soviet missile attacks launched from thousands of miles away. Yet I was welcome. But not in Ankara where a special pass admitted me only to perform.

My pad was a room on the second floor of a new hotel near Kizilay Square, a sunny room with a balcony. Carnations and roses grew along the narrow strip that lined the entrance. I liked the hotel food, especially the spiced meat balls fried with nuts and capped with yogurt.

When I studied the world map that I'd taped to the wall, Russia beckoned. I'd never be this close again. I ran my palms over that massive stretch of land like it belonged to me. I could board a ship to Odessa. Take a train to Moscow. Leave the best to the last—Leningrad, home of Tchaikovsky. Imagine! Just the Black Sea between Russia and me.

The taxi dropped me at the Russian Embassy on a muggy August afternoon. The stark gray building stood on a quiet street. No offices, no shops, no people. Nothing but the embassy. In the reception room, an expressionless man behind a glass window slid a pane to speak through a narrow opening.

"Madame?"

"I want a visa for Russia."

"A visa?"

"Yes."

"Wait." He pointed to a brown leather chair. "Sit."

The waiting room seemed sinister. Dark and dismal. No pictures, no magazines, no plants. Was I their first customer? I waited ten minutes before a door opened. A tall, slender man in his early forties strode in with an air of dignity.

"Lev Frolov, Third Secretary." A gentle voice.

"My name is Shirley Deane. I'm American. I came for a visa."

He seated himself across from me. "Why do you want to go to Russia?"

"To visit the homes of great composers. Tchaikovsky, Korsakoff, Rachmaninoff. I want to feel the vibrations where Tchaikovsky composed *Swan Lake.* These men inspire me. They've taught me."

"May I ask what you do in Turkey?"

"I play accordion. I'm working my way around the world."

"Around the world? Alone?"

"Alone. I've played Europe, Africa, and American bases here in Turkey. Now I'm playing at the Ankara Officers Club."

He sat quiet while he processed what I said. An attractive man. Gentle.

"Will it be possible to get a visa?" I asked.

"Probably not."

"Why?"

His glance held my eyes. "It is not easy," he said. "We don't issue visas like that."

"But one of the functions of an embassy is to issue visas."

"Of course. But rarely does anyone apply from here."

"I'll be the exception."

His voice was barely audible. "It is not likely, I'm afraid."

"Can I show you my bona fides? Would that help?"

He grinned. "I don't think so."

I felt disinclined to go. If I left, there'd be no chance to know him. While I hesitated, he said what I thought he'd never say. "Will you dine with me tonight?"

"I'd like to. And tonight is my night off."

At six p.m. I waited on my balcony, my eyes following a long black car that slowed down and parked in front of my hotel. My heart beat noisily, like it did on my first date. *He's just another man*, I told myself. But he wasn't, of course.

In his small cluttered apartment, Lev introduced me to the Russian diplomat who shared his living space. Perhaps they weren't permitted to live alone. His roommate looked forlorn, a heavyset man with a raspy voice. "You would like a drink?" he asked.

"Thank you, yes."

"Vodka?"

"Fine. I like Bloody Mary's."

"Bloody what?" Lev asked.

"Vodka with tomato juice."

They laughed. "That's an insult to vodka. We take it straight."

"*Nasdrovia*," they toasted.

A chessboard lay on an end table. "Oh, my favorite game."

"Want to play?" Lev asked.

"Oh, yes."

He set up the pieces, closed his palms around a white and black pawn, and extended his arms. I touched his left hand, pressed my palm over his knuckles, and kept it there. He opened his palm. White pawn.

Playing with white made no difference. Two queens wouldn't have made a difference. He beat me in eight moves.

Lev fascinated me. His aura of mystery, the gentleness.

He held my coat. "We'll dine at a famous restaurant," he said. "Good food. The Americans' favorite."

His roommate waved goodbye as we descended the stone steps to Lev's car. While Lev drove carefully and silently, I imaged a cozy, dimly lit supper club with soft background music like The Red Carpet on Park Avenue. But he ushered me into a neon lit room the size of a skating rink. A circular balcony overlooked the dance floor packed with loud, drunk American GIs.

We took a table along the railing. "Drunken American soldiers embarrass me," I said.

"Russian soldiers act worse when they drink."

Lev asked me what countries I'd visited, and what I was searching for. He was a pensive, patient listener.

After dinner, he drove me around Ankara, parked along a lakefront, and turned on the *Voice of America.* A little too loud. "I always wanted to see America," he said softly. I strained to hear him. "I'd love a post in Washington."

"Can you request it?"

"I can, but my wife and son wouldn't be able to join me."

That disappointed me. I didn't think he had a family. He didn't wear a ring. "Why not?"

Lev didn't reply. Dumb question. If he brought his family, they'd probably defect.

He put his arm around me. "May I kiss you?"

His kiss was soft. "You're so gentle," I said.

"Many would disagree."

"Lev, is a visa really impossible?"

"Impossible. No Russian official would believe you want to feel the vibrations where Tchaikovsky composed *Swan Lake.* They'd think you have another purpose."

"You think so?"

"No. I see the honesty in your eyes, but I don't make the decisions."

"Can't you influence those who do?"

"Who would believe me? They'd say it's impossible. How can a woman work her way around the world on an accordion? If I suggest a visa, they'll say your accordion is a cover-up, that you're a CIA agent. That's how they think."

"I can't imagine how anybody would suspect me of that."

The Voice of America played The Four Freshmen's recording of "Graduation Day."

"Ah! My favorite group," he said. "My favorite song." He turned up the volume.

"I like your taste. That's the kind of jazz I play."

"I never heard an accordionist play jazz. Russian accordionists play folk music."

"My accordion sounds like an orchestra. I use an amplifier, not for volume but to round out the tone."

"Amplifier? Our accordionists never use such things. My government would be very suspicious of an accordionist who uses an electronic box."

"I'd love to play 'Graduation Day' for you. If I get permission from the captain of the Officers Club, would you be our guest? Say, Thursday evening?"

"I'd love to, but would they let me in? I don't want to cause you any trouble."

Captain McGill, who ran the Officers Club, took everything lightly. A waiter or musician who didn't show up; a shortage of beef or beer—he'd grin. "The only problem in the world is thinking that we shouldn't have problems."

I told him about Lev.

"A real Russian? Here at our club?" His eyes danced. "I never met a Russian. We could serve vodka and caviar. The caviar comes from Iran, but he wouldn't know the difference. The band could play "The Volga Boatmen."

"Lev is lovely, Captain," I said.

McGill checked the vodka supply and conferred with the cook. "Everything will be ready," he told me. "The MPs at the gate will expect him."

On Thursday at five, I began to dress. Lev would pick me up at six. I'd change into a gown at the club, but what should I wear coming and going? My navy dress seemed too dark. I donned an ochre suit. Too loud. I tried three garments, settling for sky blue. I checked my eyebrows, lashes, and lips three times. Polished my nails with strawberry red. Lev might think it too bright. Wiped it off, and applied neutral.

I stood on the balcony at six. No black car. It wasn't like Lev to be late. Six-fifteen, six-twenty, six-thirty. I'd start playing at seven. Maybe he got stuck in traffic.

I wrote a note: *Lev, Please drive to the Base. The MPs at the gate expect you. They'll lead you to the officers club.* I gave my note to the hotel clerk. "When Mr. Frolov comes, give him this note, please. Tell him it won't matter if he's late."

"Mr. who?"

I pointed to the name on the envelope. "*Fro-lov.*"

A taxi rushed me to the club. My heart beat fast. What if Lev didn't show up after all the preparations McGill made? The club packed with his friends, eager to meet a Russian. The band playing "The Volga Boatmen." Vodka and caviar on the tables.

I slammed the door of the taxi, paid the driver, pulled the club door open and stopped cold. The room was empty. The bandstand, bare. An unfamiliar face greeted me.

"What's going on? Where's the band? Where's Captain McGill?"

The man stood before me like a sentencing judge, his eyes narrow slits. "There is no band. There is no Captain McGill. *I'm* the boss."

"What? Captain McGill was here yesterday. An important guest is coming."

"An important guest *was* coming."

"I don't understand."

"You don't have to. Get your instruments and get out."

"What?"

"You want it in writing? You're fired!"

I cleared out in a daze, taxied back to the hotel, and sat on the edge of my bed like someone who got off a train at the wrong station. The hostile face of that man haunted me. Why? What did I do that was wrong? What happened to McGill? Did the Air Force transfer him for setting up the event? What happened to Lev? Did he get into trouble because he wanted to hear me play?

My mind whirled, flitted from question to unanswerable question. I couldn't sleep.

Next morning I called the Russian Embassy. "Mr. Frolov, please."

"Mr. Frolov has left."

"Left? For where?"

"I don't know."

"He was transferred?"

"I don't know."

Maybe Lev's car was tapped. Maybe his government heard us. No wonder he spoke softly. If his boss heard him say that he wants to see America, that his government would keep his family in Moscow, that he lives in an environment of suspicion, they'd ship him to Siberia. My fault! If only I could find out where he was. I should have checked the name of his street and house number. If I knew it, I'd go. I'd find out what went wrong.

I couldn't make sense of anything that happened. Worst of all, it swelled the burden of guilt that I hauled around like a ball and chain. The two-hundred bucks in New York. The red dress in Mozambique. Ahmed's hand. Now, an American captain lost his job because of me. Because of me, a Russian diplomat vanished. Maybe to Siberia.

If you can't stand someone, you stay away from the guy. But what do you do when you can't stand yourself?

29

ANKARA

Next Day

Russia was out, but the rest of the world remained to be seen—the East. First, I'd go back to Germany to pick up my stored luggage. The Orient Express was the way to go, the most famous train in the world. For no extra fare I could see Sofia, Bulgaria. Book a room at the railway station and board the train again the next day.

I needed a visa. On an August morning, I walked up the dozen stone steps that led to the Bulgarian Embassy. Turned the doorknob, but it was locked. I peeked into a window beside the stairs when a woman's voice startled me. I spun around.

"If you don't mind, you will come with me." She stood on the step below, dressed like a college student of twenty. Neat, with bangs. She didn't smile, but didn't look mean.

"I do mind."

She pointed to three cars parked in front. How did I miss them? Four men sat in the first and third cars, doors closed, engines running, eyes fixed on me. The doors of the middle car were open. Two men sat in front, waiting.

"If you don't mind, you'll come with me," the woman repeated.

Even if I bolted down the steps and ran, I wouldn't have gotten far. I followed her to the middle car, and sat in the back. "What's this all about? Where are you taking me? Who are you?"

A bald man in the front seat said something in Turkish. "You will see," the woman translated. The three cars drove in convoy like a funeral procession around parts of Ankara I hadn't seen.

"This is illegal. It's kidnapping. I'll report you to the American Embassy."

They said nothing. We rode in circles around the city and its outskirts, slowed down in a deserted industrial area, and stopped in front of an abandoned brick building, twelve stories high. We entered the lifeless hall, footsteps echoing on concrete, and took a cargo lift to the eighth floor.

The men were silent and grim as they led us to the end of the corridor. They opened a door to a large room with a high ceiling, neon lights and olive green walls like in old American hospitals. Eight stone-faced men looked surreal sitting silently around a rectangular table covered with files. They eyed me with scorn.

"Where am I?" I asked. "And who are you? What's going on?"

One pointed to a chair on the left end of the table. I sat with my back to the door, facing ugly, high uncurtained windows.

A bald man on my right drew himself up. "We are officials of the Turkish Government. You have been associating with a leading Russian intelligence agent. We believe you are a danger to our country."

"Me? A danger to your country? Lev? A leading intelligence agent? This is ridiculous. Where's the phone? I want to call the American Embassy. Now!"

"No telephone," said a man with flashing black eyes. "See these?" He tapped his files. "Complete documentation. Evidence you cannot deny."

"Evidence of what? What are you talking about?"

He opened a folder, took out a photograph of me in front of the Piper Cub that I flew in Waukegan, Illinois. "Jesus! Where in hell did you get that?"

"We ask *you* the questions," a translator said. "You do not ask *us*. You fly Piper Cubs. Very interesting. What do Piper Cubs have to do with music?"

"They have nothing to do with music."

"Exactly! For what reason you fly them?"

"What a ridiculous question!"

"You want to answer questions here or behind bars?"

"I don't believe this."

"You want to answer the questions—"

"Your question is dumb. I flew a Piper Cub like most Americans fly Piper Cubs. For recreation."

They talked Turkish. "Recreational pastime? To fly a plane?"

"Correct."

"You own this plane?"

"Hardly. Student pilots pay by the hour."

"When you last flew this plane?"

"1953."

"You have not flown this plane in six years?"

"Correct."

"Where you parked it?"

"Waukegan airport near Chicago."

More talk.

An emaciated little man opened a folder of photographs. He took out my professional photo in a fishtail gown with the accordion and amplifier. "You are this person?"

"I am that person."

"What is this equipment?"

"A Gibson amplifier."

"What does an amplifier have to do with an accordion?"

"It amplifies the sound."

Animated talk.

"Turkish accordion players do not use amplifiers. Why do you?"

"To make the sound louder."

The man showed me another photograph. I gasped. The contents of the box in which I carried electronic accessories had been laid out on a rug. Extension cords, microphones, converters, transformers, adapters, recording equipment. They must have taken the photo in my hotel room. No wonder the hotel clerk eyed me curiously.

"What are these?" he pointed.

"Extension cords. I use them when I play far from electrical outlets."

"This?"

"A microphone for the top of my accordion. I use it when I sing and walk around, and can't use a standard mike."

"These?"

"Converters, transformers, and adapters for ships, and in countries that have 220 current instead of 110. Adapters are for different kinds of outlets. That recording equipment tapes my performances."

A lengthy discussion followed. A man with a mustache like a walrus showed me copies of my university transcripts. "You were student at New York University?"

"Correct."

"Also University of Munich?"

"Correct."

"Why you did not complete in New York?"

"Not enough money."

Animated talk. "Enough money to travel? Not enough to study?"

"Correct."

"Why did you come to Turkey?"

"To earn money."

"How?"

"Playing accordion for military bases. In Adana, Erzerum, Izmir, Ankara."

"Why?"

"I have to eat."

Animated discussion. The emaciated man said, "This is not a meeting for jokes. You will respect us or we will not respect you."

"What the hell does that mean?"

"You understand English. Answer the question. You are playing at classified American bases. Why?"

"I told you. I have to eat. I'm working my way around the world. I play the accordion for room and food. I play for military installations. Classified or not, Americans want to be entertained by Americans."

"Where else you have worked?"

"With that ton of notes, you have to ask?"

"Answer the question!" he pounded. "Where did you work?"

"New York, New Jersey, Chicago, Palm Beach, Atlantic City, Kansas City, Memphis. On a ship to Curacao, Puerto Rico, Venezuela, the Virgin Islands. In Norway, Sweden, Germany, France, Italy, Spain, England, South Africa, Rhodesia, the Congo, Ethiopia."

Turkish talk. Shuffling papers. Searching for documents to verify or dispute what I said. "Where in Ethiopia did you work?"

"Kagnew Air Base in Asmara."

"Why you choose Ethiopia?"

"Because it lies between the Sudan where I came from, and Somaliland where I was going."

More Turkish.

"You were seen walking into the Russian Embassy. What purpose?"

I recalled how eerily quiet the street was, how devoid of life. I'd had a fleeting thought—was someone watching? "I went to get a visa."

"Why?"

"To visit the birthplace of Russia's great composers."

"What happened when you went in?"

"The third secretary introduced himself."

"His name?"

"Lev Frolov."

"Ahh." More Turkish talk.

"What did he say?"

"He asked what I wanted. I said a visa. He said it wouldn't be possible."

"What happened then?"

"Nothing."

He pulled out a photograph showing the back of me as I walked into Lev's apartment building.

"My God!"

"This is you?"

"Yes."

"What did you do in this apartment?"

"What business is it of yours?"

"We ask *you* the questions," the crusty one barked. "You do not ask *us*. What did you do there?"

"Played chess."

"And?"

"He won."

"That's not what I mean. What else did you do?"

"Drank vodka."

"Were other persons present?"

"Yes."

"Name them."

"A man. I don't recall his name."

"What happened then?"

"Nothing."

He hauled out another photograph. "Is this you?"

Jesus! There I was, laughing, holding Lev's arm as he opened the door of his car.

"That's me."

"Where did you go?"

"A big restaurant with lots of American GIs."

"Where did you go after?"

"Nowhere."

"You had to go somewhere."

"For a ride."

"Where?"

"I don't know street names."

He hauled out another photo. "This is you?"

The picture was taken when Lev pulled up in front of my hotel and got out to open my door. I kissed him on the cheek which embarrassed him. The camera caught the kiss. "Yes, me. Where is a telephone? I want to call the U.S. Embassy."

"No telephone here."

"I'm hungry."

"We are hungry, too."

Questions continued for eight hours, followed by a heated exchange in Turkish. The man with steel features said, "We will bring you back to your hotel. But you must leave Turkey within forty-eight hours."

My hotel room felt weird. I scanned the ceiling, walls, and furniture for hidden cameras. Did they see me? Were they recording every movement? For the first time, I realized how strange I must appear to natives. A woman alone, playing the accordion around the world. Americans get it straight away. But to natives, it must be a cover-up.

Next day, I walked up the steps again to the Bulgarian Embassy. Before I tried the door I checked the streets. No cars this time, but a man who looked Turkish stood twenty feet from the steps and turned the other way when I glanced. He must have followed me. A man twenty feet behind him looked American. Maybe he was following the Turk.

The Bulgarian Embassy issued my visa in ten minutes. The U.S. Embassy on Ataturk Boulevard was next. First, for mail. Then to the ambassador to report the detention. I'd tell him that I played the accordion at the Officers Club. That Turkish security police hauled me to an empty building where they questioned me for eight hours. No food, no phone. A woman taking me to the toilet when I had to go. He should report it to the prime minister. Or was it the president? Turks should never do that again to an American.

The pretty mail clerk on the ground floor, a Turkish American, checked my name on her list. "Your mail is in the ambassador's office."

"The ambassador's office? Why?"

She shrugged, smiled, dialed. I heard his voice. "Send her up."

I climbed the big, wide steps. What right did he have to hold my mail? That was his door, the Honorable Ambassador William Fletcher Warren. Captain McGill knew him. Said he often dined at the Officers Club. That he came from Texas. That his name had big adjectives—"Ambassador Extraordinary," "Ambassador Plenipotentiary." That means that he wields all the power he wants, politically and financially.

"Come in." I thought he was standing until he stood to extend his hand. A giant of a Texan. Glasses, gray hair, calculating eyes. Probably so immersed in intrigue he didn't know anything existed outside of it.

"I was held against my will, Mr. Warren. Captured by Turkish Security Police. Hauled to an abandoned building. Questioned for eight hours. No food, no phone."

He smiled a theatrical smile. "We know, Miss Deane. I'm so sorry."

"You knew? And you did nothing to stop them?"

"We couldn't, Miss Deane. They're the host country. We're just guests."

"But you're here to protect American citizens."

He waved off my comment with a swish of his hand. He might as well have said that protection was no priority. He sat straight, hands clasped on the desk, cold eyes on mine. I glared back. He knew about my friendship with Lev. He knew about the interrogation. He did nothing to stop it. I wondered—*son of a bitch!*—I wondered if *he* engineered it. *Son of a bitch!*

"Mr. Warren, where is Lev Frolov now?"

"I have no idea, Miss Deane."

"Where's Captain McGill?"

"Who's McGill?"

If I were a man, I'd have knocked him on his smug ass. "He ran the Officers Club."

"I have no idea, Miss Deane."

"You're so helpful, Mr. Warren. Thank you. I'll take my mail."

He handed me a tidy pile of letters. I had no doubt that he'd read every one. The giant stood. "By the way, Miss Deane, isn't Lev charming?"

"Indeed he is, Mr. Warren. In *every* way."

30

THE ORIENT EXPRESS

1959

Since the 1880s, the Orient Express had carted royalty, diplomats, businessmen, spies, courtesans, arms dealers, and well-heeled newlyweds from Paris to Constantinople (Istanbul). They slept in oak-paneled compartments that converted to daytime, carpeted sitting rooms with velvet-covered sofas. They toasted champagne in the restaurant car beneath crystal chandeliers. Ordered their hot hors d'oeuvres, frog legs, and *Poulet a la Marengo* from gourmet chefs garbed in silk breeches. The sofas of velvet, the breeches of silk, and the panels of oak had gone. But the Orient Express remained the world's most famous train.

My route would take me from Ankara to Istanbul where Asia meets Europe. Then to Sofia, Belgrade, and Milan for a train to Nuremberg. I didn't buy a sleeper, just a second-class window seat that reclined.

We rumbled past high-rise hotels, broad boulevards and mosques with minarets gilded by bright afternoon sunlight. A man on the other side of the aisle with patched eyeglasses read a book that bore the familiar Koran inscription on its cover: *There is no god but Allah, and Mohammed is His prophet*.

I wished I could share his faith. Not his religion, not any religion. Just faith in something beyond myself to help me bear my guilt.

A robust man opposite me, my age, read a German book. I leaned forward. "*Sie sind Deutsch?*"

"*Jawohl! Sie?*"

"*Amerikanische*. My German is rusty. Haven't spoken in a year."

He leaned across, covered his mouth, and whispered, “That man on the other side of the aisle in the gray suit, he’s watching every move you make.”

I stole a sideways glance. He was the man who’d followed me to the Bulgarian Embassy. “Oh, shit!”

“Something wrong?”

“Look, sorry if I seem forward, but can we have coffee in the dining car?”

We moved past the man. Three rows behind him was the other man I saw following the first one. I wondered if they were spying on me or on each other.

We ordered coffee at a corner table. He handed me his card.

Dr. Klaus Hoffman
Anthropologist
Düsseldorf

“Call me Klaus.”

“*Ich heisse* Shirley Deane. I’m a musician, an accordionist, working my way around the world. Boy, am I pleased you’re here!”

“That man back there. You know him? He is chasing you?”

“It’s a long story. I’d been in Africa and the Mid-East, and was playing for U.S. Forces in Turkey. I wanted to see Russia; it was so close, just over the Black Sea. The fiasco began when I went to the Russian Embassy for a visa.”

“Ooh! You never studied history?”

“I wasn’t a great history student. Why?”

“Animosity between Russians and Turks goes back centuries. They spy on each other like hawks. Cameras would be all over that street.”

“They were.” I told him about Lev, the chess game, the dinner and drive. About our plan for the Officers Club, and Captain McGill. “You think Frolov was sincere?”

“*Ja!* Sounds like your naiveté broke through his defenses. Most Americans he meets are agents with double agendas.”

“Why would he take the chance of going to the American Officers Club?”

“To taste freedom.”

"But why would he take the risk? His government could easily track him."

"He'd say he was on a mission."

"I wonder what happened to him."

"Siberia, maybe."

"That's what I fear. What do you think happened to McGill?"

"What happens in Germany when Americans get into trouble. They get transferred to Supplies. Counting sheets or cans of beans."

"Two lives ruined because of me."

"In anthropology, we have a saying: A man's destiny unfolds from the inside out. Not the other way."

"That doesn't ease my guilt," I told him. "You know, Klaus, I'd planned to get off in Bulgaria and stay overnight at the railway hotel in Sofia. But with these two men on board, I'm anxious. What do you think?"

"Don't do it. It's a risk."

When we crossed into Bulgaria the conductor asked for our passports. My concertina additions fanned out.

"*Ach, Du liebes Bisschen!*" Klaus said. "Even your passport is an accordion!"

We rode through poverty stricken villages toward Sofia. When the train pulled in, Klaus and I walked around the station. Red banners were strung throughout the main square. Loudspeakers blared from every corner. "What's going on?" I asked a policeman.

"National celebration. Today is fifteenth anniversary of Communism. The coups was September ninth, 1944."

"What do these banners say?"

"Long live the prosperity!"

"What prosperity?" Klaus whispered.

Across the broad street, a dozen people clothed in tattered garments waited on a long queue outside a bakery. They'd wait an hour, maybe two, for a loaf of bread. I wished I could walk into the bakery, buy all the bread they had, and hand it out.

En route to Belgrade we played chess on Klaus' portable magnetic set. Neither of us noticed when the two men disembarked, but they were gone when we reached Zagreb.

We parted in Germany. Klaus was bound for Westphalia. I was bound for Bavaria, the home of bockwurst and beer halls.

At seven p.m. I arrived at the U.S. Army Hotel in Nuremberg, happy to be back in the same lobby with the same chairs, telephone booths, lamps, side-tables. The same portrait of President Eisenhower on the back wall. The commanding generals of the U.S. Army on another. All looked the same, yet something was different. People came and went like they did in Broadway hotels that booked rooms by the hour.

I'd wired the new officer in charge to say I was coming. "Where do I find Captain Costello?" I asked a desk clerk. He gestured toward a man rushing to the desk with a stack of papers in his hand. He walked fast, like he was the hub of life, and others were spokes. "Excuse me, Captain Costello. I'm Shirley Deane."

"Oh, yes, the accordionist. We need someone fast, five nights a week. Can you start tomorrow?"

"Sure."

He hurried off.

"Captain." He turned and frowned. An extra second of his time seemed unreasonable. "The contract, the terms."

"Same as before. The contract will be in your mailbox tomorrow."

"My room is reserved?"

"Yes, yes. See the desk."

Unpacking luggage and the bags I'd stored took a few hours. Then a stack of mail to go through. Offers from agents to play Italy and France. TV offers for Milan and Vienna. A letter from Mom. *It's time to come home.*

My room was fine for rests between performances, but I wanted to live away from the hotel.

I found a furnished one-bedroom flat on Essenheim Street. The white chenille bedspread reminded me of my mother's, and I loved the wall paintings. A nineteenth-century castle built for King Ludwig II. The Ruhr River Valley. Fir trees in the mountains of the Black Forest.

Someone knocked at ten on my first Sunday morning. Three short, hard knocks. A slight, unsmiling man tipped his hat and handed me his card:

Eric Benedetti

U.S. Central Intelligence Agency

For a moment I stood still. "Come in."

Benedetti took a sofa seat and removed his hat. Pockmarks covered his face like tiny potholes on an empty road. "You like your new apartment?" he asked.

"It's fine. Why did you come?"

"First things first. Let's have your PX card, Miss Deane."

How does he know about the PX card I got in Ethiopia? Suppose he's guessing. Handing it over would prove my guilt. Why do that? But remember the dossiers compiled by the Turkish Security Police? These guys know plenty.

"I only use it to get Noxzema and Kleenex."

"I don't care if you use it for toilet paper. I want it."

I gave it to him.

"Next item—Lev Frolov. We understand you met him."

"So?"

"Did you meet him?"

Why should this man intimidate me? Who is he to demand a reply? I'm not beholden to the CIA.

"Well?"

"Yes."

"Good starting point. What kind of a man is he?"

"A gentle man."

"Listen, Shirley, I'll come clean with you. We've tried to get the lowdown on this guy for a long time. We couldn't even get close. You did. We want info. Anything you can tell us will help."

"Like what?"

"Anything. What kind of music does he like?"

I thought back to Lev's words, how he loved The Four Freshmen's song, "Graduation Day." "I don't know," I said.

"C'mon. Give us an idea. Does he like jazz, classical, Russian folk music?"

"All of it."

"What does he drink?"

"What every Russian drinks. Vodka."

"Straight?"

"Like every Russian. Only an American will drink a Bloody Mary."

"What did you talk about?"

"When we had dinner, I told him I was embarrassed to see GIs make drunken fools of themselves. He said Russian solders act worse when they drink."

"What did you do with him?"

"Played chess."

"And?"

"He won."

"That's not what I mean."

"I don't care what you mean."

"I doubt that, but fine. Point three. You're in a perfect position to help us. You've gotten around half the world with your accordion. The CIA wants to offer you a job. We'll pay you more than anything you're used to."

"Mr. Benedetti, I'd rather collect empty milk bottles from the streets of Nuremberg than work for the CIA."

He stood. "You need your sails trimmed," he said, and stomped out.

If Benedetti had offered me a hundred bucks a day, I would have refused. I'd be unable to live with myself.

31

NEW YORK

1959

Only a few guests lounged in the lobby of Nuremberg's Army Hotel at eight p.m. on October twenty-ninth. Relaxed on a couch before my next performance, I mentally rehearsed, "The Flight of the Bumble Bee." In the middle, a rare, lucid image of my father sprang into my mind.

I should call him, but that's silly. What would I say—Hi Dad, how are you? He'd say, Fine, how are you? The public phone booths were empty, but I didn't have enough change anyway.

On the bandstand, Dad's face floated through my brain again. *I'd better call. But that's foolish, calling halfway around the world with no reason. What would he think?*

Captain Costello came to the bandstand. "You have an overseas call."

Mom wailed. "Dad's dead. He had a heart attack."

Tears flowed in torrents as I packed a small suitcase for an early morning flight to New York. The funeral would be held when I arrived.

Tears blinded my eyes as I stroked my father's casket. *Oh, Dad, I loved you so much. Sometimes I thought you didn't care for me, but that didn't matter. I loved you terribly. I always will.*

Three and a half years had passed since I'd left America. Yet everything in my parents' apartment that I'd lived with as a child and teen seemed unconnected to me. The living room chandelier with its missing pendulants. The faded sofa cover. My parents' dancing trophies on the fake mantel.

"Make yourself at home," Mom said. "Change your room any way you like." She assumed that I'd come to stay.

"I need to work, Mom. I can't make a living here."

"Sure you can," she said. "You can go back to show business."

"Play from nine to three in the morning again? Wiggle in fishtails? No way!"

"Then work days like everybody else," she said.

"A nine-to-five job? Like in an office?"

"Office. Department store. Anywhere."

"A department store saleswoman? An office clerk? I'd go insane," I said.

"Others don't go insane. Why should you?"

"I don't know why. I'm different. I can't live that way, never could."

"Then what will you do?"

"I have to go back, Mom. I'm on contract in Germany."

She froze. "You'll leave me *alone*?"

"Mom—" That wasn't the time to talk. "I'm going out for a while."

Most of the elms on our street had been chopped down to make room for driveways to new apartment buildings. Stores beneath our windows had changed hands. The corner bakery had become a bookstore.

Commuters on the local subway to Roosevelt Avenue, and the F express to Manhattan, read small, folded sections of the *Times*. Some read *The Daily News*. Others focused absentmindedly on the multi-colored graffiti scrawled on ads above the seats.

At Forty-Ninth Street I headed east. The sun was barely visible on that November day. Narrow cross-town streets struck me like tunnels between high ridges. I turned north, then east again, past silent, faceless figures. New buildings lined the gray-hued streets. I entered one with turnstile doorways, newspaper kiosks, drug stores with soda fountains, and smart new elevators. The old gray-gloved operators had vanished.

New York depressed me, yet I was grateful to it. It gave me the best accordion lessons in the world. Exposed me to radio, clubs, and TV. A leading designer created my wardrobe, though I didn't like his fishtails. Renowned cameramen photographed me. Walter Winchell and Earl Wilson reviewed my performances. Still, New York depressed me. For the cost of a sandwich, I could live in Naples for a week.

The street where I lived before I left America, East Forty-Ninth between Lexington and Third, had changed. The Bazaar Club beneath my flat was gone. Too many police raids, perhaps. Or maybe a cop didn't get his promised cut.

Near the western boundary of Central Park, facing the swank San Remo apartments, leashed poodles with red bows heeled alongside chic women. My mind reversed to Khartoum, where dogs' ribs protruded grotesquely beyond their skin. Where shriveled men and women in rags paced dry and dusty streets in search of scraps of food.

The edge of the lake called up memories of Sunday afternoons in canoes with my father. He would sing Irish songs as he paddled. How I loved him!

The sight of a caged camel at the zoo saddened me. "I rode your brother," I told her, "in Egypt. You'd like it there." I pitied the lions and apes. "You'd love Kruger National Park," I told them. "You'd be free to do whatever you like."

Another subway took me to NYU. Four years had passed since the day I walked out bawling because I couldn't keep working nights and studying days. But I'd learned things in Europe, Africa and the Middle East that I could never have learned at NYU.

Washington Square Park, where I'd played chess, was deserted. No players. No drinkers. No bums. Just policemen on horseback. I trekked west toward the setting sun with a sense of disquiet. Clubs in Greenwich Village where I'd played jam sessions and listened to musicians like Dave Brubeck were vacant, their windows smashed and taped. Even the Village Gate was closed. Gay clubs were shuttered.

"What happened to this area?" I asked a policeman.

"Racial hatred," he said. "Negroes and Italians."

Many Italian immigrants had settled in the Village, opening restaurants and bars along its narrow meandering streets.

"It's getting dark," he said. "I advise you to get out of the area."

A black man in a zoot suit climbed up the subway steps as I walked down. He stopped halfway. "Hey, white baby. If you ain't been fucked by a spade, you ain't been fucked."

I hurried down. I'd never been afraid in New York. Even the night I drove to Harlem and walked into a club alone with my accordion and amp, I felt no fear. Now I was scared.

Like other New Yorkers I read the paper on the train to Queens. An article about the Village Mafia caught my eye. Some gangs carried sharp knives, some carried screwdrivers. Clubs that refused to pay the twenty-five percent required for police protection had closed.

When I returned to the apartment, Mom sat sullen, eyes red. If I left her alone, I'd carry more guilt, moving through the rest of my life like the loaded donkeys of the Middle East. But if I stayed in New York, I'd go insane. I didn't know what to do. I yearned to talk to somebody. Somebody like Bill Hastings, my old psychiatrist friend.

I called Bellevue Hospital. "May I speak to Dr. Bill Hastings?"

The clerk checked files. "He was transferred to California."

I thought to myself that nobody can pick up from where they left off.

An idea struck me, energized me. Why didn't I think of it before? Mom will come with me! From now on, I'll take care of her. Life is easier and cheaper overseas. I'll get her a new passport. We'll clear the apartment together. We'll pack. That's the right thing to do. Care for her like she cared for me.

Arm in arm, we strolled to an Italian restaurant in Jackson Heights. Brightly lit, crowded, noisy. A strong odor of olive oil and pasta. Accordion music in the background. At the table, I told her. "I've got it, Mom. You're going to travel with me. I'm going to take care of you."

"Travel? Where?"

"Germany, first. I have a furnished flat in Nuremberg. You'll like it. You'll take the bedroom, I'll sleep on the couch. We'll have fun together, Mom. You'll come to the Army Hotel every night, and I'll play all your favorites. You won't be lonely, Mom."

"Nuremberg? Me?"

"Yes, Mom. You."

"That's where the concentration camps are."

"*Were*, not *are*. The war's over, Mom. Long ago."

"How can I go where they gassed Jews?"

"The gassers are gone. Americans are there."

"I don't speak German."

"You don't need to. Germans speak English. Listen, we'll go everywhere. I'll rent a car and show you Paris. Outdoor cafés—you'll love them. And shops! We'll go to Venice and ride a gondola together. Oh, Mom, it'll be so good to have you with me!"

Her eyes wandered as she tried to picture it. "I'll think about it."

The best thing I could do was to assume she'd go. "Tomorrow morning I'll get you a passport. Bring your old one. Next week, we'll go through your stuff. See what we can give away, sell or store. Then we'll clear the apartment."

"Clear my apartment? It's my home. I don't want to clear it."

"But Mom, you don't want to pay rent while we travel the world. We'll sell the furniture, pack what you want to bring, put the rest in storage."

"Sell my satin drapes? My cornice that you can't get anywhere in the world? Put my things in storage?"

"What does it matter, Mom? Drapes and a cornice?"

"It matters. My maroon velvet sofa matters."

"I never saw the maroon velvet. You kept it covered since I was born."

"Of course. That's why it's in such good condition."

"The hell with the sofa. You'll see the world with me. Doesn't that matter? A sofa can't make you happy."

"My chandelier. How can I leave it?"

"Half the pendulants are gone."

"Nobody notices. The chandelier is precious."

"Bugger the chandelier. I want you with me, Mom. Being together means more than chandeliers and a covered sofa. Please, Mom."

"I'll see, I'll see," she said.

Next morning I asked, "Where's your passport, Mom?"

"God knows."

"Okay, never mind. Give me your birth certificate."

"Never had one." My mother never told me when she was born.

"I won't look at it, Mom. I promise. I'll just hand it to the passport officer."

"I don't know where it is."

"Where do you keep legal papers?"

"I don't know."

"Okay. Just come with me. Bring your social security card and all your IDs."

Our coats were on. Ready to go. At last, I was doing something right! "C'mon, Mom, let's go."

Wearing her pillbox hat and raccoon coat, she strode into the living room instead of toward the door. Plopped herself on the covered sofa. Leaned back. "I'm not going."

That was it. No point trying anymore. She wouldn't go, and I couldn't stay.

"You know what, Mom? You can type and do secretarial work. If you get a job, you'll meet interesting folks. You'll have an income. You could wear all your clothes. Imagine, a different dress every day!"

For the first time, Mon smiled. A place to wear the designer dresses she'd bought in Klein's basement. New friends. An income.

Her facial muscles relaxed. "I like that," she said. Thank God Mom liked something.

Back in Nuremberg, in the lobby of the Army Hotel, the telephone booths grabbed my eyes. *Why didn't I call Dad when his face floated through my mind? The telephone booths were empty. The desk would have given me change. Why didn't I?*

Dad knew he was dying. Maybe he wanted to tell me that he loved me, for the first time in his life, and for the last time in his life. I didn't hear him say it. I didn't hear it because I paid no heed to that quiet inner voice. *Oh, Dad, I am so sorry!*

32

NUREMBERG

1959-60

Monday morning dawned wet and cold. The heater in my Essenheim Street flat was on "high," but the thermometer read fourteen degrees Celsius. I wore a warm Norwegian sweater to clean and cook.

Someone knocked. A short, plump man in a London Fog coat with his hat in his hand gave me his card: *Sydney Messner, Reporter, Time Magazine.*

"*Time*? Come in. Have a seat." We faced one another, Messner on the couch, me, on the easy chair. He had a round, reddened face. Reddened from the cold.

"Why on earth would a *Time* reporter visit me?"

"We'd like your story, Miss Deane." He spoke with a New York accent.

"My story? *What* story?"

"The Russian Intelligence agent you met in Turkey. And the visit from the CIA."

"How in hell do you know about that?"

"We don't disclose our sources, Miss Deane."

"You must have gotten it from the CIA. But why would they tell *you*? Why would they want to advertise it in *Time*?"

"I didn't say they told me."

"Then how do you know?"

"Like I said, Miss Deane, we don't disclose our sources. Look, we're prepared to make a lucrative offer."

"What kind of an offer?"

"That depends on what you can tell us."

He baffled me. Why would the CIA agent inform *Time* that he visited me? To embarrass me? To ruin my reputation? But I'm no VIP. Why would my reputation matter? And why would the CIA tell *Time* about Lev? Maybe the U.S. Government tapped our talk in Ankara, not just the Russians. But why would they want to advertise it?

Oh. Maybe I *do* get it. If *Time* wrote that Lev wants to come to America, that he fears the Soviet government would keep his family behind so he wouldn't defect, that his government suspects every move he makes, the article would embarrass the Soviets. Perhaps that's the purpose. To embarrass the Soviets.

Suppose I give *Time* the story. What might the Soviets do to Lev that they hadn't already done? How much more guilt can I carry on my head?

"No dice, sir."

"Not interested in money, Miss Deane?"

"Not interested in *your* kind of money, Mr. Messner."

When he left, I felt good about myself. The same goodness I felt when I got the desire to bring Mom around the world with me. I needed good feelings about myself. I'd need a lot more to offset the bad ones.

Lieutenant Bowen drank beer at the Army Hotel bar every night. After his third, he'd sing "Danny Boy," his oversized ears turning a fiery red on the high notes. We'd sit next to each other between my sets.

I told him that the hotel had changed since I'd gone to Africa. More civilians than military men patronized it. Room guests held rowdy parties, and sometimes fought. It didn't function like an army hotel anymore. What happened, I wanted to know.

"See that room at the back?" he whispered.

"Next to the john? That's a storage room."

"That *was* a storage room. Peek, next time the door opens."

On the way to the restroom, I paused. When someone opened the storage room door, I craned my neck. Rows of slot machines! Officers, privates, German civilians. How could Costello get away with it?

"I'm stunned," I told Bowen at the bar.

"Not just gambling," he whispered. "But freeloading. Unauthorized Germans booking rooms. Gifts from civilians for favors. Even women, if you know what I mean. The hotel's going to pot."

"Can you talk to Costello? Tell him that people know what's going on?"

"You kidding? He's a captain, I'm a lieutenant. A civilian could talk to him, someone like you."

I caught up with Costello as he rushed to an elevator. "Captain, can we talk for a moment?"

"What's up?"

"Can we talk in the corner where no one will hear us?"

Before he answered, I darted toward the corner like I was the hub, and he was a spoke. "Sir, this hotel has been my home for years. Now it's like a Vegas casino, not an army hotel anymore. It's getting a bad name."

He thrust his index finger in my face. "Keep your fuckin' nose out of my business. I'm givin' you notice, and I'll put it in writing. Your contract's up Friday."

I sat in the dark in my apartment, replaying that scene again in my head. Should I have ignored what I saw in the back room? I couldn't. But my action cost my job. Well, the Kalb Officers club might book me. They'd offered me a contract in the past.

I called Captain Strydom, told him I had a run-in with Costello, and that if his offer was still good, I'd take it. "Good timing," he said. "We need you for a month."

Next morning, Strydom called back. "Hate to tell you, but we have to cancel. Costello sent a memo to all clubs in Germany. Says you're a prostitute and dope addict."

"That bastard!"

"You have two options," he told me. "Call it quits and leave, but your reputation will tail you like a shadow. Or attack it. Head on."

My typed report took three hours, and filled five pages. I posted it Special Delivery to the Commanding General of the U.S. Army in Europe. The letter closed with my overriding concern: *My name must be cleared, and I must be granted the right to earn a living in the only way I can.*

After posting it, I questioned whether it was the right thing to do. Perhaps it would have been better to drop the matter. Let it go. Leave Germany. But that wasn't me.

Action happened fast. General Edelman, General Gates, the entire Inspector General section, and a huge contingent of military police flocked to the hotel. General Edelman asked to see me in the manager's office.

The left side of his jacket was blanketed with five or six rows of ribbons, their bold colors a stark contrast to the paleness of his face. He asked about my background, life and travels. About my association with the Army Hotel and Captain Costello. I told him everything, including what happened in Ankara.

"Miss Deane, I want to be frank," he said. "We know what civilians can do to us. I want to ask you, I want to beg you. *Please* don't write to your senator. This dirty chapter in our history doesn't need any more broadcasting. Will my apology suffice?"

A general? Pleading with me?

"Sir, I have no intention of writing to my senator. Your apology will be more than enough, if you clear my name and guarantee me the right to earn my living as an entertainer and musician."

"I'll send out a memo today to clear your name across the board. And I'll give you a private number to call should you need my help in the future."

A major shakedown followed. The Army transferred Captain Costello to a supply office, and shipped three Majors to Munich. Colonels were reprimanded. A court martial scheduled. Local police arrested slot machine salesmen living in the hotel. The Board of Governors was dismissed, and a new one formed. Hotel policies were overhauled.

The time had come to continue my quest. The next leg of my journey, to the East, would take several years if I worked in every country. I'd need all my luggage. The bags I took through Africa, and those I'd stored at the hotel. I dreaded carting all that on trains, ships, and planes. I wondered—could I drive? Had anyone ever driven around the world?

On my battered world map, I drew a line eastward through Europe, the Mid-East, Iraq, Iran, Pakistan, India, Burma and Malaya. Maybe I could find a job in a medical mission in Malaya. Twelve-thousand miles. I'd have to ferry a car twice. Across the English Channel, and across the Bosporus.

The library carried a few books about overland journeys. An Oxford and Cambridge team had driven to the Far East in Land Rovers. They had mechanics, a medic, photographers, a writer, and subsidies. Peter Townsend did it in a Land Rover. But as Princess Margaret's ex-boyfriend, an aide to the King, and a World War II hero, he had ace contacts wherever he went.

Could I do it alone? Without a mechanic, contacts, or money?

I wrote to Land Rover in Birmingham, England. Did they think that such a trip was possible for a woman or did they think I was nuts? They replied by return post.

> We are delighted to learn of your plans and your interest in the Land Rover. You will, no doubt, be the first woman to drive around the world. We feel certain that our vehicle will meet your needs.

The directors invited me to be their guest at a local hotel.

On a cold December night, two porters at the Nuremberg Bahnhof loaded my luggage into the baggage compartment of a train to London. The train huffed, puffed, and pulled away. *Auf Wiedersehen,* I waved to the city and country that had been my home.

If only I could leave my guilt behind. Drop it in a bin like waste. But maybe nobody deserves to live guilt-free.

33

ENGLAND

1960-61

My hotel room in Solihull, Birmingham was Land Rover's gift. Cozy, but so tiny that I had to rent the room next door for my luggage.

I walked the short distance to the factory in bitter cold. The sky was clear, the sun shone, but the airways of my lungs had narrowed. I exhaled pure white puffs, and wheezed.

Three directors introduced themselves in Land Rover's sunny reception room. A Bromley, a Bacon, and a Knight. Very proper, very British. I tried to remember who was who. Bacon had a beard. Bromley wore a bowtie. The Knight was skin and bone. They served hot tea, showed me photographs of Land Rovers, and wall maps with bold, black lines marking overland routes.

"We pictured you a tough, lorry type, Miss Deane," Bacon said, "We're surprised to see a stunning young woman. As we wrote, you'd be the first woman to drive overland alone."

"I'll be the poorest. I have to work my way on my accordion."

"Work your way on an accordion?" they asked in unison. "We want to sell you a Land Rover," Bromley said, "but a woman alone? Playing her way on an accordion? That would worry us."

I tried to imagine the directors of Willys' Jeep putting me up in a hotel, and worried more about my safety than a sale.

"You've got pluck," Knight said. "Oxford and Cambridge had six men and subsidies. Peter Townsend had money and contacts. You're going with nobody and nothing. Of course, we'll help in every way we can."

"I'll need help with routes. Would I follow Townsend's?"

"No. He took the northern route because of the Suez crisis—Turkey into Iran. The southern route is safer." He slid his finger along a marked route on a wall map. "Through Turkey to Beirut. East to Damascus. Across the Jordanian desert to Baghdad. Then Iran, Pakistan, India."

"What's the toughest part of the drive?"

"Iran," Bacon said. "Desert roads are corrugated. You have to skim the tips at eighty kilometers an hour or dip into the ruts at eight."

"Is it true that brigands roam the deserts and rob foreign drivers? I'm worried about my accordion and amp."

"We've heard a few stories," Knight said, "but we don't know if they're true. We can build you a false floor to cover your instruments. No one will see it. We'll send a chap to your hotel to measure them, and anything else you want to conceal."

"People will see what I have through the windows."

"We'll install metal shields behind them, and build a partition between the front and back."

My list lengthened. A shelf that would slide out of the glove compartment for my portable Royal typewriter. A self-propelling winch. Four jerry cans, two on each side of the winch to carry petrol for long desert stretches where you can't get any. Blue color. Hard white detachable top. And, of course, left-hand drive.

The tab for the eighty-eight-inch wheel-base, custom-built Rover came to three thousand dollars. I gave Land Rover a three-hundred dollar deposit.

"You'll be the best advertisement that Land Rover ever had," Bacon said.

A hundred thousand Americans lived in England, most of them with the air force. I would launch my act in Norfolk, with ten thousand Yanks at Sculthorpe Air Base.

Captain Poe booked entertainment, and filled in for comedians, mimicking Winston Churchill with a faultless Oxford accent. He perused my portfolio. Yes, indeed, the Officers Club would love to have me. They prefer American entertainment. American everything. Launderettes, schools, stores, churches, chaplains, cars, movies, magazines, women. "American across the board," he said. "When can you start?"

"Tonight," I told him.

The pay was good. I'd live on base, and send Land Rover half of what I earned every month.

I was unpacking in my room at the Bachelor Officers' Quarters, when Poe knocked. He faced the floor. "We have to cancel. You'll have to go. I'm sorry."

"What do you mean? Why? What happened?"

"I can't tell you, I'm sorry. You'll have to go."

"If you don't tell me, I won't go."

"I got a wire. You're—you can't play here."

"I'm what? Tell me or I won't budge."

"You're tinted pink."

"Tinted pink?" What was he talking about? "What's that?"

"Means you're a commie."

"Oh, for Chris' sake!"

"I'm sorry but you'll have to—"

"Like hell I will."

I flipped through the cards in my wallet. There it was, General Edelman's number. He said I should call him if I had a problem.

"I need to phone General Edelman."

"Oh, come on, not that crap. Leave, please. Otherwise, I'll get into trouble."

"I'm going nowhere. Just to phone General Edelman."

"You're gonna phone a general? C'mon. Tell me another one."

"I want to use a phone."

"Even if you get him, which you can't, it won't matter. We don't take orders from him. We take orders from the Joint Chiefs of Staff in the States."

"Say what you want. His word will matter."

I reached Edelman in ten minutes. "General, I'm at Sculthorpe. Captain Poe said he got a memo that I'm tinted pink. That Nuremberg captain, Costello, must have done it. Probably dug up what he could. I told you about the incident in Turkey—"

"Put Poe on."

Poe straightened as if Edelman were sizing him up. "Yes, sir. Certainly, sir. Oh, sorry, sir. The post commander—"

Edelman had asked to speak to the post commander.

One week later, I played to a room packed with top brass. Captain Poe had become my booking agent, arranging contracts throughout England. All it took was a phone call. Poe would never know that Edelman acted fast only out of gratitude for my promise not to go public with the scandal.

Land Rover's directors urged me to consider a partner for the trip. For safety, they said, and to share expenses. They were right about expenses. I'd been told that the "GB" I'd carry on my license plate didn't mean *Great Britain*. It meant *Gas Burner*.

My ad in the *London Observer* for a traveling companion drew thirty weird responses and one promising letter from a portrait artist. We arranged to meet at the Eros statue in Piccadilly Circus.

I spotted Erica Suttill with ease. My age, flat-chested, bony. No makeup.

"Shall we have tea at Lyons?" she asked in a highbrow accent. I had hoped to go to a pub. "Sure," I said.

Erica placed snapshots of her portraits on our table. They were stunning. She said that she longed to see the world, not as a tourist, but as an artist. We shared interests—classical music, literature, art. I told her that I hoped to stay in the East for a while. Perhaps in Malaya, working in a medical mission. She'd like that, too, she said.

I suggested that we test our relationship to see if we could get along.

Erica arrived at the air force base where I performed, stepped into my room, and gasped. "Good grief! All this will go with you?"

"I'm afraid so. I live out of suitcases."

"Whew! You'd have space for me?"

"What would you carry?"

"Two suitcases, art supplies, one bucket, a pup tent, a sleeping bag, a kerosene stove, a dish, knife, and spoon."

I wished I could travel like Erica, but I couldn't get along with one knife, one spoon, one bucket. I needed a bucket to wash vegetables in, and another for clothes. We differed, but we might get along better that way than if we were alike.

Visas and vaccinations topped our task list. Visas were easy to get when you flew into a country, but not when driving. No country would grant us a visa unless we could prove that we were in transit, and wouldn't sell the car. The only way to do that was to display a visa for the country we'd travel to next.

We uncovered a daisy chain of rules. Turkey wouldn't grant a visa until Syria did. Syria wouldn't, until Lebanon did. Lebanon insisted on a Jordanian visa, and Jordan insisted on a visa from Iraq. Iraq, Iran, Pakistan, India—all demanding to see the next country's visa before they'd issue their own. India would not grant us visas until Burma did. That's where the buck stopped. Burma wouldn't let us in.

The only country that would accept us from India was Nepal. But Nepal would not issue a visa until they knew where we were going next. Without Burma, there was no next. We'd have to play it by ear.

Vaccinations followed. Bruises over our arms bore as much testimony as our signed vaccination cards. Smallpox, yellow fever, diphtheria, typhoid.

We compiled lists: Land Rover depots, military installations, camping sites, historical sites, spare Rover parts to carry. But with all the preparations, I wasn't ready. What if we found a medical mission? What could I do besides sweep the floor? Perhaps a university could teach me something useful. In Germany, I walked into the University of Munich medical school, and got in. Why not try the London School of Tropical Medicine? They'd think I was mad, but I had nothing to lose.

On the winter afternoon that I reached the stone façade of the school, I almost turned back. The building looked like a World War II bunker, buttressed to withstand assaults by the forces of ignorance like me. *This won't work, kid. But you're here, so try.*

I mounted the stone steps, entered the bunker, and passed the registrar's office. No use talking to a registrar. He'd think my mission bizarre. A faculty member might be receptive. I knocked on the door of Dr. Buckley Hughes.

"Come in," the voice said.

Hughes was a sallow-skinned man seated at an enormous walnut desk, smoking a pipe. I spoke fast.

"Sir, I'm going to drive a Land Rover from here to Malaya. Somewhere in the East, I want to volunteer in a medical mission. Could somebody teach me something that might be useful?"

You'd think I'd asked him to flout his Hippocratic Oath. Well, maybe I did. He motioned for me to sit, and picked up his phone. "Send Dr. Lloyd, please."

The tall, white-haired man with a bow tie and dignified manner stepped in, grinning. I liked him before he uttered a word.

"Tell him," Hughes said. "Tell him what you told me." I did. Lloyd burst into laughter. "Fascinating!"

"Highly unusual," Hughes said, knitting his brows and packing his pipe.

They discussed possibilities, these stately men surrounded by massive, leather-bound volumes on every shelf.

"Malariology could be useful," Lloyd said.

"It's a course?" I asked.

"Certainly. Why?"

"Ethiopians cure malaria overnight with garlic cloves taped to their wrists."

"God help us if we prescribed garlic!"

"How long would the course take?" I asked.

"We'll go as fast or as slow as you like. Three months if slow. One month if fast."

Dr. Lloyd and I sat in a high-ceilinged lecture room every day like a comedy team. He, with his vest and bow tie and Oxford accent, as though ready to address a graduate assembly. Me, in slacks, trying to grasp in two months what students study in two years, so that some day I might do something in some mission, somewhere.

I adored the informality. I giggled freely, and asked questions without the fear of sounding dumb. The course was easy, but enough to get me into a mission door.

On my last day, I recalled what a New York friend had advised for my roach phobia. "Professor, a psychiatrist once told me that the best way to overcome my fear of roaches is to carry them around in a test-tube, and study their habits."

Lloyd brought a test-tube with two hefty roaches. "They're from Texas," he told me. "The female is pregnant. We call them Alice and Ben-Hur."

Their chunky bodies and moving antennae repelled me. "How do I feed them?"

"Put the test-tube in a refrigerator once a day. Leave it for ten minutes, no more. Take it out, remove the cork, and insert tiny bits of moistened crackers. Replace the cork. Within a few minutes, they'll defreeze and eat."

That night, I wrapped the test-tube in a brown paper bag and carried it in my handbag to the club where I was booked.

"Sir," I asked the bartender. "Can you refrigerate my rose?" I handed him the bag. "It's in a glass vase, so please be careful."

Ten minutes later, I took it to the ladies' toilet with the roach food. The look of their thick brown bodies panicked me even while frozen.

Our travel brochure featured our photographs. Me in my fishtail with the accordion. Erica on the floor, painting a portrait of a small boy in a high chair. A striking likeness. A map she had sketched showed our route through every continent. She hoped that after our medical work in Malaya, we would tour Indonesia, Australia, New Zealand, and the Pacific Islands. For some reason, my mind could not get past Malaya.

Captain Poe read our brochure. His wife's birthday was coming up, he told us. "What a unique gift my portrait would be!" That launched Erica's first military commission.

One night, I dreamt I was driving in a strange country. An army of men who had no hands pursued me. I pressed my pedal to the floor, reached a crater, braked, threw open the door, and leapt to the precipice. Serpents undulated along the crater walls above a blazing fire. The army caught up. I screamed out loud and woke in a sweat.

I would have to dump my guilt before I left.

34

LONDON
1961-62

Maybe a nun could help. The American priest I met in Lourdes had told me about a convent where the nuns were converted Jews.

The sign read, "Convent of our Lady of Sion."

A Sister opened the door and led me to a reception room with a long table, eight chairs, and a fire blazing in a cast-iron fireplace. The aroma and crackling sound of burning embers relaxed me.

Sister Sarah entered. Fiftyish, garbed in a black robe with a head cover. I'd come at "high tea" time, she told me. She brought a pot of tea with raisin tea cakes. What had I come for, she asked.

"To confess my sins, Sister. To anyone. They're too heavy for me."

"Good, my child. Our Chaplain, Father William Kahle, hears confessions."

"Can I see him?"

"He's on retreat." She paused. "You're Catholic?"

"Jewish."

"You came to the right place. We were Jewish, too. Of course, you'll have to become a Catholic to confess."

"Just to confess?"

"Not *just*. Your sins must be washed away by the Blood of Christ."

"I must be Catholic for that?"

"Of course. Only the Catholic Church has apostolic authority."

"Sounds complicated, Sister. All I want to do is confess the sins that press my mind so hard I can't sleep."

"Only baptism can wipe your slate clean."

"People of other religions can't clean up their act?"

"They can't."

"Makes no sense, Sister. Religion is too intertwined with geography. Folks born in Egypt are Muslim. In China, Taoist. In India, Hindu. How can one religion be right for the whole world?"

"We're blessed, my child. They're not."

"I can't buy it, Sister. All I want to do is to share the blisters on my soul."

A blues song drifted through my mind. While Sister left for the kitchen to fill the teapot, I drew a five-lined staff on a paper napkin. I could hear Sarah Vaughn sing it.

Wash my sins away, Sister, wash 'em far away
Take 'em down the river by the bright light of day,
Roll 'em off my shoulders cause I can't bear the weight,
Take 'em Sister, take 'em, 'fore it gets too late.
Wash my sins away, Sister, wash 'em far away.

"When can I see Father Kahle, Sister?"

"Next week, but you can't just confess. You need instruction, the catechism. Jesus gave His Life to erase our sins. You must be incorporated into His Body, the One True Holy Apostolic Church. You must learn the liturgy, the Mass."

"It's not me, Sister."

She edged her chair close. "Think. Are the fires of purgatory, you? St. Augustine said that purgatory fire is worse than anything you can suffer in life...*gravior erit ignis quam quidquid potest homo pati in hac vita.*"

A loud popping sound of embers pulled my eyes to the flames. Sister's voice was grave. "Unbearable it is. And the prayers of the living can't intercede."

I took the course. Three weeks later, I blasted Father's ears in the confessional. The pot I'd smoked in Chicago, and played nineteen choruses of "Tea for Two." The red dress I wore in Mozambique, returned it, and got my money back. The two hundred-dollar lie in New York. The five bucks that cost Ahmed his hand. The mess I caused Lev Frolov and Captain McGill in Turkey.

I quit. Father sat in the confessional like a statue. Had he never heard worse? In a solemn voice, he told me to repeat the *Hail Mary* and *Our Father* forty times each.

Sisters from The Lady of Sion gathered around the baptismal pool. Father Kahle placed a white shawl on my shoulders, and prayed. I repeated the prayers, leaned forward and turned my head toward him. He scooped water from the pool, and poured it on my forehead. "I baptize you in the Name of the Father, the Son, and the Holy Ghost."

I wished he'd said "Spirit" instead of "Ghost."

"Here's a crucifix," Father said. "And a rosary. Keep the rosary in your pocket and the crucifix in your bag."

I slept well that night.

My new Land Rover sat like a queen in the factory showroom. Short, compact, mighty. I'd owned a Chrysler and a Mercedes. I'd ridden in a Rolls Royce. But nothing could compare with my Land Rover. No challenge would overwhelm its self-propelling winch. The four belted jerry cans would carry enough petrol to get us through any desert.

I ran my palms across the sides, the hatch back, the windshield and hood, and kissed it. I'd never loved a car so much.

"Want to drive?" Bromley asked.

I had only a few shillings, not enough for gas. "Don't worry," he said. "Land Rover is giving you a gift. A full tank, and four full jerry cans."

"You guys are more family than business," I said.

I climbed in. "Oh! Second floor!"

"You'll get used to the height," Bromley said. He demonstrated the gears: eight forwards and two reverse. I circled the factory. The Rover felt like a tank.

Bromley took the wheel, and drove to the licensing office. My license plate—6066UE—could only be used in England, the clerk informed me. I'd have to exchange it for an international plate before I left.

Land Rover's directors arranged for me to take a self-maintenance course at their London school. I dreaded it, but I'd have to learn how to clean my air filter so I could do it in the desert.

On a Monday morning, I pulled into Land Rover's spacious London school. Three mechanics trained on one side of the room. Derek Rowland taught on the other. "I'm your teacher," he said. Heavy build, huge hands, ruddy skin.

"Sir, I have no aptitude for mechanics. I'm just a musician."

"This is easy stuff. What to do if the Land Rover won't start. How to change your tires. How to clean your air filter. The course takes three weeks. Not to worry."

Every morning Derek lifted the hood, pointed, and talked fast in a thick Cockney accent. On Friday he tested me. "Turn on the ignition," he said. "The Land Rover won't start. Figure out why." He leaned on the door of the Rover, arms folded.

I turned the key. Nothing happened. I picked up the hood and looked.

"Do something," Rowland ordered.

"I'm scared."

"Oh, for Chris' sakes. Do *something!*"

I didn't know what to do. Derek stomped out. The mechanics howled and pointed out the window. "There goes Derek in the pub."

"Please, would you help? Derek did something to the engine so it wouldn't start. Wants me to figure out what it is. Help me, please."

"Hell no, we ain't helpin'. You want us to lose our job?"

I scanned everything, but dared not touch anything. Derek returned, reeking of beer. "Do something!" he hollered.

I unscrewed the first screw I saw.

"Listen to me," he shouted. "*This* is the battery. *That* is the generator." The mechanics roared with laughter.

"Derek, nothing will happen to this Land Rover. It's new. I won't need to fix anything," I told him.

"I ain't here to play games. My job is to teach. Now for Chris' sakes, what would you do if the Land Rover didn't start? Show me!"

I stood, shaken. Touched something that had two parts which looked like they didn't belong together, and tried to pull them apart.

"*Lis-ten!*" Derek waved his arms like the religious fanatics on Orators' Corner in Hyde Park. "Everything in an engine either goes up and down or all around!"

By the end of the third week, I knew what to do if the engine didn't start. And I knew how to clean my air filter.

Derek handed me a small, square box. "You deserve a gift."

I tore off the wrapper and removed the lid, but couldn't fathom what I saw. A pair of four joined metal rings with pointed steel projections.

"Knuckle-busters," Derek said. "If anybody gets fresh, put 'em on your fingers, and sock 'em good."

Erica painted a map and the words *Eastward Ho!* on the Land Rover doors. Our photos appeared in the press with a picture of the Rover, and a long article. A Pan Am advertising agent read it, and phoned.

"We'll pay you to carry a sign: *Next time I'll fly Pan Am!*"

"Thanks," I told him, "but this trip is no ad campaign."

I was ready, but Erica was still painting Captain Poe's portrait. I'd set out alone. She'd meet me in Frankfurt.

The digits on my international license plate—QJ4499—added up to an eight. Good sign. All important numbers in my life were eights.

I packed. Everything fit, even my portable toilet. But what would customs officials say if they spotted Frau Hildegaard, my human skull? Or my knuckle-busters? Or worse—Ben-Hur with his pregnant mate.

An Unreasonable Woman

In search of meaning around the globe

PART III

35

EASTWARD HO!

June, 1962

My Land Rover was one of many cars rolling up the ferry ramp to cross the English Channel, but probably the only one embarking on a twelve-thousand-mile trek.

A driver with a GB plate popped his head out. "Hey, *Eastward Ho!* Jolly good!"

My house-on-wheels *was* jolly good. Rooted nowhere. Anchored to nothing. Nothing but freedom.

Eastward Ho! rolled off the ramp onto French soil in Calais. What a pleasure to be alone! Erica was still painting a portrait in London. I liked her company but if she were with me, we'd stop at every gallery on route. Alone, I was free. Besides, I was no tourist in France. I knew it well. Germany, too. Italy, Greece, Turkey, Lebanon, Jordan, too. But Iraq would be new, strange, exotic. Baghdad! I could hardly wait.

Driving into Frankfurt was like coming home. Every military club booked me, and by the end of my second week, almost every enlisted man, NCO and officer had examined the engine, undersides and body of my Land Rover. Reporters from five newspapers had interviewed me.

The Stars and Stripes captioned its front-page article, "A Driving Ambition," and printed a wide-angled photo of my Land Rover with the belted jerry cans and self-propelling winch. I waved from the driver's seat.

> A 30-year-old American girl and her British companion are about to begin a round-the-world trip by jeep-like truck. If they succeed, they will be the first women to circumnavigate the globe entirely by car and ship...

The American journalist who wrote that article said I'd joined the Musicians' Union when I was ten. If Americans wrote such fiction, what might I read about myself around the rest of the world?

Overseas Family captioned its article, "Artist Sings Way Round World."

> What jazz musician would abandon engagements at New York's swank St. Regis and Park Sheraton Hotels for a tiny native club somewhere in Africa? Crazy? Maybe. But it's all what you want out of life, says Shirley Deane, who did just that…

Frankfurter Rundschau's caption read, "Weltreise mit zehn Gangen"—"World Journey with Ten Gears."

> … Since a few days, you have seen an unusual vehicle on the streets of Frankfurt…This monster is driven by a woman. This woman is able not only to drive this machine, but can also, in just a few hours, take it apart and put it back together.

I posted that article with a translation to Derek Rowland, my teacher at Land Rover's self-maintenance school in London. He wrote back that he stuck it on the cartoon bulletin board.

The Frankfurt Officers Club was swinging. A dozen officers and their wives toasted drinks at a corner table, singing "Happy Birthday" to a Major. I chatted at the packed bar with Fritz, a portly German bartender. At 8 p.m., feeding time, I reached in my purse for the brown paper bag with Alice and Ben-Hur.

"Fritz, put this rose in the fridge, please. I want to keep it fresh. It's in a glass vase, so be careful."

After ten minutes I told him I was going to my room. "I'll take it now, thanks." Fritz was shaking a cocktail with one hand. With the other, he opened the fridge and took out the bag. It slipped. The test-tube crashed.

"Oh, my God!" I shrieked, crouching over the bar. Alice and Ben-Hur lay immobile on the floor amidst shards of glass. "Look what you did, Fritz!"

He stared down, lifted his heavy shoe and stomped the life out of the frozen creatures.

"Oh, shit, Fritz!"

"Vas shit? You have no right to put roaches in my fridge!"

"It's not *your* fridge."

"I am in charge. You said it was a rose."

"Roach, not rose."

"Roaches are verboten. Verboten! This is restaurant and bar. Roaches are verboten. Against law."

"Show me where the law says roaches are verboten."

He ranted in German while I stomped out. I felt bad. I'd begun to see Alice and Ben-Hur as creatures whose lives depended on me. Now my phobia would last forever.

Pigeons and people prattled noisily on the wooden platform of the Frankfurt railway station while I waited for Erica. I spotted her as she stepped off the train. She grabbed me in a warm, bony embrace, we picked up her luggage, and drove to the U.S. airbase, catching up on news.

Erica painted and I played accordion until mid-June when we left Frankfurt for southern Germany and Italy. Military clubs booked me for two weeks to a month, and most club managers were able to convince someone on base that their greatest need was a portrait. We stayed in Bachelors' Officers' Quarters, relishing hot-water showers, clean toilets and toilet paper. Between jobs, we camped out.

Erica was a better camper than I. She'd pitch our tents, light the petrol stove, set plates and utensils, open packets of soup, wash salad vegetables and cook. Fair exchange, I thought. I got portrait commissions for her, did all the driving, and checked the battery, radiator, oil, and tires every day. We got along well, not in spite of being different but because of it. Details intrigued her like the braided hair buns of Italian women, which she'd sketch in restaurants. Broader pictures intrigued me like the readiness of Italians to break into song on the streets, and just as spontaneously, into fights. We dressed differently, too. Erica wore long-sleeved blouses tucked into neat pleated English skirts or slacks. I wore sloppy blue jeans and men's cotton shirts because they had big pockets.

One afternoon at an air force base in Italy, a club captain asked me to dinner in front of Erica. I told him that we only went out on double dates so he'd have to find a friend. "In that case," he said, "forget it," and walked off.

"Please don't do that again," Erica told me. "I'm used to being alone." After that, I was careful to discourage liaisons that didn't include her.

From southern Italy, we drove onto a ship to cross the Ionian Sea to Greece. I sat next to Erica on deck as she set up her easel and painted a vivid portrait of the clear turquoise waters. She painted effortlessly in a thought-free state as though some silent inner guide were moving her hands.

We drove along Athens' broad streets past the Hilton with its marble exterior and balconies that overlooked the Acropolis. A narrow winding side street led us to a small, pinkish stone hotel. Parked in front was a Willy's jeep with an Australian plate.

The desk clerk, the owner's handsome black-eyed son, gave us forms to fill out. "Why are you here? Where are you going? What is your work?"

Erica wrote "artist."

"Artist?" he asked.

"Yes," she said.

"Painter?"

She nodded. "Portrait painter."

He eyed her like she'd transformed into Marilyn Monroe. Picked up her bags and led her to her room while a porter carried mine to an adjoining room. Erica's cheeks had crimsoned.

Paintings of fishing villages hung on the walls of the hotel restaurant. Pictures of mythological figures, and traditional homes with inner courtyards. We sat at a table near a window from where I could see my Land Rover. Bazooki background music reminded me of my Greek TV show in Chicago.

While we ate soup, beef, mushrooms, grilled feta cheese and baklava for two dollars each, we shared plans. The Land Rover depot was first on my list. The Acropolis was first on Erica's. As we drank our strong, black coffee, a chunky man in his twenties strode to our table. He nodded toward my Land Rover.

"That's your 'jobbie'?" he asked with an Australian accent.

"It is. That's your jeep in front of mine?"

"Right. Me and my friend are headed west to Britain. You?"

"East."

"My name's Philip."

"Have a seat," I said. "We're Erica and Shirley. Tell us about the route you took."

"Me and my mate shipped from Adelaide to Singapore."

"Then north to Burma?" I asked.

"Nope. Couldn't get a visa," he said. "Road's bad, bridges are down."

"Townsend did it," I said. "If he can do it, so can we."

"Townsend can do anything," he told us. "The British Embassy paid locals to get him through the rough spots. Me and my buddy are just ordinary blokes."

If Burma wouldn't let us in, we'd have a problem at the Indian border. The daisy chain problem. But I refused to dwell on what *could* happen.

"What's the Iranian desert like?" I asked Philip.

He whistled. "Desert of Death. That's where an Aussie before us got beheaded." Erica put her coffee cup down. The color drained from her face like oil from the sump of my Land Rover.

The hotel owner's son left his shift at 6 p.m. and knocked on Erica's door. I heard him. "May I have the pleasure of your company for dinner?"

"Oh, wait, please." She knocked on my door. "Shirl? Mind if I go out to dinner?"

"Not at all, Erica. Enjoy yourself."

Down the steps they walked, and out the door to his Mercedes. I wondered if that was her first date in years. We seldom discussed men. Erica was so properly British that I rarely brought up the subject.

At 10 p.m., she knocked. "Shirl? You up?"

"Sure. Come in."

A radiant woman walked in, happy in her skin, sure of her gait. All it took to transform a straight-laced Limey into a vibrant female was a man's interest.

"Shirl, Costas wants me to paint his portrait. Shirl, ever had a Greek man?"

"It would be more correct to say a Greek man had *me*."

She hesitated. "I need to tell you something, and I don't know how to say it."

"You want to stay here."

Erica nodded.

"You're quitting the trip."

Another nod.

"No problem, Erica. I'd planned to drive alone, anyhow. I don't mind at all."

She hugged me. "Any advice you can give me?"

"Get the money before you start to paint."

"Oh, I couldn't. That's not ethical."

"Then get a lawyer to draw up a contract. You know—'This is to state that I accept the commission to do Costas' portrait for such and such a fee.'"

"He'd think I'm commercial."

"Take my advice. If you want the relationship to work, put your work on a business basis."

I lay in bed in the dark. It didn't matter that Erica dropped out. I preferred to do the trip myself. No compromises to make. Besides, if beheading was going to happen, better one head than two.

Next morning, Costas took Erica's belongings out of my Land Rover. His eyes betrayed him. He schemed while she dreamed.

Alone again. If I ever write a book, I'll call it *Alone Again*. No matter how close you are to somebody, parting is inevitable. Atoms bumping into atoms, and going their separate ways. *Alone*.

36

TURKEY REVISITED

1962

A ferry across the narrow Bosporus brought me to Asia, phase two of my trek. Drowsiness assailed me on the stretch from Istanbul to Ankara. When Land Rover's directors suggested a metal partition to close off the back, I didn't know how hot the front could get. To keep from dozing, I stopped for coffee every hour.

Each stop was a trumpet call. Dozens of men and boys appeared from out of nowhere, encircling the car. At one café, a boy of ten pointed to *Eastward Ho!*

"What is mean?"

"Means"—I pointed—"I go this way. East."

"Where is man?"

"Home."

"What work you?"

"Drive."

On the outskirts of Ankara, I checked into a small hotel, but couldn't sleep. Erica's face popped into my mind, the way it glowed with hope. She was living a fantasy, believing what she wanted to believe like most of us do. We fall in love and tell ourselves that we'll press our bliss into permanence and live happily ever after. Even when our glass house shatters, we feel sure we can put it together again and restore the bliss. It seldom works, but we spend our lives trying.

I drove along the familiar broad, tree-lined streets of Ankara, past the railway station where I'd boarded the Orient Express back to

Germany. What if I stopped at the Russian Embassy to ask what happened to Lev Frolov? The thought tempted me, but thousands of miles lay ahead. I couldn't afford another incident.

With a small American flag tied to my left side-view mirror, I pulled up to the U.S. air base. An MP stopped me. "Your pass?"

"I don't have one. I'm an American entertainer. I'll work at the Officers' Club."

"You're expected?"

"Expected, no. Welcome, yes."

"Your I.D, Miss."

I gave him my passport. And the letter of introduction from General Edelman.

The club had new paint, new furniture, a new captain. Captain Fischer looked through my brochures. Before he spoke, I did.

"I have contracts lined up around the world, Captain. I can only stay two weeks." Without a pause, I asked, "By the way, where's Captain McGill?"

"Who's he?"

"Used to run this club."

Fischer shrugged. "Never heard of him." Once known, now unknown.

Two men in civilian clothes walked in. "Hey, Captain! D'ya see that crazy jeep outside?"

Turkish military officers and reporters from the *Hurriyet* newspaper were invited to my opening night. I had to laugh when I saw my photograph with the Land Rover on the front page. On my first visit to Ankara, I was a captive. On my second, a star.

The road that ran southeast from Ankara was the best highway in Turkey. I could see for miles ahead, and drove at fifty miles an hour. I promised myself I'd cook meals on my camp stove, but I was too impatient to open the hatch, get the utensils, light the stove, cook, eat, wash, and pack up. To stop for kebab was easier.

Next time someone asked what I missed most about America, I'd say "toilets." Public toilets reeked. A Red Cross worker once told me that a few drops of perfumed oil in my nostrils would take care of the worst odors. I wished I'd thought of it sooner.

The rough road dipped, then climbed through the passes of the Taurus Mountains where Saint Paul was born. It led through the narrow gorges of the Cicilian Gates, the same gorges that invaders and traders used for centuries. A bitter taste of dust filled my mouth. My chest felt tight. I reached for my asthma inhaler, fourth time that day. The Rover climbed the rocky road in progressively lower gear, winding its way around U-shaped bends.

My stomach sank. The engine quit. There I was, alone in the Taurus Mountains. Why couldn't the Rover have stopped in Ankara? Within minutes, air force mechanics would have fixed it. But I was stuck on the ancient roads that the Crusaders had trekked. Stuck in the corridors of history. Tears fell.

Get out, Deane, I told myself. *You learned a few things in London while you drove your teacher nuts. Get out and lift the hood.* I got out, lifted the hood, saw nothing. Tears flowed. *Open your notebook, kid. You took a ton of notes at the London school.*

My notebook said: "If you've traveled on a dusty, unpaved road…climbing in low gear, and the engine sputters and stops, check carburetor jets (the things that mix fuel and air to combust)." A self-drawn diagram showed how to dismantle the jets. "Clean them with solvent." My maintenance kit was in back, the solvent on top. I poured a few drops into the jets to dissolve the dirt, then put them back together. I sat behind the wheel, scared to turn the key. What if it wouldn't start?

Turn the key, kid. The Rover started. I felt like standing on the rooftop, beating my chest like an ape. Shouting to the mountains, *Hey, look what I did!*

In Adana, in southeast Turkey, a few officers at Incirlik base remembered me from three years back, and gave me a two-week contract. Good fee, bright room, clean toilet, toilet paper, hot water, three meals a day. A holiday.

On the road again, the route south from the Syrian border ran through Aleppo to Homs. The Rover crawled in lowest gear over old roads. If Erica were with me, she'd have wanted to visit the Crusaders' castles. I'd like to have seen a castle but the road was too bumpy. Before I saw the bumps, I hit them, and the Rover bounced.

From Homs, I drove southwest to Beirut. Only in Beirut could I get a major Rover service, wash a mound of laundry, get a haircut, pick up mail, answer my growing stack of it, add pages to my passport, develop film, and buy tinned food for the road.

After lunch at a roadside café, the Rover wouldn't start. Customers, waiters and cooks came out and shouted in Arabic and English, "Open. We fix."

"No thanks. No, no."

My notebook said: "When the car bounces up and down on bumpy roads and stops, check the generator." Next to my diagram were the words: "Do wires rub against each other? If so, you have a short. Tape them up."

Men milling around me watched every move I made, their bellies quaking with laughter. With tape from my maintenance box, I covered the ends of the wires so they wouldn't touch. The Rover started, and the men applauded. I bowed.

The Commodore Hotel stood in the center of town, and at the center of Beirut life. A few minutes after I checked in, three young British men knocked. The short one, a man with a glossy complexion that looked like he'd just scrubbed it with ivory soap, asked, "You're *Eastward Ho!*?"

"That's me."

"My name's Clyde. We're goin' eastward, too. Australia."

Brent, older, with a low-pitched voice and the hint of a beard, said they'd planned the trip for five years.

Rolf introduced himself as the baby of the three. He spoke with an unlit cigarette dangling from his mouth. "I only got a learner's permit so I don't drive. I do the routes."

"What luck to meet you chaps! You got a Rover?"

"Nah," Clyde said. "A cheapie. Willy's convertible soft-top. Hey, could we convoy?"

To convoy would be fun. Besides, Brent was cute. “Maybe to India,” I said. “I don’t know what’ll happen after that. I’d like to go to Burma, but I don’t have a visa.”

“We don’t either,” Brent said. “Let’s convoy to Calcutta.”

I laid my route map on the rug. We squatted, sharing plans for the next stretch. I pointed to the three roads that ran from Beirut to Baghdad. “Top and middle ones are bad, I hear. I plan to take the bottom one, the oil pipeline road. It’s tarmac, well maintained.”

“We planned that, too.” Rolf ran his forefinger across the route. “From here, east to Damascus. South into Jordan. Straight east across the desert. Seven hundred miles later, Baghdad. *Bagh-dad!* I can’t wait.”

Next morning, a journalist and a photographer from *Al-Mujtama* magazine came to the Commodore. They sat with the Brits and me in a corner of the spacious lobby to photograph and question the four of us.

The journalist took out his notebook and peppered me with questions. “What secret drives you from one place to another? Where have you been? How far will you go? Have you no fear? What was your childhood like? What if something goes wrong with the engine? Ever been in love? What happened to him? What do you think of marriage?”

“Look, here,” I told him. “These three guys are also driving around the world. Why don’t you question them?”

He grinned. “Men are not as interesting as women.”

Next morning, the two-page Arabic article appeared in the *Al-Mujtama* on all newsstands. I thought the hotel manager was joking when he translated it.

> …. She left New York in 1956 with an English female friend…who was a maid…. Shirley was rooted in wealth… She found herself in need of money while she was in Belgrade… Submitted writing work until she accumulated what she needed…. She says love is beautiful… Marriage is a prison… Shirley’s eyes are green…

Only one statement in the *Al-Mujtama* was true: I did say that marriage is a prison.

On our last morning in Beirut, a Friday, another article appeared. This time, in the English language paper, *The Daily Star.* My photo with the Land Rover was captioned, "Young Woman on World Tour Leaves Beirut Today, Eastward."

> The globe-trotting feat of a young woman who will be leaving Beirut Friday morning is painfully slow when contrasted with U.S. astronaut Walter Schirra's six orbits in nine hours Wednesday.

For the first time, a reporter got it right.

37

THE JORDANIAN DESERT

September, 1962

My Rover kicked up so much dust that the jeep had to stay too far behind to call us a convoy. Still, it was good to know that three guys were riding behind me. If I stopped, they'd catch up. Eventually.

We were out of Damascus, riding east through the Syrian Desert. Beyond the frontier of Jordan, I pulled over to wait. Twenty minutes later they showed up, hungry. They laid a cloth, cooked tinned stew, and boiled a pot of water to pour over spoonfuls of black Bovril, a British yeast extract. With a little imagination, it tastes like soup.

We lay on mats after our meal. The October evening was cool and clear, and the moon was full. "You know, guys, this silence is more than an absence of noise. It's a presence of something subtle."

Loud shrieks pierced the stillness. "What the hell was that?" Brent cried.

"Hyenas," Clyde said.

"They'll attack?" I asked.

"They could. Their jaws would tear us apart."

We were ready in seconds. I was climbing into the Rover when Brent said he'd like to ride with me. "Isn't it your turn to drive?" I asked.

"It's okay," Clyde said. "I'm not tired. Besides, Rolf keeps me awake. He talks non-stop."

I ignored my feeling of uneasiness when Brent climbed in.

"The three of us went to school together," he told me. "When we heard about the Oxford-Cambridge overland tour, we figured if those blokes could do it, so could we.

He turned to me. "Can I put my arm around you?"

"Sure."

A perfect moment. Alone on a tarmac desert road, narrow like a ribbon. White sands, an attractive man, stillness.

"What's the real reason you're doing this trip?" Brent asked.

"Searching for meaning," I told him. "Most of the time, we chase castles in the air. I want to know if there's anything that's real, that lasts."

Brent pointed to a concrete mile-marker on the side of the road showing the number of kilometers to the next checkpoint and gas pump. "That's the final checkpoint before the Iraqi border," he said. "Let's pull over and wait for them."

When the engine shut off, we heard the desert silence again. Brent kissed me gently. Maybe Clyde would drive slowly so we'd have a half-hour together. Maybe an hour. As our bodies touched, the only sounds we heard were our breaths.

Time passed. Brent moved to the window to check his watch by the light of the moon. "Something's wrong," he worried. "An hour, and they haven't caught up. Let's go back."

I started the engine, turned the Rover around and pressed the pedal. We rode in silence, uneasy. The moon looked hard now, not mysterious or romantic.

Suddenly Brent screamed, and my mind shut down. I slammed the brakes so hard that we lurched toward the windshield. The jeep was upside down. Six Arabs stood in a semi-circle around it, snatching cigarettes, radios, cameras. Stuffing them into the waist pockets of their white robes. In the glare of my headlights, their eyes were big with shock. "Here, lean on the horn," I told Brent.

"My God! My God!" he cried.

I took his left elbow and pressed it to the horn. "Keep it there."

I grabbed the fire extinguisher and ran out, pointing my extinguisher at the Arabs' faces like it was a machine gun. They galloped off.

"Bastards! Bastards!" I roared, running in my man's hat, oversized shirt and jeans. The glare of my headlights, the loud sustained horn, my fierce shouts and fire extinguisher, spraying as I ran, moved them with speed. Their white robes flapped in the air like sails of a ship in a wild wind. Wallets fell from their robes. Cigarettes. Beer cans.

"Bastards! Bastards!" I ran and shouted, spraying liquid in the air and on the sand. When they were out of sight, I ran back. The horn still howled, the headlights glared. Clyde and Rolf lay still, faces down.

"Clyde? Clyde! You okay?"

His pulse raced. He picked up his head. "What happened?"

I wiped sand off his eyelids and mouth. "Rolf, are you all right? Rolf, talk to me."

He turned and moaned. His eyelids fluttered. "What happened?"

I opened the right door to the Rover. Brent still had his elbow on the horn. "My God, my God!" he repeated.

"Get out, Brent. Stay with them. I'll be right back."

He climbed out, eyed the men, the upturned jeep and wailed. "My God, my God!"

I got in the Rover, turned around and raced to the checkpoint. The light was on.

"Help, help," I told a policeman. "Accident. Three men need doctor. Where is doctor?"

He dialed a number, said a few words in Arabic, and handed me the phone.

"Doctor Hassan here," a voice said.

"Doctor, a jeep was ambushed, it's overturned. Two men are lying there. Another in shock."

"The men are on the tarmac?"

"No. Sand. They're in shock. Hurry, quick."

The officer and doctor spoke briefly. "Doctor come with stretchers," the officer told me. "Police coming. Why you say ambush? No ambush here."

"I saw them. I saw the ambushers. Six Arabs, pilfering."

"What is pil—?"

"Stealing."

"You go back. We come."

"You don't know where."

"One road only."

I drove fast. Brent sat in the sand near his buddies, bawling like a baby. Clyde and Rolf lay as I left them. "Are you all right?"

Clyde stirred. "Where are we?"

"You'll be okay. A doctor is coming."

"Doctor?"

"Rolf, are you okay?"

"Where is...? Where is...? What happened?"

A truck pulled up. Three men jumped out. "I'm Dr. Hassan," said a short man in a white coat. He took the men's pulse, checked for injuries, and ordered his men to bring stretchers. They put the two in back of the truck, and helped Brent to a seat in front.

"Police will come now," Hassan said. "They'll pick everything up and store it at the station. Why did you tell police the jeep was ambushed?"

"Because I saw them. I saw the ambushers. Six Arabs, pilfering cigarettes, wallets, radios, beer."

Dr. Hassan put a hand on my shoulder and swiveled me around. "See?"

The concrete mileage marker on the side of the road was split in half, the top part hanging down like the side of a triangle. At the middle break point, bent steel wires held the halves together.

"The driver must have fallen asleep," he said. "The jeep veered, crashed into the concrete marker and flipped. Bedouins heard the impact and took advantage. But God was with these men. If they'd been thrown on the road, they'd be dead."

I burst out crying.

"It's okay," he said, "It will be okay." He left with the truck.

I wept. My fault, my fault. If I hadn't wanted Brent's company, he would have driven the jeep. This wouldn't have happened. I'd never forgive myself. I turned to the mess sprawled on the sand. The bitter end of their dreams. *My fault.*

A police van pulled up. Three officers sprang out, rounded up car parts, radios, clothes, cans of food, flasks, blankets, shaving cream, toiletries, first-aid kits. I followed the van to the police station where they locked everything in a storeroom. An officer rode with me to a one-floor mission hospital.

"The men are all right," a male nurse told me. "They're in shock. They took medicine. Sleeping now.

"Your room," he pointed. It was next to theirs. I lay on a narrow iron cot, re-living what happened. That moment, that awful moment when Brent asked if he could ride with me. I knew it was wrong. It was unfair to Clyde who had driven many hours and needed a break. But Brent's brown eyes, the soft mouth, the hint of a beard fired a longing I couldn't quash. I'd quashed the prick of guilt. But not the fire in my loins.

Hour after hour, the greedy grabbing arms of the white-hooded Arabs paraded through my mind. Clyde and Rolf, face down in the sands. Brent, repeating "My God!" like a man gone mad. Their dreams in ruins because of me.

In the morning, I saw a way to assuage my guilt. I dressed quickly, and followed a nurse who carried a tray of tea to their room. They sat up on their iron-framed beds, one next to the other. Their features were strained, fixed, rigid.

"I'm so sorry. So sorry! Forgive me, please," I blurted, and burst into tears. They didn't hear, they didn't speak, they didn't move. They looked like beaten men.

"I know what to do. I figured it out. You'll come with me. I'll send my stuff to India so you'll have the back of the Rover. We'll keep the hatch up for air. No cost to you. I'll pay the gas. I'll pay everything."

They said nothing. Just stared at the sheet and their hands.

"Talk to me, please. I feel sick. It's my fault, I take the blame. I want to make up for it. Please…"

"It's my fault," Brent said slowly. "I wanted to ride with you."

"I should've stopped when I felt drowsy," Clyde said.

"Come with me, guys, please. No cost, nothing. I'll buy gas, food, everything. Please. Let me make up for it. *Please!*"

"Five years. Five years we planned. Five years!" Brent said.

"*Please* come with me. We can do it."

"We're going home," Clyde said.

"Home? How?"

"Dr. Hassan will arrange truck rides back to Mafraq. From there, shared taxis to Damascus. A bus to Beirut, a ship to Turkey."

I knew those ships. I could still see the peasants and smell the chickens on the ship I took from Haifa to southern Turkey.

"In Turkey, we'll get the Orient Express back to Europe," Clyde said.

Three days later, I watched them climb like worn-out men into the back of a lorry. They carried sacks with remnants of their trip. Shaving kits. A few packs of cigarettes. A camera with a broken lens.

I felt like a laborer shoveling piles of debris into a kiln. But the piles weren't debris. They were guilt. And there was no kiln. I was shoveling the guilt straight into my heart.

38

BAGHDAD & TEHERAN

1962

Alone again. Alone hereafter. *No more men!*

A Jordanian guard stamped an exit visa in my passport and pointed straight ahead. I didn't know why. I saw no other way to go.

On the Iraqi side of the border post, an unshaven guard in a one-room office shack flipped through my passport, checked my Iraqi visa, and stamped an entry visa. He asked to see all my permits. International vaccination card. International driver's license. Car ownership. Lloyds of London documents.

"North, not go," he said. "Problem."

"What problem?"

He turned a dial on his desk radio to Voice of America but the static was so heavy I heard only bits. Kurds revolted, they wanted autonomy. Negotiations failed, violence broke out. They'd gained control over some oil fields. Fighting was fierce.

"I won't go north," I assured him.

Along the desert road to Baghdad, the mental images of the accident were as vivid as passing camel caravans. The overturned jeep. The Bedouins' greedy eyes and grabbing hands. Clyde and Rolf face down in the sand. Brent, bawling like a baby. The mission hospital, the narrow iron beds, the torn white sheets. Three faces disfigured by bitterness. I wanted to blank it out but couldn't.

At a New York bar, a Manhattan cocktail would have helped. I could taste the red liquid lining my mouth and stomach. Anesthetizing my memory like Novocain numbs the gums. But what could I do on a desert road to Baghdad?

Rutbah Wells, on a high plateau, was an oasis in the desert. A police checkpoint, gas pumps, comfort stations, first aid help, good food. After supper, I washed in the rest room and slept across my front seats.

Before dawn I headed east. Unlike Europe, where border posts and customs are at the same place, hundreds of miles separate them in the Middle East. At Ramadi near the Euphrates River, a customs guard stood at a *Halt* sign, motioning for me to come out. He pointed to the back hatch. “Open.”

When I lifted the hatch, a duffel bag of clothing, bedding and towels toppled out, and barely missed his head. He cursed in Arabic. “Too much baggages!”

“Sorry.”

“Camera. Where is camera?”

The American Embassy in London had told me that customs in these countries often sealed cameras on entering, and unsealed them when exiting. I’d squeezed my Voigtlander between the back of the driver’s seat and the partition.

“Don’t know. Can’t find.”

He pointed to the portable typewriter. I took out the Royal.

“You from newspaper.”

“No. I type letters to Mama.”

Inside his office, he perused my documents again, asked the same questions, and handed me a permit. He had written a single line of English following the Arabic: *May take baggages but must takes same when leaving Iraq.*

I’m going to Baghdad, I reminded myself as I rolled into the outskirts of the mystical city, listening to muezzins chant through the slender minarets of mosques. I turned into Al Rashid Street, the main thoroughfare, but it looked like a stage set. Times Square with high-rise buildings, and a stream of Buicks, Pontiacs, and Fords idling bumper to bumper. Or London with its double-decker trams.

But I couldn’t forget that this was a modern metropolis in the heart of the Middle East. Not with those black-veiled women giggling on queues outside movie houses that featured western films.

It wasn't just the incongruity that struck me. The moment was frozen in time. Nothing moved. Everything was stuck behind everything else. And everywhere, between vehicles, on sidewalks, standing on trucks, were armed police. *This is Baghdad?*

I had stopped behind a truck. A policeman in a shabby uniform came to my window, and stuck out his hand. "Passaport, passaport." He turned to the page with my picture on it, looked at it, then at me, closed the passport and handed it back. "Go," he said. But the truck in front had not budged.

My gas gauge showed almost empty. If Kurds had seized oil fields, petrol would be scarce. I drove a little, halted, drove a little more, stopped. A long line of cars waited at a pump near the Land Rover Depot. The cost was twice what I had budgeted. I'd have to choose between fuel and food.

What would I do if I had Aladdin's lamp? I'd rub it for a filet mignon, string beans, a baked potato with a pat of butter, salt and ketchup. Another rub for a Manhattan cocktail with a cherry, the stem resting on the rim. I'd sip it, cut the meat and bite into a hunk of thick, juicy flesh. But I didn't have a lamp. I only had a choice of filling my stomach or my tank.

I wanted a good night's sleep in a clean hotel with a hot water bath instead of a cold water wash in a toilet. What was I doing this for? Because I had nothing else to do. Make a living, that's all. That was the point of my quest. Is life only about making a living? I felt hungry, dirty, lonely, depressed. But suppose I was in New York, working from 9 to 5 in an office, or 9 to 3 a.m. in a club. I'd feel worse.

There was no answer. Just keep going.

The U.S. Embassy was a fortress. Marine guards surrounded the building and grounds. An advisory notice at the mailroom instructed Americans to leave the country or "stay at your own risk." Attached was a list of approved travel agents and safe hotels, four-or five-star. One night would cost my whole month's budget.

Mom had written,

> I don't like you traveling in those countries. It's unsafe. Where do you sleep? Eat? Who do you

> talk to? I am nervous, here on my own, my only child running around the world by herself. I still type and file papers in an accounting office. When are you coming home?

Mom had enclosed three bank checks for fifty dollars each so I only needed to change fifty bucks at a time. If I changed a hundred-dollar check, I might get stuck with foreign currency at the border and have to buy dollars back at a loss. Bless Mom. Now I could eat a meal instead of dried crackers and a packet of Lebanese chicken soup.

The road climbed into the mountains of Iran. The air got cold and thin. I pumped my inhaler every two hours instead of three times a day.

Teheran was a sprawling city with broad boulevards lined with cypress trees and statues of heroes I'd never heard of. Colorful billboard ads along the main bazaar featured silk, gems, orchids, and carpets with intricate designs. Rice, spices, dates, caviar, unleavened bread, and all kinds of fruit. And Crest toothpaste.

Rich as Teheran appeared to be on Takhte Jamshid Road, you couldn't miss the littered side streets where squatting beggars stretched out bony arms for coins. I'd read that only fifteen percent of Iranians were literate. That half the babies died before they reached the age of five. That the average peasant's lifespan was forty years. A waiter whose wife lost three of her six babies said the Shah didn't worry about such small things, especially since he'd become Washington's closest ally in that part of the world.

The Teheran Palace Hotel would have been ideal, but the tab was too high. I settled for a modest hotel near the main bazaar. While checking in at the desk, a lean European woman with no makeup strode into the lobby.

"Erica! Erica Suttill! Here, in Teheran!"

We embraced, and relaxed on a worn brown couch in a corner. She told me that Athens was a disaster. She should have heeded my advice. She'd never make the same mistake again. The Greek she met was depraved. Corrupt. A villain. She didn't want to talk about it.

"But how did you get here?"

"By bus," she said. "The Nairn overland bus."

"And now?" I asked. "You'll join me?"

"Can't, Shirl. I have a commission for the British Ambassador. Met him in Athens." She sighed. "The only good thing that happened to me in Greece."

"After his portrait, where will you go?"

"I'll have enough cash to fly to Pakistan. From there, I'll hop a bus to India. But tell me about you."

"Well, when I left you, I drove north to Turkey. Played some bases. Drove south to Beirut where I met three Brits in a jeep. We convoyed—"

"How lucky! All the way here?"

I couldn't tell her. I longed to. I longed to tell somebody, but it hurt too much. Like something got stuck in my throat that wouldn't go down and couldn't come up.

"No. Part way. Let's have lunch."

Arm-in-arm we strolled to a bustling restaurant for chelo kebab, a tasty meat dish served with rice, raw eggs and pickles. On the way back to the hotel, Erica pointed. "Oh, look. They've spotted *Eastward Ho!*"

The *Kayhan* newspaper van had parked behind my Rover. A photographer was taking pictures of the front and sides. A reporter waited for me at the desk.

"How did you find out about me?" I asked him.

"Hotel managers call the press when celebrities come."

"I'm no celebrity."

"To us you are. How many women drive around the world alone?"

Erica left for her room while the journalist and I sat on the couch. Why was I doing this? How did I support myself? What's inside that fantastic vehicle? What if it breaks down? Who was the woman with the British accent? What do I eat on the road?

On Monday, October 15, the two-column article appeared, captioned, "Entertainer Turns To Globe Trotting."

> A young American woman, equipped with a Land Rover, a course in mechanics, ... a makeshift kitchen, an accordion and an ability to sing is presently passing through Iran...Shirley Deane will probably be the first woman to complete her globe-girdling tour by car and ship...Miss Deane talks knowingly of spark plugs and crankshafts...

The reporter got it right, except for the word "knowingly."

A day after the article appeared, a Mr. Smith from the U.S. Embassy called. He wanted to see me. The matter was urgent. He couldn't discuss it on the phone.

I fretted as I drove to the Embassy. Did Smith want to discuss my friendship with Lev Frolov? My illegal license plate as Rose Shapiro? My illegal military I.D. as Rose Anderson? But even if he knew, why would that matter now?

Smith's secretary ushered me into his office. He stood, a man who resembled Abe Lincoln. The *Kayhan* article lay across his desk.

"His Imperial Majesty read this," Smith said. "He advised our Honorable Ambassador that you must change your plans. You can't drive through the desert alone."

"His Imperial Majesty must be joking," I told him. "The desert's the only route to Pakistan."

"It's for your own good, Miss Deane. It's not safe for anyone. Let alone a woman."

"What am I supposed to do? Stay here?"

"His Majesty says that if you insist on going, you must accept an escort. Two armed Iranian soldiers can accompany you from here to the Pakistan border. The trip will be a gift from His Imperial Majesty. All expenses paid."

Erica and I dined on Iranian caviar and soft drinks. My treat.

"Why would the Shah provide you with escorts, and pay the tab for your trip?" Erica asked. "What's in it for him?"

"Ask the question the other way," I told her. "What's in it for him if he doesn't? With the notoriety that follows me, imagine the consequences if the first woman to drive around the world—an American—got beheaded in Iran!"

"Oh! Beholden as he is to Washington, that *would* be awkward."

Erica raised her glass of apricot juice. "Here's to your trek through the Desert of Death. And far beyond!"

39

IRAN & THE DESERT OF DEATH

1962

Iran is massive. You don't grasp it when somebody tells you that it's bigger than England, France and Germany put together. You know it only when you drive across country. When it suddenly hits that this will be the longest stretch of your trek. Two thousand miles to the nearest city in Pakistan, the distance from New York to Santa Fe without turnpikes. You know it when you see the snow-capped Elburz Mountains fade from sight as you head south out of Teheran toward the great desert.

Glee shown in the faces of my escorts. Rostam, near the window. Sami, near me. In their thirties, with khaki uniforms, rifles pointed up, waistband pockets bulging with ammunition. For me it was a thrill, but I wondered how they felt. Armed soldiers driven by a woman in a country where women hide behind robes. Where they stand on trains while their men sit. Where they lug heavy parcels alongside men whose hands are free.

I wished we could talk. I'd ask how it felt to be driven by an American woman. I'd tell them about New York. How the maple leaves were turning crimson and gold in those October days. But my phrase books wouldn't translate that.

"Food?" I asked. We stopped. Our box of food, a gift from the Shah, contained tins of meat, fish, vegetables, and fruit. Packets of milk powder, cold cereals imported from America. Dried fruit, dry bread, biscuits, pistachio nuts, cans of juice, Nescafé and tea. The guards laid out the meal, ahhing and oohing.

They sang army songs as we drove over the corrugated surfaces of the desert road, sometimes skimming the crests at sixty miles an hour, sometimes dipping into the corrugations at six. Skimming worked better than dipping as my Land Rover teacher had told me in England. Dipping made Rostam nauseous.

All that worry about the Desert of Death. Yet nothing about it seemed sinister. But I was sitting inches away from rifles that would blow anything sinister to bits.

The Shah was right. No one should cross this desert alone. Not just because of hostile tribes, but because deserts had nothing to keep you awake. Nothing like Howard Johnson's from New York to Chicago. You could use the restroom, wolf down one of twenty flavors of ice cream, and go, fortified.

In the desert, only an occasional herd of goats, their owners perched on donkeys in back, broke the monotony. We'd stop and wait for them to cross like you wait for a train. Men and women in colorful robes glanced at me, then peered at the guards whose rifles glinted in the burning sun.

Halfway to Isfahan we spotted a jeep headed west. I stopped, and they stopped. Four young Australian men greeted me like we were old friends. We shared a meal, and posed in a queue for a camera shot. I stood in front, holding the lid of my portable john.

Off again over desert sands, hot during the day and cold at night. At dusk I felt relieved to see the *Welcome to Isfahan* sign. Isfahan, the ancient Persian capital.

We pulled up at the *Maidan Palace Hotel* on the Maidan-I-Shah town square. They expected us (thanks to His Imperial Majesty). We checked in, ate, then piled into the hotel manager's van for a sightseeing tour. He drove us past mosques, their sky-blue domes tiled with intricate designs. He weaved down ancient streets, pointing out intriguing arcades, old palaces, and courtyards.

Sami and Rostam behaved like kids at Disneyland. "Their first time here," the manager translated. "They were never out of Teheran. They also want to see Persepolis."

"Tell them I plan to go," I said. "It's just a short drive off the main route."

I, too, wanted to see the columns built twenty-five centuries earlier that still stood, despite Alexander's rampage. What did we learn from that carnage? Does history teach anything? Despite the lessons of centuries, Hitler rose in my time. World War II and the Korean War happened in my time. Now we were on the brink of another war, this time with the Soviets. History repeats itself but we learn nothing.

Near Persepolis, Rostam raised his hand. "Sick. Stop." He flung the door open and threw up. I gave him a marzine pill from my medicine kit while he sat on the sand, his skin and lips pale. "Shiraz got doctor," he said. "No doctor in Persepolis."

We drove toward Shiraz. More corrugations, more nausea, more goat crossings. "Okay now," Rostam said. "Food, please."

We opened sardine tins and a packet of salt biscuits. Color returned to his face.

Near Shiraz, the simplicity and elegance of a mud and stone hut with a gentle dome intrigued me. I stopped to take a photo, and a veiled woman opened the door, her dark eyes glowing like diamonds through a thin black veil. She said, "Ghabel na-dareh." I found it on page two of my phrase book: "You are welcome."

I had to bend to pass through the short door into the front room, bare except for a thick Persian carpet on the floor, and a carpet on the back wall that neither matched nor clashed. The woman lifted her veil. She had lustrous black hair and flashing black eyes with long, thick lashes. Her smile was like an innocent child's, yet sensuous.

"Me, Farah. America you?"

"Yes. American."

"Where you go?"

"Shiraz."

"Hotel you?

"Hotel three," I pointed to the men.

"You stay here. Mens go hotel. Please, please."

Two unveiled younger women walked in through a curtain at the back. One who looked sixteen called herself Niki. An older one with a wide space between her front teeth said her name was Tara. "You Ameerican?"

"Yes."

"You stay," Farah said. She led me to a back room with the biggest bed I'd ever seen, a thick Persian carpet, and four trunks along the back wall. Old-fashioned trunks like my parents took to Europe when I was three.

"Bed, you," she said.

"For me? Where do you sleep?"

"Here, floor. All three."

"Oh, no. I can't sleep on that big bed while you three sleep on the floor. No."

"You guest. Koran say, welcome guest like Allah."

A white-haired, heavy-set man strode in. Baggy white pants, striped cotton shirt open at the collar. "Welcome. I, Ali."

"Shirley."

"Sheerlee. Sheerlee." The women giggled. "Your Land Rover?" he asked.

"Mine, yes."

"Coming from? Going to?"

"From London. Going to Malaya."

"Oh, *khosh amadi*. Welcome. We are Muslim," Ali said. "You our guest. You eat and stay night." He pointed outside. "I get place for mens."

"Thank you, but we have hotel reservations in Shiraz. One room for them, one for me."

"No, no. You our guest. We have guest bed."

"I can't sleep on that bed while the women sleep on the floor."

"No. By Allah's will, no." He turned to Farah to give cooking orders. "Women cook. We go Shiraz."

He walked ahead. I wanted to tell him that the front of the Rover only seated three. In fact, it only seated two, but the guards were skinny.

Ali plopped himself on the right front fender, legs folded. "Go," he signaled.

I'd never driven with anyone on the fender. Surely it wasn't legal. I was so afraid he'd fall off that I crept in first gear. He turned. "Fast, fast go," he shouted. I drove faster, shifted to second, then third. He stayed perched on the fender like a hood ornament as we wove our way along the rutted road to Shiraz, and down a main street to the Hotel Park where rooms were reserved. (Thanks to His Imperial Majesty.)

The guards got out with their bags and rifles, ecstatic to be on their own.

"I take you sight-see," Ali said, dropping his bulk on the empty front seat.

He held up a hand as we drove past a long bazaar. "Stop." Inside, he led me to the stalls that he owned, managed by his nephews. They sold handmade wooden boxes painted with Persian motifs, and porcelain bowls for puffing water pipes.

We drove past magnificent gardens laid out two centuries earlier. Roses and jasmine, citrus and cypress, vineyards stretching as far as my eyes could see. Cotton plantations, rice fields, palaces framed by the Zagros Mountains. Past the tomb of poet Sa'di, with turquoise tiles covering its dome, and the tomb of poet Hafiz.

I'd read Hafiz' poems in an English class at NYU. I recalled his words, "In the rushing of water, witness the transience of life." He must have searched like me for permanence, and never found it.

We passed the American hospital, a million-dollar building with modern surgical and medical equipment, and luxury rooms like New York hospitals. American builders made the same mistake there that they'd made in a modern hotel in Teheran. They built the toilets facing Mecca so nobody could use them. Tearing them down and rebuilding had cost another million.

On the way back to Ali's hut, I asked about the women. "Your relations?"

"Wives," he grinned.

How did it work? Did he sleep with a different one each night except Friday, the Islamic Sabbath? Two at a time? All three? Where did the others sleep when he made love to one? Were they voyeurs? Did the women get along? I wished I could ask.

Farah and Niki laid a large thick dining cloth over the carpet in the front room. Ali and I sat on the floor while his women brought trays of meat kebabs, stews with beans, rice and butter. Yogurt, cherries, grapes.

"You treat me like a queen," I said. "I'm just a traveler."

"All guests are kings and queens," Ali said. He served me a liqueur. Thick, fruity, and strong.

In the bedroom, the women lay on the floor and ordered me into bed. I felt absurd on that six-by-six-foot bed with the women side by side on the floor. When the light went out, I giggled and couldn't stop. My body rocked with laughter when Farah snored, and when a loud flute-like sound whistled through Tara's front teeth. I was convulsed with laughter. I had to cover my head with the top sheet, and stuff a wad of it in my mouth.

In the morning, I picked up the guards at their Shiraz hotel. Next stop was Kerman in southeast Iran.

We drove through desert roads, arid valleys, bare plains, hills, long stretches of sand-covered roads and parched riverbeds. At times, the back wheels spun. Sometimes, the front wheels spun. Often I saw only a foot ahead through the dust. Hardly anyone passed. Occasionally we saw the sun. When it slipped behind the mountain peaks, the world got dismal.

One afternoon, I wondered if we'd make it. The land became barren and hostile. Dust filled our mouths with a bitter taste. If we died there, who would find us? When we stopped to relieve ourselves—the guards on their side of the car, me on mine—I poured water on my hands, searched for the rosary I got at Westminster Cathedral, and prayed. Rostam and Sami stretched out on a tarpaulin, fingering their beads, murmuring, "Allah."

A camel caravan passed the opposite way, kicking up mounds of dust. Thank God we had water. Water for the Rover, boiled water for us. I fell asleep, while the men waited outside.

It was almost dawn when we reached the desert oasis of Kerman, the carpet city. The cruel city. There, in 1794, Agha Muhammad Khan sold twenty thousand inhabitants into slavery, and gouged out the eyes of twenty thousand more.

While we ate from our food stocks, a mechanic in Kerman checked the Rover springs, topped the oil, cleaned sparkplugs and air filter, filled the tank and jerry cans.

We were off again past the snow-capped peaks of the Kuh-i-Hazar Mountains, heading for Bam on the rim of the Dasht-i-Lut, the great Sand Desert. How many faces the desert had! It frightened, terrorized, beguiled. Why should a desert beguile? Space, I thought. Limitless expanse of space.

We stopped for the night at the oasis of Bam. The men set up their tent next to the Rover. I slept across the seats. At dawn we were off for the last stretch, the road to Zahedan, the official border post between Iran and Pakistan.

Rostam's face lit up when he saw the *Welcome to Zahedan* sign at dusk. "By the Will of Allah, we here!"

The worst was over. Asad, manager of a government-owned rest house, had been informed of our expected arrival. (Thanks to His Imperial Majesty.) Rooms were tiny. Baths had stone floors and buckets of hot water.

We celebrated with fresh food and wine imported from the vineyards of Shiraz. Sami and Rostam relaxed, giggled, and drank.

Next morning we breakfasted together. The usual packs of young men gathered around the inn. On their way out, Sami and Rostam answered their questions, proud to convey vital data. Where I came from, what I did, where I was going.

A government representative would arrange the guards' return to Teheran by trucks and army jeeps. No money or gifts should be given to them, I was told. But I gave them all the rials I had left, and the food.

My do-list for Zahedan included the usual Land Rover service, border clearance documents, visa updates, vaccinations, food supplies, a haircut by anyone who'd cut a woman's hair. And the inevitable frontier bureaucracy.

Border officials had so little to do that when a foreigner, especially an American woman, passed through their portals, they made the most of it. Every official document I possessed was studied. Not once, not twice, but a dozen times. My passport was marked with words, squibbles and stamps that covered five pages.

On a cold gray morning I took off. No guards. No rifles. Just alone as I crossed the frontier into Pakistan. The road to Nok Kundi, the official Pakistan customs post, was a hundred-mile stretch of fierce, barren desert that gave me a sinking feeling.

Odd, how accustomed we become to companions. When I left Erica in Greece, I missed her. In Beirut, the company of the Brits had buoyed me up. After the accident, I got lonely again. In Iran I got used to Rostam and Sami. Now, in Pakistan, I craved human companionship. But, I reminded myself, everything is temporary. And some things are more temporary than others.

40

PAKISTAN

1962

Nok Kundi was the official Pakistan frontier with the usual formalities. Inspection of property, passport stamps, money exchange.

After a night's rest in a traveler's bungalow, I left for Quetta, a straight stretch of dusty, barren tarmac with winds that twisted the dust in circles. I'd read that when God built the world, He raked the debris together, dumped it there, and called it Baluchistan.

The air grew cold as the road climbed through mountains. Nomadic tribes headed south toward the plains, perhaps Kuchi nomads who farmed in the valleys of Afghanistan during summer and the Indus River plains during winter. I wished they wouldn't work their camels like that. The poor beasts carried mountainous loads. Old people, sheep, tents, water.

An attendant at the Ahmad Wal petrol depot snapped my picture in front of the sign: *London, 5,876 miles.* Men who manned the petrol stations and checkpoints spoke English well. No wonder. Only fifteen years had passed since India was partitioned into Hindu and Muslim nations. Before then, all students were schooled in English.

The higher I climbed, the colder it got, the harder it was to breathe. When the sun set, I stopped at a rest house with old-fashioned room heaters and a twelve-year-old cook. In the morning, I wore every sweater I had on the rocky, desolate road to the old British garrison town of Quetta, where a trained Land Rover mechanic completed my check list. Had it been Friday, the Muslim Sabbath, I'd have waited a day. This was Thursday.

I drove south to Karachi, the capital on the Arabian Sea where I would pick up mail at the U.S. Embassy, shop and rest. I wouldn't stay long. Peshawar, my next workplace up the Indus River, was still far away.

Traveling from mountains to prairies, I traded cold, rocky desolation for farmland, villages, and oxen carts. Each geographical setting was like a stage with a unique backdrop and costumes.

Badaber Air Base in Peshawar was never meant to be famous. The secret base was built beneath the Soviet belly to provide an ideal platform for Cold War reconnaissance flights. But on the first of May, 1960, when Captain Gary Powers' U2 plane took off from Badaber, the whole world learned of it. The Soviets shot him down over Sverdlovsk, convicted him of espionage, and sentenced him to prison and hard labor.

The Soviet attitude toward Pakistan soured, as did Pakistan's attitude toward America. Pakistan claimed it knew nothing about America's spy missions when America leased its land.

An MP at the entrance gate to Badaber Air Base rang an officer. "I swear," he said, "her jeep looks like it's from Mars. Covered with soot, sealed windows, roof rack piled high. *Eastward Ho!* painted on it. Never saw anything like it." He listened. "I'm not kiddin'."

A brief pause. "Hey, miss. Captain Franks wants to know where you drove from."

"London."

"London, she says." Pause. "That's what I told her. She'd get her feet wet."

I butted in. "My feet got wet three times. The English Channel, the Ionian, and the Bosporus."

"What's that, Captain?" Pause. "I'll tell her."

"Miss, Captain Franks wants to see your passport and the letter you said you got from a general. If they're okay, he'll show it to Colonel Goerder, base commander."

Three hours later, I'd signed contracts to play all the clubs and all the private parties planned for Christmas, New Year, birthdays, anniversaries, promotions. I'd been interviewed by *The Mystic Lamp*, the base newspaper, and the base radio station.

I was back in swing where life was predictable. Where everything was as everything always was. In Ethiopia, Turkey, Germany, England, France, Italy. Back with Noxzema and Kleenex. I was grateful to earn, and spend nothing. Honored to be the focus of so much male attention. But boredom set in, and the same self-disgust I always felt when I made my living as an entertainer. My heart yearned for something else.

Captain Franks invited me to a film of the spy swap in Berlin involving Soviet spy Rudolf Abel and Gary Powers. Powers walked west across the River Havel bridge, passing Rudolf Abel coming east. Abel, a master Soviet spy, had been caught in New York and detained for several years. I held my breath as they passed each other, hoping they'd dared to shake hands. But they glanced at one another, and moved on.

"Powers did hard labor in the Soviet Union," Franks said. "Know what he got for it? The CIA never forgave him because he didn't kill himself like he was supposed to. He had the poison on board."

How could anybody work for an organization with so little regard for human life? I'd never forget the face of the agent who visited me in Nuremberg. Or his snide arrogance when I turned down his request to work for the CIA.

By January of 1963, I'd had enough. I'd earned money and saved it, but I couldn't bear another day of show business. How would I support myself in the future?

Lahore, my last stop in Pakistan, was its cultural and intellectual hub. I drove along the tree-lined Mall past chic cafés, hotels, stately government offices, horse-drawn carts, and crowds. I passed the famous fort built by Akbar, the great Mogul emperor. Modern bazaars had sprouted beneath it, selling "all you get on Broadway."

I drove past Aitchison College, the embodiment of the British colonial era. A sprawling structure crowned with a domed tower that the British had built to educate the children of Maharajahs. A nearby hotel boasted reasonable rates. I checked in.

Next morning, a servant brought up a tray of fried eggs, toast, and tea. "Reporter here to see Memsaab," he said. "Waiting lobby."

"Reporter? Already?" I glanced out the window. Photographers swarmed around my Land Rover, snapping pictures of the front, back, sides.

Later in the lobby, the journalist handed me his card:

Nafees, The Pakistan Times, founded by Quaid-I-Azam,
Mohammad Ali Jinnah, founder of the nation.

We settled into easy chairs along the back wall. What was I searching for, Nafees asked. What was the real mystery of my soul? Nobody had ever asked me about the mystery of my soul. Maybe that's what I was searching for.

His three-column article appeared in *The Pakistan Times* a few days later. A photograph of me in my fishtails with the accordion had been superimposed on my Land Rover, captioned, "Introducing…The Lonely American."

> A pretty 25-year-old American girl, prowling the world in a Land Rover, would be a usual enough thing … but it is not the sheer boredom of life which has thrown her on the long and winding road to nowhere.

I was the type, he said, who belonged everywhere. The world was my village. He wrote that what distinguished me from average globe trotters was a "quiet, self-consuming and exceedingly sensitive personality behind the debonair face and its ready smile." His closing statement awed me: "It is so nice meeting Miss Shirley Deane, scouting the world in search of herself."

I didn't know that I was seeking myself. I thought I sought meaning. Something real and permanent that was worth living for.

Before I finished packing, the hotel manager rang. "A sahib in lobby to see Madame. He read the article."

"What's a sahib?"

"Pukka sahib, Madam. Tribal chief, like prince, Madam. Prince from Baluchistan. Mohammed Bugti."

I started down the steps. The man leaned against the desk, arms folded, his eyes sweeping my form. Curly black hair. Short, but well proportioned. A trim mustache and beard. A cocky smile.

We shook hands. He clasped my hand in both of his. He was a brazen man. "I want to show you Lahore," he said. "Shalimar Gardens. Jahangir's tomb. A good dinner." He pointed to a black chauffeured limousine outside the entrance.

"Thank you, but I'm packing."

"Please, Madame. Pack later." He took my arm. "Lahore is magnificent. You must see it."

"No thanks." I pulled my arm from his. He took my arm again.

There I was, walking out with this man whose smile I didn't trust. Out the door with him. Stepping into the back of his Ambassador. What was wrong with me? I swore that I'd live without men forever. Men were no good for me, and I was no good for them. Did I forget Nick in Chicago? Alvar in Nuremberg? Lev Frolov? Captain McGill? The three Brits in Jordan?

Yet there I sat, in the back of his car. Warmed by his presence on my right, by the biochemical effect of his proximity. Maybe every interaction has a biochemical effect. Falling in love. Winning a chess game. A standing ovation. Maybe nothing has value in itself. Maybe the sole value of anything lies in our biochemical reaction to it.

Over steaming rice, mutton curry, and chapattis, Mohammed studied me like a specimen in his lab. His cool, unflappable manner both disgusted and attracted me.

"Black hair and blue eyes. Hmm. Rare," he mused.

A waiter stood behind him, ready for his next command.

"You'd like a drink?" Mohammed asked.

"Scotch-on-the-rocks."

After dinner he said, "We'll have coffee in my suite."

I disliked him, and hated myself for being attracted.

Mohammed lived in a two-room suite in a residential hotel. His lounge looked like a meeting room. Two sofas, four armchairs. At a round table near a window, he poured coffee from a carafe.

"You drove through Baluchistan, my area," he said. "What did you think of it?"

"Inhospitable, arid, lifeless. How do your people live without rain?"

"We have oases and riverbeds. And channels that carry water to cultivated fields."

"How do most Baluchis make a living?" I asked.

"Many are nomads. They herd sheep and goats south in winter, north in summer."

"You speak English well. You went to Aitchison College?"

"Aitchison? Me? Never went to college. A Cambridge student came to Baluchistan some years ago for research. I housed him and fed him and took him all over. In return, he taught me English. And look here."

Bugti led me to his bedroom where stacks of books lined the wall. Hitler's *Mein Kampf.* Marx' *Das Capital*. Plato's *Republic*. Tolstoy's *War and Peace*. Books by Toynbee, Dostoyevsky, T.S. Eliot. Oxford dictionaries. He pointed to a stack of notebooks. "When I see a word I don't know, I look it up, and write it in a notebook."

I respected that, but felt uncomfortable. The enormous bed with its cozy netting made me edgy. "I must go, Mohammed."

"You will dine with me tomorrow?"

"I'm leaving Pakistan tomorrow."

"Stay one more day, please."

"All right. One more day."

"You'll wear that?"

My eyes searched my slacks and over-blouse. "Something's wrong with it?"

"Pants don't flatter women," he said. "Tomorrow morning, my driver will take you to a fabric shop. Buy a silk sari, and fabric for a blouse and slip. He'll take you to a tailor. Get sandals, too."

"But I'm only staying a day."

"Take it with you."

Next morning, I bought a jade silk sari, matching fabric for a blouse, and white cotton for the slip. *"Salaam alekum,"* the owner said when I left. It occurred to me that I wasn't the first woman whom Mohammed had sent to that shop.

The driver scooted down "tailor" street where tailors sat in open stalls with old-fashioned manual sewing machines. A tailor measured me shoulder-to-shoulder, bust, waist, height. "One hour you comes back."

"You can make a blouse and slip in one hour?"

He showed a toothless grin. "I makes anything in one hour, Memsaab."

I asked the chauffeur to drive me to the US Consulate to pick up my mail.

"Yes, Memsaab. Anything, Memsaab."

My room maid draped my sari. I barely recognized me in the full-length mirror. Broad shouldered. A bust that appeared larger than 34B in the skin-tight sari blouse. Slim waist, seductive hipline. Modest, yet provocative. Six and a half yards, and not one seam.

I walked back and forth. Interesting, how a garment dictates carriage. In driving togs, jeans and men's shirts, I felt assertive and masculine. In a sari, I held my head high, shoulders back, and took dainty steps in flat-heeled sandals. A proper lady.

As promised, I delayed my departure for a day. Two days. Three days. A month into my stay, Mohammed spotted my chessboard. "You play?"

"I do. My favorite game."

"I want to learn. You teach me?"

I set up the board with my plastic pieces on a writing table. "Chess is a war game," I said. "Two armies fight each other with pawns as front-line soldiers. They advance in a forward motion, one square at a time. When they want to capture an enemy, they take him from the side. Like this."

"What's the rationale for that?"

"Many years ago, soldiers wore suits of armor, and couldn't be hurt in the front or back. Only their sides were vulnerable, the part the armor didn't cover."

Mohammed took a card from his shirt pocket and wrote, "*Vulner-able = can be harmed.*" I admired that.

"What about this piece?" he asked.

"Bishop. It moves diagonally."

"Rationale?"

"You never get a straight answer from a bishop."

We played every afternoon.

One day, I found a gift in my room. An inlaid rosewood chessboard with hand-carved ivory pieces. Never had I seen a set like it. I wrote Mom that my life had transformed from denim to silk, jeans to saris, and plastic to ivory.

Mohammed's chauffeur picked me up every day, drove me to shops, to the Consulate to pick up mail, and to Mohammed's suite for chess. We played and drank vodka. At six, I returned to my hotel to shower, and spend twenty minutes draping one of my three silk saris.

Where did Mohammed get his money? Did he work? Was he on someone's payroll for the title of tribal prince? Why did he live in Lahore and not in Baluchistan? Often he eyed me like a cat eyes a mouse, but he never kissed me. What would I do if he asked me to sleep with him? I'd tell him, no. *No more men*, I promised myself. So why was I there? I left America to find answers to questions that plagued me. I wouldn't find them with Bugti. Well, two more weeks, and I'd be off to India.

We were munching chicken curry and drinking vodka in his suite. "Ever go back to your homeland, Mohammed?"

"Occasionally."

"What are your tribal customs like? Marriage, for example."

"We Muslims can have four wives. I have three."

"Three!"

He winked. "I can have one more."

"How do three wives get along?"

"They don't. But the senior wife, the first married, has authority over the others. What she says, goes. We marry first cousins, so our wives know each other from childhood."

"Why first cousins?"

"Land is precious, especially land with access to water. Such land must be kept within a family. Secondly, our women aren't free like Americans to meet strange men. They never leave home. They can't show their faces to strangers, just family members."

"What if a marriage doesn't work? Can they divorce?"

"A law was just passed that permits divorce, but what would a woman gain? Who would take a divorced woman?"

"That's cruel."

"Not cruel. Our men deserve virgins."

What gall the man had!

"I have six children," he said.

"Six! You're responsible for nine people?"

"I'm responsible for hundreds. My family, my tribe, my servants. Descendants of servants who worked for my ancestors."

"How do you support hundreds of people?"

"We're land-owners," he said. "Let me tell you about Baluchis. We come from Iran, but in the late nineteenth century the British created a boundary between Iran and British Baluchistan, which split our families and divided our tribes. Some tribes perished because they couldn't cross the border to reach their source of water and food. The British also pitted our leaders against each other for their own advantage."

"They did that in Africa, too," I said.

"The British tool. Divide and conquer."

"Do Baluchis follow their own laws or Pakistan's?"

"Tribal laws," he said. "If a man from another tribe kills someone in my tribe, we must revenge the killing. We don't involve the Pakistan police."

"How primitive! An eye for an eye. A tooth for a tooth!"

"Call it what you will. That's the law of my land. Honor reigns supreme. For honor we live, for honor we die, for honor we kill. If a wife is caught in bed with another man, we kill them both. Pakistan law won't interfere. We must kill them, for honor."

Surely Mohammed wouldn't kill. He was too civilized, sophisticated, smart. His heart was too big. He talked like that because I come from the west. Tribal pride, they call it. But a killer? No way.

41

MOHAMMED BUGTI, LAHORE

1962-63

Part of me wanted to leave Pakistan to continue my journey eastward. Another part wanted to solve the mystery. The mystery of Mohammed.

We were sitting on his sofa drinking vodka. "May I kiss you?" he asked. His kiss was tender, not passionate. "We're not like Westerners," he whispered. "A bit here, a bit there."

He took my hand, lifted me to my feet, and pulled me to his bedroom. Unwound my sari, let it slip to the floor, and rolled down my slip. What was I doing? No more sex, I'd told myself. He was unhooking my bra, flinging it to the floor, and I was letting him do it. What's wrong with me?

I lay on the bed, nude as he undressed. I had time to say, *No, I don't want it*, but I couldn't. I felt like a band without a conductor. Trumpets blowing their own tunes. Drummers beating their own rhythms. Does anyone live with a conductor?

Thoughts ceased. Mohammed lay next to me, rubbed himself against me. Skin on skin. To hell with a conductor. Let the trumpets blare. Let the drums roll. We were animals. Wild, passionate, forgetful of the world.

Chess, vodka, and sex became a daily routine. Mohammed made swift progress in chess. He studied openings from a chess book, and once, he almost beat me.

He taught me about the politics of the east. Did I know about India's war with China? Yes. Did I know that the United States rushed to India's side with massive arms? Yes. Did I know that the United States ignored Pakistan's pleas to pressure India to settle the Kashmir dispute before India used arms to settle it? I didn't know. Had I ever seen an ant thumb its nose at an elephant? I hadn't.

"That's what Pakistan did. Thumbed its nose at the U.S., and turned to China with both hands out."

"But Americans are still in Peshawar, spying on the Russians."

"Because the U.S. has a lease," he said. "When it ends, Pakistan won't renew it."

"This government, is it a democracy?"

"Can a dictatorship be a democracy? Ayub Khan is a dictator. A fool. For four years we lived under martial law. Last year, a new constitution gave Ayub Khan the same powers that your president, government departments and Congress have, combined. Can you imagine such power? We Baluchis hate him. We have sources of great wealth. Copper, bauxite, iron ore. But is it ours? No. The central government sends Punjabis to settle our land and mine our resources. We're too uneducated to fight back.

"Even if we had the power and wits to fight, the Shah of Iran would stop us. He'd think if the Baluchis of Pakistan assert themselves, so will the Baluchis of Iran. You know what he'd do? Call Washington for help, and he'd get it. He's DC's puppet."

Alone in my hotel room, I tried to put the pieces together. Learned Punjabis rule the country with political, military, and economic might. They show no interest in the backward folks of outlying provinces like Baluchis. Baluchi women have no rights, but Punjabi women who live in cities do. They're rich, unveiled. Other tribes like the Pashtuns undergo the same discrimination.

The dynamic was familiar. Baluch culture differed from Punjabi culture just as the traditions of Native Americans were alien to those of European descent who controlled the power structure in America, and with similarly catastrophic results for the indigenous people.

I understood that. But where did Mohammed fit in?

One night in his hotel room, our passions spent, I got out of bed to dress. His chauffeur waited downstairs for me.

Mohammed's nude body, so still on that massive bed, looked like it was floating on water.

A sharp knock on the door roused him. He sat alert, pulled a brown silk robe from a chair. "Stay here," he said. He walked through the heavy curtains that separated the bedroom from the lounge.

I sat on the edge of the bed, my feet stuck to the floor. Could it be his wife, the senior one? All three? But he told me they never left Baluchistan.

Someone walked into the lounge. Two, maybe three hushed male voices. They weren't speaking Baluchi. Maybe this was Urdu, the national language of Pakistan.

I peered into the slit that divided the heavy curtains. Two men in Pakistan army uniforms, their rifles straight up beside them, sat cross-legged at Mohammed's feet. Mohammed reposed on an easy chair, listening and responding in measured tones.

As I stepped back, the curtain shifted and pulled their eyes toward me. My Western face traumatized them. Mohammed said something, maybe, "It's all right, pay no attention."

A half-hour later we were alone again. With one step, he was in the bedroom. He clasped my arms, his eyes wide. "Will you marry me? Will you?"

His grip was tight and tense. "I—I don't know," I said. "An American woman, the junior wife in a harem. That would be hard."

"You can stay in Lahore with me."

"I'll think about it. Why do you ask now?"

He paced. "I need you. If you don't become my wife, I may lose you. I need you for love, for chess, for…"

"For what?"

"Pour a vodka. Big one."

He pulled a rusted trunk from under the bed and unlocked it. Papers, letters, news clippings. With a penknife he pried up a false cardboard bottom, pulled out a map and laid it on the bed. "Don't tell anyone," he warned. "What do you see?"

"A map with no names."

"What's this country?" he pointed.

"Pakistan, but smaller than it is."

"This?"

"Part of Iran."

"This?"

"Afghanistan, without the bottom part."

"And *this*?" He pointed to a huge area.

"A big Baluchistan."

"Correct! A big Baluchistan."

"I don't get it."

"Pour more vodka."

His copper skin darkened with the drink. "That's the goal," he whispered. "One Baluchistan! One nation, independent, with the Baluchis of Pakistan, Iran and Afghanistan!" He searched my face. "Well?"

"You mean secession? From all three countries?"

"*Se-cess-ion.* From all three countries!"

"That's a cockeyed dream," I said.

"It's not!" he shouted.

"How can you fight three governments?"

"You can't. You don't. You strategize underground."

Why would he impart such secrets to me? Vodka, maybe.

"You work slowly," he continued. "Quietly. At the final hour there is…." He whispered in my ear. "*In-sur-rec-tion.*"

"You mean military rebellion?"

"Military rebellion."

"Simultaneous rebellions in Iran, Afghanistan and here? Impossible," I said.

"Don't use that word!" he roared. "Look at American history. How many thought it was impossible to beat the British with their military might? But Washington and his men had faith. More faith than weapons. They held on, and outmaneuvered the enemy.

"Before Pakistan was born, Muslims told Jinnah that a Muslim state was impossible. Gandhi didn't want it. Nehru didn't want it. Mountbatten didn't want it. But Jinnah believed in it. He rejected Gandhi's offer of Prime Minister of a united India because he believed in a separate Muslim nation. Like that, an independent Baluchistan *is* possible. I know it. My people know it." He clasped my arms. "You will help."

"Me? What in the world could *I* do?"

"Pour vodka. You won't talk about this to nobody. Yes?"

I nodded.

"I tell you *what* and *why*," he whispered. "Not *who*, *where* or *when*. Understand?"

"Yes."

"Baluchis are pariahs in our country. How Native Americans were treated, like that, we're treated. Subjects of a government that speaks a different language, that has a different culture. Nothing in common but Islam. We don't get good jobs. Foreign aid doesn't reach us. It goes to the rich to make them richer. We have minerals in Baluchistan, but no training to turn them into cash. The central government sends Punjabis, the hated ruling class, to settle our areas and mine our wealth. Pariahs we are! Understand?"

A tiger was talking. He alarmed me, but I sympathized. Repression and oppression had always triggered my rage.

Bugti pointed to East Pakistan on the map. "They're separated from West Pakistan by a thousand miles. We have our language and culture, they have theirs. East Pakistanis make jute. You know what's jute? Burlap. Biggest factories in the world, they have. Who profits? *West* Pakistan. Who gets the best jobs in East Pakistan? *West* Pakistanis. Who gets American imports? *West* Pakistan. How long you think this will go on? Tell me!"

"Don't shout at me. Not long. The East will rebel."

"Correct. They will re-*bel*. Pour vodka."

I filled a glass. He whispered. "Freedom fighters are training. Money is there. It won't be long. Bloodshed will happen, but so will freedom. Mark my words. In three years, by 1966, East Pakistan will be independent with a new name. Governed by themselves. Not by crooks a thousand miles away!"

"But what does East Pakistan have to do with Baluchistan?"

"Ahh! Everything!"

He rummaged through a pile of books on the floor to find the poems of T.S. Eliot. "Look at this line: *'Distracted from distraction by distraction.'*"

Strange that he quoted that line. I'd read T.S. Eliot at NYU.

On the subway to Queens, when I'd gape at the multi-colored ads defaced with graffiti, that line would repeat itself in my head.

"Timing is key," he said. "We bide our time. We prepare underground. When East Pakistan rises in flames toward victory, we act. West Pakistan will be distracted from distraction. See?"

"Clever."

"We need your help."

"Me? How?"

"You must be my wife."

"How would that help?"

"If you marry me, you will stay. If not, you will go. I need you."

"What could *I* do?"

"The world doesn't know what Baluchistan is or where it is. We must teach them, so when the final hour comes, we'll have friends. I'm writing articles. You will edit."

"What are the articles about?"

"Our land, people, history. They'll be published in America, Canada, England, Germany, Italy, France."

"Who will get them published?"

"Friends in those countries."

"Show me the articles."

He opened the trunk. "My notes," he said proudly, showing me a sea of paper.

"But the articles?"

"Not written yet."

"Then the first thing we must do is organize your notes. Can you get a file cabinet?"

"No, no. No papers must leave this trunk!"

"Then we'll turn your trunk into a file cabinet. We'll stand up file folders and keep papers in them. We'll need file pockets, files, labels, colored crayons."

Next morning, his chauffeur drove me to Lahore's largest stationery store. As Mohammed instructed, we put the parcels in a suitcase so hotel staff wouldn't get curious.

Back in his suite, Bugti fretted. "Last night I drank too much vodka. What did I say? Tell me."

"You said you want to tell the world about Baluchistan. You'll write magazine articles that you want me to edit."

"What more?"

I was careful, though I didn't know why. "You said East Pakistan makes jute."

"Good. You know what is jute?"

"Burlap."

"Good."

I squatted on the bedroom floor in a sea of paper. French, Urdu and Arabic notes I put aside. I labeled file folders *Land, People, History, Cities & Towns.* Under *Land,* I collected notes on scanty rainfall, barren soil, picturesque mountains, the Bolan Pass, juniper forests, rivers, valleys, eight thousand-foot plateaus, marble, iron ore, coal.

In the *People* folder were notes on nomads, migrations north in summer and south in winter. Their goats, sheep and camels. Pictures of nomadic tents, huts made of branches and grass, primitive stringed instruments, colorful dress, songs.

Under *History* I filed clippings and notes that dated back to Alexander the Great, the Mughal Empire. The bloody birth of Pakistan as six million Muslims crossed into the new nation that could neither feed nor house them, and four million Hindus and Sikhs crossed into India. Two million were slaughtered in that blood bath of migration.

Mohammed's source of funds baffled me. Who would bankroll such a colossal task? Who paid for my hotel room? My silk saris? Our vodka?

"Sure must be hard to find funds for this mission," I said.

"When you need funds for anything, you ask yourself a question: Who would profit from the outcome? Answer that, and you have your donors."

Would the Soviet Union profit? Could an independent Baluchistan grant them access to the Arabian Sea? But that was a far-fetched idea, and Bugti's source of funds didn't matter. Nobody should be a pariah in his own country.

My push to leave Pakistan was strong. I wanted to go before the monsoons in India and further east made roads impassable. But I wanted to help Mohammed, too. I was a good organizer. A natural.

"I'll organize your notes," I told him, "which could take two weeks. Meantime, start writing. I'll edit, and outline the rest of your material. Then I'll go."

"Go?" He glared. "You will leave with my secrets? You won't marry me?"

"I won't marry you, but I won't leave with your secrets. I'll leave them behind." He said nothing, and I felt uneasy. Silly, I told myself. Organizing his papers is the least I can do.

Each day began with papers and articles, and ended with vodka, chess, and sex. One evening, Mohammed asked if I'd like to see a private showing of a foreign film.

"What's the film?"

"Hitler. His life."

"Hell, no! Why would I want to see that?"

"It's important. We must understand his mentality. The making of the man."

"I know enough about Hitler's mentality."

For the first time, I questioned Bugti's motives. Was freedom for his people what he wanted? The right to govern themselves? To profit from their own resources? Or did he crave power? I couldn't believe that his only motive was a quest for power.

At dinner, high and excited, he said, "They did it in Iraq!"

"Who? What?"

"The Baath Party took over!"

"What's the big deal about that?"

"Hear me. When you thought, 'I'll drive around the world,' how did you know it was possible?"

"Because Oxford and Cambridge did it. And Peter Townsend. If they could do it, so could I."

"Exactly! If Iraq can do it, so can we. The Baaths worked underground for years. They worked from *inside* the army. Understand? Now they command the nation!"

So that's what the Pakistani soldiers were doing. Planning,

reporting to Mohammed. This scheme, this operation—whatever it was—was bigger than I thought. I wondered what I'd gotten myself into.

Mohammed's chauffeur stopped in front of the American Consulate in Bank Square. He'd wait in the parking area, he said.

"My mail, please," I asked a petite woman at the Consulate mail window. She checked her name list. "It's in that office," she pointed, "the Consul."

If I ever write a book, I'll call it, "*The Consul Has Your Mail.*"

"Come in, Miss Deane."

David Bane had an open, kindly face with a neatly trimmed moustache. He wore an immaculate blue blazer. A patient man. Anybody who takes the trouble to put cufflinks into French cuffs on a Wednesday afternoon has to be.

"Your mail," Bane said, handing me a stack. I had no doubt that he'd read it. The question was *why*.

"Why the sudden interest in me, sir?"

"It's not just interest. It's concern."

"For what?"

"For you, Miss Deane."

"Call me Shirley, please. You probably know more about me than I know about myself."

"You're involved in a risky situation."

"Risky? I'm slightly infatuated. That's risky?"

"Mohammed Bugti is risky."

"He loves me. He proposed. Said he has three wives and can have four."

"It doesn't look good, an American in a harem."

"I don't live for what looks good."

"Shirley, listen to me. You're living with dynamite whether you know it or not. Everything Mohammed does and everybody he knows is a risk for you."

"I don't understand. He wants to improve the lot of his people. Like Gandhi."

"Bugti is no Gandhi. Baluchis live by tribal law. If he suspects you of the least infidelity, he'll kill you. Then he'll kill another man, strip the clothes off both of you, and lay you in bed side by side. No one will punish him. He'll do it to preserve his honor."

"I don't believe he'd do that."

"I can't help your disbelief. My duty is to warn you. His colleagues think you come to the Consulate to report what you know. Not for mail."

"Colleagues? What colleagues?" Did he mean Mohammed's army friends?

"Shirley, the danger isn't just for you, it's for us."

Bane paced the floor. "An incident like that would make world headlines. The U.S. government would be forced to initiate a thorough investigation and make public statements. Who do you think would be at the center of it? Me!"

I tried to grasp what he was saying. Dead in bed. Nude beside a strange dead man. World headlines. U.S. government investigation. Public statements. It sounded ludicrous.

"By the way, how did you know I'm involved with Bugti?" Bane's smug smile made me feel like a fool. "Sorry. I know better than to ask that. You chaps are omniscient."

"I wish we were. Where's your Land Rover?"

"In Kahn's garage near my hotel."

He wrote a phone number on a scrap of paper without his name. "In an emergency, call me. Any time of day or night."

When I stepped into Mohammed's car, his chauffeur didn't turn and smile as usual. Perhaps he was annoyed that I'd stayed so long.

Mohammed was setting up the chess pieces in his lounge. My breath had gotten shallow. Nervousness, perhaps. I fished through my handbag for my ephedrine inhaler but couldn't find it. My chest felt tight. I turned the handbag upside down on the floor. The inhaler wasn't there.

"What are you looking for?"

"My inhaler."

"You have asthma?"

"Yes."

"Why you didn't tell me?"

"I need my inhaler!"

He took it from his pocket. "This is what you want? Why you didn't tell me? This is bad for me. You could compromise me, hurt me. You know who I am? First president of Baluchistan! If someone says to you, 'Tell me what Bugti does, and I will give you your inhaler,' you will tell him!"

"Give me my inhaler. Now!"

He threw it, and I saw the truth of him. The Consul was right but I had to be careful. An underlined sentence in one of Mohammed's textbooks came to mind: *Danger multiplies when you let an enemy know your enmity*. I smiled a look of forgive and forget, and silently planned to leave next day.

An elderly doctor scanned my international vaccination card at a local hospital. "You need yellow fever," he said.

"I don't want it. Vaccinations make me sick." I showed him a ten-dollar bill. "Will this buy the stamp and your initials?" He signed.

When I got back to my hotel room, I started packing. I dreaded ringing Mohammed, but I had to. "I'll skip dinner tonight, Mohammed. I don't feel well."

I ordered a glass of wine, eased myself into an armchair, and sipped slowly. How had I missed the signals? Because commitment to freedom for the oppressed had moved me. My mind saw a man prepared to die for a cause, not a man drunk with power. With Nick the Greek, my mind saw a man who was God's gift to the world. The real man escaped me then as now.

This was awful, this growing list of male blunders. Men were either a disaster for me, or I was a disaster for them. Nick, the psychopath, and his three women. Alvar Olsson, who landed me in a German jail. Mostafa Lotfy, with whom my imprudence had cost a man his hand. Lev Frolov doing hard labor in Siberia. Captain McGill counting cans of beans. The Brits' adventure down the drain because of me. The American Consul nervous because of what could happen.

Enough. Tomorrow, I'd leave Pakistan. And with it, men. For the rest of my life.

Someone knocked. The waiter, perhaps, to ask if I wanted another drink. Without a thought, I opened it.

Every nerve in my body quickened. Mohammed stepped in, slammed the door behind him, sat heavily on my chair.

"What's wrong, Mohammed? What happened?"

His face twisted into a hyena's snarl. He grabbed my wine glass, smashed it against the floor lamp, and tightened his fist around the base of the shattered crystal. Jagged spears of glittering glass extended toward my throat from his clenched hand. Terror swept through my body.

"You told the American Consul. Told him everything!"

"I didn't. I swear!"

"My driver said you stayed thirty minutes. Thirty minutes to get mail? Tell me! Tell me!" He did not wait for an answer. He tensed, raised himself, and lunged at me with the broken glass in his grip.

I threw myself at his feet. "No, no. Please, please don't hurt me," I sobbed hysterically. "I did nothing wrong. Please don't hurt me, please!" My hands clutched his ankles, my head down on his feet. He threw the glass at the wall, kicked me and rose. "Liar! Liar!" he roared. He pulled the door open and stalked out. Tears blinded me.

The scrap of paper with the Consul's telephone number was on my dresser. Sobbing, I told Bane what happened, what Mohammed did, what I did.

"Listen carefully, Shirley. Pack. Be ready to leave at 6 a.m. Under no circumstances should you open your door before then. At six, two men who work for the Consulate will come to your room. They will slip my card under your door. Give them your luggage and follow them out. You'll see two jeeps. Get into the first one. The driver will bring you to Kahn's garage, and put your bags in your car.

"From Kahn's, follow the first jeep to the Indian border. Drive behind him at the same pace. The other jeep will follow you. If you need a restroom or if your car has problems, flash your lights three times, use a hand signal, and pull to the side. Don't get out until the two men come to your door to accompany you. Do what you have to do, and get back fast. When you reach the Indian border, the jeeps will leave you. Don't give the men any money."

They knocked at six. I opened the door, gave them my luggage, and followed them out. I got into the first jeep. We rode to Khan's Garage where the men packed my Rover. Driving in front and in back of me, they escorted me to the Indian border. One got out of his jeep and handed me an envelope. "From the Consul," he said. Scrawled on the outside were the words, "Read later."

Amritsar was on the other side of the border, the site of the holy Golden Temple of the Sikhs. The temperature was one hundred and five degrees. I felt too ill and too hot to drive. Twice an hour, I used my inhaler. A cool place like Kashmir might help.

I garaged the Rover with my luggage locked inside. Carrying one suitcase, I hailed a taxi to the airport, and boarded the next flight to Kashmir. In the plane, I leaned forward to ease my lungs, using my inhaler steadily.

A bald man across the aisle tapped my shoulder. "I am doctor. You must not use inhaler like this. Three times a day only."

"Thank you, doctor."

I put the inhaler in my bag, took out the Consul's envelope and opened it with a metal nail file. He had penned a note on plain paper.

> Shirley, the following paragraph comes from an information sheet on the Baluchi tribe. I found it under the heading, "Tribal Codes of Honour."
>
> "Tribal codes of honour demand revenge for the slightest offense. If, however, a man or woman about to be victimized for an offense should beg for mercy, he or she will be spared. Begging for mercy is tantamount to acknowledging the superiority of the offended one. That acknowledgement restores his honor."
>
> You came within a hair's breadth of death. Had you not thrown yourself at his feet, we would have shipped your body home today. Clearly, Somebody-Up-There is watching over you. Saving you for something. Good luck, Shirley.

He signed his initial, *D.*

Tears streaked my face all the way to Srinagar. But I never made a sound.

42

KASHMIR

1963

The green and scarlet houseboat on Dal Lake was called *Srinagar* like the town. Five furnished rooms, servants' quarters on board, and a full-time servant cost less than my hotel in Lahore. I was the only guest.

A tourist agency's brochure lay on a lamp table.

> *Tour the luscious valley of Kashmir surrounded by the Himalayas. Visit jasmine and lotus gardens, Mogul palaces, gold-domed temples. Buy handmade Kashmir shawls, silk saris, and handcrafted copper and gold.*

Not for me. I thought my asthma would abate in cooler weather. It didn't. Sometimes I crouched on the floor like a dog. It was too hard to breathe standing up.

Jamal, the houseboat servant, said, "Memsaab not well. I sees it." He wore an old white tunic and baggy trousers. About eighteen years old, I guessed. He told me he was twenty-eight.

"I can't breathe, Jamal."

"As-ta-ma, Memsaab?"

"Asthma, yes."

"Memsaab, we are having good *hakim* in Srinagar. He fixes astama."

"What is *hakim*?"

"Doctor."

"Jamal, I come from New York. Biggest city in the world. In New York, London, Paris, everywhere, doctors can't cure it. What can anyone do here?"

"*Hakim* is doctor of *Unani* medicine. Cures all peoples with astama. Arabic system very old, Memsaab. Not like west. My brother was having very bad astama. Worse like you. Now he is good. I takes you tomorrow."

When Jamal turned the lights off, I nestled my arms and head in a pillow on the dining table. I couldn't sleep lying down anymore.

Next morning, we set out. I didn't want to go. I went for Jamal's sake.

In some areas of the lake, you need a *shikhara* to reach the shore, a water taxi that looks like a covered gondola. But the *Srinagar* was moored near a dozen stone steps that led to the embankment. My breath was so shallow I had to pause on each step.

We moved slowly along the embankment. "How far, Jamal?"

He nodded toward a junction. "We takes bus there."

An hour later, we walked down a flight of steps to the basement hall of a residential building. More than a hundred people, men on one side, women on the other, sat on the floor of the large, bare room. The *hakim*, a shrunken old man in a white turban and tunic, squatted on a mat in front. His soft, black eyes beckoned us.

The hakim spoke to Jamal in Kashmiri, then motioned for me to squat. I could only kneel. He felt my pulse, moving his hand around different parts of my wrist. Jamal translated. How long did I have astama? What did I eat? Did I drink cold drinks? No good. He felt my pulse again, moving his fingers all around my wrist, and scribbled what looked like a prescription.

"*Hakim* says you must take medicine for four days. Then astama finish."

"Sure," I nodded. Sixteen years I'd had it, and a floor squatter tells me he'll cure me in four days. I smiled a thank you, and gave the *hakim* his two-rupee fee. Twenty American cents.

"We go back, Jamal?"

"First, medicine store."

We climbed a steep path to the medicine store, a darkish room with a bench along one wall, and shelves on the opposite wall stacked with roots, bark, red and brown powders, pestles, mortars, copper pots. While I sat on the bench, the Kashmiri medicine man pounded, beat, and sifted.

"Four glasses a day I prepares," Jamal said. "I steep bark and leaves. Memsaab drink one tea every three and one-half hours. Four days, then you well."

I would do it to please him. I wanted to tell him that doctors around the world say, "Once an asthmatic, always an asthmatic." But I didn't want to hurt him.

Back on the houseboat, Jamal brought the first cup of tea to my room. "Drink, Memsaab." The taste was bitter, but that didn't matter. The next tea was a different concoction, darker than the first, and very bitter. "What is this stuff?"

"Bark of Chinese tree, Memsaab."

By evening, I'd had four teas. I didn't feel as breathless as usual, but that was probably my imagination. I wished I could lie down instead of sleeping at the table, but I wouldn't try. Within minutes, I'd be crawling on all fours.

On day two, Jamal prepared teas as cautiously as an American pharmacist prepares pills. By nightfall, I wondered if I should lie down. Silly. I'd be crawling on the floor, crying for cortisone. Good old cortisone. Shakes your body up for six hours, but at least you can breathe.

By noon on the third day, I hadn't used my inhaler. Must be psychological, a kind of placebo effect. Breathlessness would return soon enough. But by 6 p.m., air was coming in and going out of my lungs like a normal person. I lay down, and fell asleep.

On the fourth morning, I opened the door of the houseboat. The acid test—twelve steps. Slowly I climbed. One, two, three, four steps. I stopped. I was breathing normally. Five, six, seven, eight steps. I stopped. Air was still coming in and going out. No tightness in my chest. Ninth, tenth, eleventh, and twelfth step. I stood poised on the top, breathing normally. Surely, I'm dreaming.

Down the steps I went, and up once more. One, two, three steps. Four, five, all the way. Did it again! Down the stairs again. Up one, up two, faster now. Three, four, five. Faster. Six, seven, eight. Faster. Ten, eleven, twelve. Jamal eyed me from below.

"Memsaab is good, now. Good, Memsaab!"

Tears streamed down my face as I ran for the first time in sixteen years. I ran toward the street where we had taken a bus to the *hakim.* Jamal tailed me, beaming like a proud parent. I ran faster. At the junction, I stopped. My lungs were free. I could breathe. That little guy had cured me!

In search of answers, I found Professor Hussain who lectured in English at the University of Kashmir. He didn't know much about Unani medicine, he said, but he could explain how it worked because his late uncle was a *hakim.*

The professor was so tall that he had to bend to clear the houseboat entrance. We climbed a narrow stairway near the kitchen to a covered terrace with canvas chairs. I hadn't noticed the exquisite beauty of Kashmir before then. The cluster of lotus beds around the front of the boat, and the Himalayan peaks that framed the lake.

Jamal served hot jasmine tea while Hussain spoke as he would in a classroom. "*Hakim* means doctor of *Unani* medicine, the world's oldest medical system. Six thousand years old, founded by Hippocrates. The system differs from Western medicine in that Western medicine treats the disease. *Unani* treats the person. Three cancer patients in the West may get the same treatment. Here, they get three different treatments.

"According to our system, the body is composed of four humours. Black bile, yellow bile, phlegm, and blood, which correspond to the elements of the universe—earth, fire, water, and air. When the humours function in harmony, good health ensues. An imbalance of the humours—too much or too little of any of them—causes illness.

"One humour predominates in all of us. For example, a person in whom black bile predominates moves slowly, gains weight fast, sleeps heavily. His temperament is called melancholic. When fire predominates, one becomes restless, burns fast in the sun, and prefers cool climates. He's called choleric."

"How does a *hakim* know what humour is out of balance?" I asked.

"By pulse. Pulse diagnosis is not the same as in the West. In the West, even a child can take your pulse because results are quantitative. Here, they're qualitative. Besides, there are several pulses, not just one. Pulse diagnosis takes many years to master."

"The *hakim* said I shouldn't eat bananas. What does food have to do with it?"

"Humours govern food, too," he said. "You have too much phlegm in your system, so you shouldn't eat mucus-producing foods like bananas or ice cream, or drink cold drinks. My predominant humour is yellow bile. I get angry fast, and I have ulcers. I love chilies, but they aggravate my condition."

"I'm taking medicine with me," I told him. "But suppose I get sick with something else. Who will help me when I leave Kashmir?"

"*Ayurveda* is practiced all over India," he said. "It's also thousands of years old, based on the same humoural system. You'll be fine," he grinned. "As long as you stay in India."

If anyone had told me they got cured in three and a half days of a sickness they'd had for sixteen years, I wouldn't believe a word. I didn't believe it now, either, but I couldn't deny that I was breathing normally.

Unani was contrary to everything I knew. It offered a new way of looking at life, a way that tied things together. Our nature, diseases, habits, food. I felt like I'd been living in a cave, unaware of the world that existed outside.

On the plane back to Amritsar to pick up my Land Rover, I asked myself why I didn't go back to the *hakim*. Why didn't I bring him money? Thank him on my knees? I'd paid Western doctors thousands of bucks to shake me up with cortisone. And gave twenty cents to the guy who cured me. Why is my wisdom so retroactive?

New Delhi, India's capital, was three hundred miles south. A three hundred-mile drive would take six hours in the States. In India, it could take two days.

The roads were zoos. Bullocks, cows, camels, horses, and donkeys were everywhere. Once, an elephant, graceful and slow, moved toward my Rover carrying a handsome young man. I poked my head out of the window.

"That man on the elephant," I asked a cyclist. "He's famous?"

"No, Madame. No famous. Today he marries."

No rules applied on India's roads. Left side of the road was official, but when it was jammed, drivers crossed to the middle.

Young men stood on top of buses. When one caught sight of me, all rushed to that corner of the bus, tipping it like it was on two wheels. Overloaded truck beds competed with overloaded donkeys, bullock carts, and rickshaws. Scooters carrying whole families skirted in and out of traffic, honking as they went. Occasionally, a cow stood still in the middle of the road, its legs missed by vehicles passing within inches.

By the time I reached New Delhi, the five-star Ambassador Hotel looked like the Waldorf. A desk clerk gave me a questionnaire to fill out. "Why was I here? How long would I stay? What was my profession?"

Ashok Krishnan, the manager, scanned it. "Musician and entertainer? Piano, Madame?"

"Accordion." I showed him my brochure.

"We'd like music for the dinner hour, Madame. Madame would like to work?"

"Yes, indeed. But my entry visa says I must not apply for a job."

"Don't worry for that," he said. "We'll take care of it."

How could a hotel manager counter visa regulations? But I was too weary to figure that out. The hotel signed me up for a month, the fastest contract I'd ever gotten. My job would be easy. One and a half hours of refined music. No vocals. No wiggles.

My room had a large bed with posts and mosquito netting, an armchair, desk, and a round table with breakfast, lunch and dinner menus. Six-course meals of fish, chicken, meat, vegetables, salads, bread, cheese, and rich desserts. Liquor was served only in the rooms. I ordered Scotch on the rocks.

"Madame lucky," the waiter said. "Most India is dry. We have permit."

I leaned into the armchair with my hand curled around a whiskey glass. Strange, I thought. I can never relax without a drink in my hand.

43

NEW DELHI

1963

The roving eyes of young men, four or five abreast, swept my body as I meandered through Connaught Place, New Delhi's popular shopping center. I'd worn the wrong garment. A nylon dress with a mandarin collar that revealed every curve and was too hot for a June day. Saris were cool, but they took too long to drape.

The other traditional female garmet, *Punjabis*, would suit me. A long tunic, baggy pants with ankle cuffs, and a soft scarf called a *deepota*. Western women called it a modesty cloth because it was worn to cover the breasts.

I bought blue cotton voile, soft as butter, for the tunic. Matching net for a modesty cloth. Heavy white cotton for pants. A tailor on "tailor lane" working outdoors on a manual sewing machine would sew it for the equivalent of two dollars.

"Two hours ready," he told me.

A turbaned palmist squatting on the corner of the street beckoned. "Memsaab, I look your hand. Come!"

He held my fingers down to study my palm. *"Aaray baapray!* You goes round and round!"

"You mean travel?"

"Travel, Memsaab. Never sees like this."

"It won't stop? The round and round?"

"No stopping, Memsaab!"

He must be wrong. Only Nepal, Burma and Malaya remained.

The Times of India reporter interviewed me on my fifth day, captioning his article "Round The World On A Musical Ride. A Young American Mixes Jazz with Mechanics." He described me as "dark-haired, tall, with a ready friendly smile." In South Africa, the *Rand Daily Mail* reporter had called me "a petite American." To Westerners, I'm petite. To Indians, tall.

The Ambassador's six-course meals added eight pounds to my weight in less than a month. A New York "Slenderella" gym could have helped, but Delhi had none.

"Try yoga," a hotel desk clerk urged. "There's a school across the street. Teacher is famous, Guru of Prime Minister Nehru."

Dhirendra Brahmacharya, a bearded yogi from Kashmir, made a remarkable appearance. Over six feet, slender, strikingly handsome with long, glossy black hair and piercing eyes. He wore a white muslin tunic, was decidedly un-Western, yet sophisticated and attuned to Western mentality. His heavily accented English was broken, but fluent.

"I came to lose weight, sir."

He told me I'd lose it, but not because of exercises. Because I'd lose the desire to eat so much. He demonstrated the sun exercise, each posture flowing into the next. "You don't get old when your spine stays supple."

Standing on his head, he told me that blood flows from the heart to the brain in that posture, so memory improves. He did the shoulder stand, bridge, fish, plough, cobra, bow, wheel, and twist. I tried each, but my body was unyielding. Then, the corpse pose. Lying on my back, legs outstretched, arms at sides, all muscles relaxed. My thoughts subsided. Scraps of hatred and guilt that had gnawed at the back of my brain like starving insects vanished. I drifted into a strange state. Half asleep, yet fully aware.

That night, I relaxed in my armchair, without a drink in my hand.

The shades were partially drawn over the windows of the long yoga studio to keep the sun out. Brahmacharya sat on a white cushion on the floor, his back as straight as the wall behind him.

His long black hair cascaded down the back of his white tunic, his black eyes flashing as he spoke.

"A sub-tle energy," he said, pronouncing the "b", pervades this universe. In man, it manifests as breath. Breath and mind are two sides of same coin. Control your breath, and you control your mind."

That's what I want! A way to control my mind. A bandleader to lead the band of my unruly thoughts.

He called this subtle energy, Prana. "Chinese call it Chi," he said. "Japanese call it Ki. Prana works our organs, tissues, muscles. Enables us to digest, breathe, speak, move, excrete, walk, run, talk. Circulates blood. Produces semen, chyle, chyme, gastric juice, saliva, bile."

"What happens to Prana when we die?"

"It withdraws," he said. "You never heard the "death rattle?"

"I didn't," I told him, "but my mother heard it when my father died, and it scared the wits out of her."

"Prana rattles when leaving body," he said. "A dead body still has organs—tissue, muscles, bone. But when Prana goes, body is like fan with power off."

How strange, I thought. Indians, Chinese and Japanese know all about Prana, and we Westerners don't.

"When Prana is wild, mind is wild." He pointed to my head. "Your mind, too busy."

He was right. My mind replayed the guilt scenes of my life like it was rehearsing for a show, and I couldn't stop it.

"And you breathe too fast," he said. "You not know that dogs breathe fifty times a minute and live for only fifteen years? Elephants breathe twenty times a minute and live to be a hundred."

He showed me exercises to slow down my breath. To cool myself in the heat, to warm myself when cold.

"Where does this strange body of knowledge come from?" I asked. "And where does it lead?"

"The answer is sub-tle," he said. He could only explain in Hindi.

"Where can I learn in English?"

"At an ashram."

"What's that?"

"A live-in center for spiritual study."

"Not another religion," I said.

He shook his head. "Religion, one thing. Spirituality, another."

"Where are these centers?"

"Best one is in foothills of Himalayas. Two hundred fifty kilometers north of Delhi. ShivaSwami, a doctor, founded it. He wrote three hundred books," the yogi said. "On medicine, nature cure, sleep, dreams, concentration, meditation, philosophy, yoga. Books about saints from East and West. Nobody compares."

"I can see him? I can ask him things?"

The yogi shook his head. "He passed last week," he said. "You can ask his successors."

44

TO THE HIMALAYAN FOOTHILLS

July, 1963

A road map of India marked my route north from Delhi. What a mass of color and grace! Women wore saris of orange, red, green and yellow, lifting them above their ankles to avoid puddles and mud. Barefooted village women, clad in multi-colors with water carafes on their heads, moved with a poise that must be inborn.

Schoolgirls wore brightly hued long skirts with matching short blouses, handmade, since few shops sold ready-made clothes. Men wore cotton shirts and *dhotis*, unseamed cloths wrapped around their bodies like sarongs. Sikh men sported turbans made of six yards of saffron, gold and white silk.

The country was a rainbow, but nothing masked its ubiquitous poverty. During siestas and nights, the homeless slept on hard pavement, their bony hands clutching the shredded cloths that covered them. When they rose, they rummaged through trashcans for scraps of food.

Often, as I got out of my Rover to eat, misshapen arms and hands tugged at my Punjabi pants. *Baksheesh, maa*. Some bodies were maimed, deliberately mutilated as babies to beg for a syndicate their whole lives. Similar syndicates operated in Mexico, South America, and Africa. I couldn't fathom the heart of a person who would maim another human being.

I didn't know who had said that India was an assault on the senses, but as I drove through the heart of the country, I saw how true it was. Bus radios and truckers' tapes played at maximum volume with windows wide open so the world would hear it. People on the street seldom spoke in moderate tones. They barked at one another, often showing red teeth, stained from chewing betel nut. On the ground, splattered pools of red spit from betel chewers looked like blood.

Public toilets assailed the nostrils. Many Indians thought it unsanitary to plunk their bare bottoms on a toilet where other bare bottoms had sat. They preferred drains. To bear the stink and sight, I coated my nostrils with a Q-tip dipped in sandalwood oil, and raised my eyes upward. Train toilets were the worst. An American woman at the Ambassador Hotel told me that before Westerners embark on a train ride, they eat half a loaf of white bread to constipate themselves.

You can't have it both ways. The East has wisdom, but assaults the senses. The West delights the senses, but often lacks the wisdom. I'd lived in the West long enough. The wisdom of the East was worth an assault.

Hell can't be hotter than India in July, and I wilted in my Rover. I needed to shower, eat, and rest. The Krishna Hotel looked adequate. Not like the Ambassador, but nothing from then on would look like the Ambassador.

"I'd like lamb," I told the waiter.

"Sorry, Memsaab. No meat."

"Chicken will do."

"Sorry, Memsaab. No chicken."

"No meat? No chicken?"

"Vege only."

The heat, fatigue, and depression that had gripped me at the maimed beggars' site got to me. "For God's sake, where can I get a decent meal?"

As soon as I said it, I felt like burying my face in my hands. The waiter, a bony kid not more than fifteen, winced. A typical "ugly American" scene.

I'd teach myself a lesson. "I'm sorry. I'll eat here." I pointed to a Hindi squiggle on the menu. "I'll take this."

"*Palak paneer*. Is good, Memsaab." His grin eased my remorse. While he was gone, I looked it up in my Hindi phrase book. Spinach and cheese. I could bear that. I was like all other Americans on the road, measuring the world by us. Every difference means a mark of inferiority. That appalled me.

The waiter brought the *palaak paneer,* which I'd enjoy if it killed me. But one bite pulverized my lips and tongue. "Good," I told him, tears rolling down from the fire.

"Pepper?" I smiled.

"*Aacha*," he grinned. "Chili pepper."

As I stepped into my room, a servant boy left with a long spray gun, the kind my parents used when I was a kid. DDT, so I guessed I wouldn't see any roaches. To check, I lifted the edge of the mattress. A mass of roach pouches!

I rushed out. "Hello, hello." I beckoned the boy back, waiting on the veranda while he swept the pouches off. In deference to Alice and Ben Hur, the roaches I carried in a test tube until a German bartender squashed them, I hoped the babies would survive. Far away.

The rocking chair squeaked as I read the little book the yoga teacher had given me. Forty watts didn't shed enough light, but I wanted to know something about ShivaSwami before I reached the ashram.

He was born in south India. Topped his class at medical school, and traveled to Malaya at twenty-six to work as a doctor on a rubber estate. Strange that he did what I'd always wanted to do.

One day, he read a book about a super-conscious state beyond the mind. He knew what it was, he wanted it, and returned to India to become a monk.

ShivaSwami meditated in a spider-infested room in the Himalayas. He treated cholera and smallpox, and carried the sick on his back to hospitals. He was a high-caste Hindu, a Brahmin, but to erase caste consciousness, he cleared fecal matter from public toilets—the task of India's lowest caste. He gave up foods he liked, returned love for hate, and bore insults with dignity.

The swami learned that our only problem lies in ourselves. That to know our higher Self, we needed to be saved from our lower one. I didn't know what a higher Self was, but I wanted to be saved from my lower one.

When the monk attained his spiritual goal, he founded an ashram. One night, in a prayer hall, a disgruntled inmate tried to strike his head with an axe. He tried three times, but the light of the oil lamp was so dim that he hit the wall instead. Police arrested him, but ShivaSwami wouldn't allow them to prosecute. He brought the prisoner fruit, clothes, books. When the man was freed, he apologized. The monk's forgiveness had transformed him.

How can a human being show love to a man who tries to kill him? Christ did, but He was Christ. Could I forgive Bugti, who lunged at me with spears of glass? Alvar, who landed me in jail? Nick, with his women and guns? If the swami were alive, I'd ask how to forgive so I don't haul my hatred to the grave.

Maybe his successors know. But I was too tired to think.

45

THE HIMALAYAN FOOTHILLS

July, 1963

The sun had not yet risen, but I ached for coffee. The little man at the corner kiosk with a scarf wrapped around his head poured hot milk into a glass, then added sugar and coffee. With arms raised high, he poured from one glass to another without spilling a drop. I drank three cups.

The breakfast menu at the Krishna Hotel was printed in Hindi. "Boiled eggs," I told the waiter.

"Eggs, no, Memsaab. Vege only."

Of course, I'd forgotten. "Okay. I'll take *uppama*," a spicy wheat breakfast cooked with vegetables. It was either that or *idly*, a kind of pancake made with wheat or rice, covered with soupy brown *sambar* that should be served with a fire extinguisher.

On the road toward Haridwar, barbers shaved heads and beards on the street. Women sold garlands of fresh flowers to offer temple deities and decorate braids. Vegetable peddlers hawked string beans, peas, carrots, eggplant, cabbage, tomatoes.

I'd reached the city of Haridwar when I wondered if I should have bought a bottle of Scotch in Delhi. I no longer needed it, but now and then I might want a glass. I doubted I could get it near an ashram.

"Bottle store?" I asked a street tailor.

"There, Memsaab," he pointed.

I stepped into a dimly lit store, shelves crammed with plastic baby bottles, rubber nipples, buckets, clothespins, Nescafé, and single cigarettes. I bought a jar of Nescafé. At least I'd be sure of morning coffee.

Haridwar, one of India's seven holiest cities, means *Door to the Lord*. If one dies there, he is cremated on the *ghats*, the steps that lead to the river, and his ashes scattered in the Ganges. Departing like that, his soul goes to the highest nether regions.

I didn't believe in nether regions. Catholic, Jewish or Hindu. What's the purpose of sitting on one's butt for eternity? When life is over, it's over. What troubled me was the point of it. Knock yourself out for love, sex, marriage, kids, profession, status, money. Then it's finished. For what?

Saffron-robed holy men, beggars, and monkeys swarmed the long bridge at the city gate. From Haridwar, millions of pilgrims and monks would begin their pilgrimage to the sacred shrines of the Himalayas where the Ganges originates.

I ordered chai at a small café, sweet spiced Indian tea with hot milk. Like magic, dozens of kids appeared within seconds, pressing their faces to the window. At such times, I missed the West. Westerners are curious for a second, then they go about their business. My waiter, who looked eight but was probably twelve, wiped the table with the bottom part of his dirty apron, grinning. Westerners meant tips.

The narrow road climbed northward toward the Himalayas with the Ganges on my right. Women and children milked cows on the street, and carried the milk home in metal buckets with full cream intact. Heaps of round cow dung cakes lay along the side of the road, drying in the sun for fuel. Indians waste nothing.

A boatman plied a canoe crammed with pilgrims crossing the Ganges. One man sang a phrase. The others repeated it. He sang another phrase. They repeated that. The rhythm accelerated with no trace of syncopation. Syncopation is the essence of jazz. The clout, the force, the engine that drives it. Yet, here was power. Right *on* the beat.

A wooden sign pointed ahead to a cluster of buildings on both sides of the road. I saw the ashram hospital on the Ganges banks. The ashram was on my left, nestled in the foothills on multiple levels up from the road.

I drove up a curved driveway, parked in an open space, and stepped out. Forested foothills encircled me, some dotted with box-like temples. Sandalwood fragrance scented the air. Somewhere, a bamboo flute played a haunting theme. The month was July. The day, Sunday. The time, 10 a.m.

Half a dozen monks appeared, some in orange, some in white, all bald as babies. They clasped their hands at their heart. "Welcome, *Mataji*." I didn't like being called "Mother," but here, it was a compliment.

"Good morning," I said, but self-consciousness stripped me of ease. My Punjabi garment was fine. My lipstick and rouge were not.

"*Mataji*, you are driving from?"

"London."

"London? You are first ever to drive from London. Come. We take you to the president, AnandSwami."

They led me down steep stone steps and along footpaths surrounded by dissimilar-shaped buildings. I waited at the open door to the office of the president, a monk squatting on the floor, surrounded by a stack of letters. My guide knelt in front of him, hands folded at his heart, whispering. The swami raised his eyes toward me. A skin-and-bone monk with soft features and brown eyes like deep, bottomless wells. Ears like the Buddha's. He folded his hands at his heart. "*Namaste, Mataji.* Come in, come in."

I removed my shoes as my guide bowed out backwards, never turning his back to the monk.

"Welcome, welcome." The swami motioned for an aide to bring a chair. But as I faced down at him, I knew it was wrong. I got off the chair and tried to sit cross-legged on the floor, but my thighs hurt. I knelt.

The monk laughed. "Be comfortable. No need for formality." He spoke with barely an accent. "At first glance," he said, "I thought you were a Punjabi lady. Many Punjabi women have fair skin."

"Thank you. That's a compliment."

"So you've driven from England in search of meaning. Right?"

"Right."

"You came to the right place at a dynamic time. ShivaSwami left his body seven days ago. We're building a *Samadhi* shrine."

"What is that?"

"When a saint passes, his body is seated in the lotus pose and lowered into a pit, its final place of rest. Sacred items like sandalwood powder, camphor and ash are poured into the pit while devotees chant holy mantras. When his body is completely lowered, the pit is closed, and a holy symbol placed above it. The shrine around it becomes a place of pilgrimage."

His words sounded weird. Everything was weird. The orange robes, bald heads, the whole place. Yet I had no doubt that this was precisely where I was meant to be. That somebody here could answer all my questions.

"May I stay awhile?"

"You may. But you must clear your stay with the General Secretary, KrishnaSwami. He's in charge of guests."

"How much does it cost?"

"We don't charge," he said.

"Surely I must pay something for room and board and classes."

"No charge. You can leave a donation at the end of every month if you like. Whatever you can afford."

KrishnaSwami sat with his legs folded on a floor cushion surrounded by books and letters. An orange shawl covered his head despite the heat. I knelt.

"What do you want?" he asked.

"I'd like to stay awhile, sir."

"For what?" His English was sharp and swift.

"To learn what I can."

"What do you expect to learn?"

"I don't know, sir."

He leaned toward me. "You have come to learn something, and you don't know what it is?"

My mind blanked.

"You wish to learn something," he repeated slowly, louder, "the nature of which you can not even ascertain?"

The man saw through me. I wanted to flee. I faced the floor. "Yes, sir, but I'd like to stay a few months to find out what it is."

"Three weeks are enough for you." He turned to the monk huddling in the doorway. "Take her to Saraswati kutir."

Three weeks are enough for you. Audacity!

Kutir means "dwelling place." Saraswati Kutir was a two-story brick-wall building near the top of the driveway. Cream colored with green doors and windows, outside toilets and baths.

Young boys darted in and out of my ground floor room with baggage from my car. I was conscience-stricken by what I possessed in the midst of India's poverty.

A narrow wooden bed with a straw mattress, and a cane chair furnished my room. Pull-strings dangled above the bed from a fan and ceiling light. I asked the novice supervising the boy "porters" where I could hang clothes. He pointed to wall hooks, and a wall-to-wall cord on which to drape saris.

My "sink" was an enamel basin on a wooden stand with a small mirror above it. Two tin buckets stood beneath. One with clean water and a scooper. The other, empty for dirty water.

"Could I have a dresser?" I asked the novice.

"Dresser? Not understanding, Mataji. What is dresser?"

"A piece of furniture with pull-out drawers."

"Not having, Mataji. So sorry. We are using floor."

I shouldn't have asked. Suitcases make perfect drawers.

The toilet down the path was the usual tiny room with a hole in the floor, canister and faucet. The "bathroom" had two wall hooks, a cold water faucet, and two metal buckets. A carrier boy would fill one with hot water for baths.

Someone knocked on my room door. "Hello! I'm Karsta from Germany. Your next door neighbor."

She leaned on my door, a blond athletic type. The sight of this normal-looking Western woman in this weird milieu reassured me. Here was someone who would understand me. Whom I could understand.

"Lucky for me! Been here long?"

"Three weeks," she said. "But I've been here before. I can help you adjust."

A dark brown object darted past her into my room. "Oh my God!" I screamed. "What was that?" The thing jumped on my bed, off my bed, and into my bucket of clean water. "A rat!" I shouted. "*Mama Mia!* Look at the size of him!"

Water splashed over the floor as the rat struggled to get out. "I'll take him out," Karsta said, calmly reaching for the bucket.

"No, no. He's a rat. Let him drown."

"He has a right to live. I'll let him out."

"Don't let him out. He'll come back."

Karsta ignored me, grabbed the bucket, and threw the water and the rat into a narrow gully a few feet from my *kutir*.

Hell of a start. The General Secretary's frosty attitude, and a rat in my bucket.

Karsta drew my eyes to the schedule tacked on my door. Meditation, yoga, breakfast, classes, lunch, rest, afternoon classes. Tea twice a day (brought to the rooms), dinner, evening programs. Classes in yoga, pranayama, philosophy, concentration, meditation, music, Sanskrit. "I want to study everything," I told her, "but I'd never make the 4 a.m. meditation. I go to bed at four."

"Me, too," she said. "I work in a bar in Stuttgart. But as Americans say, you're a free agent here. You can go to every lecture, or spend the day on the Ganges."

We toured the library, printing press, lecture hall, yoga hall, the shrine hall that buzzed with builders and craftsmen, and across the road, the hospital and Ayurvedic pharmacy. Cows lingered on the walkways. Monkeys chased us for handouts. Scrawny dogs tailed us. "Indian dogs love Westerners," Karsta said. "We feed and pet them."

When the lunch bell rang, we climbed a hundred stone steps to the dining hall entrance, removed our shoes, and stepped into a queue of inmates and guests, many foreign. Men sat on one side of the spacious dining room, women on the other—all on straw mats laid over a concrete floor. Framed epigrams hung on the walls. *Forget an unkind word. Bear Insult, Bear Injury.*

Monks and guests chanted Sanskrit prayers. Waiters in monastic robes handed out round steel plates with partitions, but no utensils. Rice followed. Then soupy lentils called *dhal*, mixed cooked vegetables and unleavened wheat bread. Indian men across from me scooped up the *dhal* with their right hands, kneaded it with the rice, and shoved it into their mouths without dropping a grain. I tried, but it spilt on my lap. Karsta stifled a laugh, and a waiter brought a spoon.

"Karsta," I whispered, "with so many Westerners here, they don't serve meat now and then?"

"No."

"Surely an egg?"

"Surely not."

"Where's the nearest restaurant?"

"For meat? Delhi. You might get an omelet in the next village up."

"Animal protein is the main part of my diet."

"You'll get used to it. I did."

After the meal, we lined up for a hand-wash. A monk poured cold water on our hands over a large metal sink. I dried my hands on my tunic.

Outside, hundreds of men in tattered clothing waited on a long queue.

"Homeless beggars," Karsta said, "the next round of guests. The ashram feeds them every day."

What a place. Feeds the homeless, charges nothing for classes, rooms, food. Just a donation, *if* you can. I never knew an organization like it.

My accordion and amp, electronics, winter clothing, and theatrical wardrobe fit under my bed. Books, maps, music, cosmetics, camping equipment, my human skull and knuckle-busters filled suitcases and boxes along a wall. My *Punjabis* hung on wall hooks. My saris lay over the wall-to-wall cord.

Swaddled in a sweater was the hand-carved wooden crucifix that Father Kahle had given me at Westminster Cathedral in London. I hung it on a wall hook.

A familiar symbol in an unfamiliar world.

46

THE LECTURE

A row of windows in the lecture hall framed the foothills. Sitting shoeless and cross-legged on the floor, I shifted my gaze from the peaks to the photographs of saints that hung high around the room. St. Francis looked down at me. I liked that. Hindus showing pictures of Catholic saints. I couldn't imagine Catholics showing pictures of Hindu saints.

About sixty monks and visitors attended the lecture. Men along one wall, women opposite. Monastic robes varied in hue from pale saffron to deep orange. Novices wore white. Foreigners had come from America, Canada, Argentina, Peru, England, Italy, France, Sweden, Germany, Australia, and Japan.

"I can't sit cross-legged for an hour," I whispered to Karsta on my right.

"Stretch your legs," she said. "But cover them with your shawl. Point them away from the speaker."

"What's the lecture on?"

"Vedanta."

"What's that?"

"End part of the Vedas, oldest scriptures in the world. Five thousand years old."

KrishnaSwami walked in on the stroke of four, seated himself on a cushion, and focused straight ahead. Flawless English words gushed out like a waterfall. He used no notes. Never paused to gather thoughts. Words flowed *through* him, unimpeded as though he were a vehicle of some otherworldly power. He mesmerized me, this monk who told me that three weeks were enough for me.

"Whatever has a beginning has an end. Things come and go.

Empires rise and fall. When nothing endures, what is the purpose of all this pageantry? If life has any meaning, it can't be what our eyes see because that passes. It's transitional, unreliable. Nothing is certain. Anything can happen at any moment. Yet we live as though nothing will happen, as though we're immortal. Tomorrow will be better than today, never worse.

"But our thoughts oppose fact. The undeniable fact is that all things will perish. Yet our disbelief that they will perish is also a fact."

That's it! The question that nagged me all my life. The fairy tale that our home, lovers, and we, ourselves will go on forever.

"We belong to two worlds at the same time. An external world—a mortal, perishable, space-time complex—and an inner world—immortal, eternal, and beyond time that summons us at every moment. That summons of immortality masquerades as a yearning for infinite wealth and endless life. Yet only the Absolute, the Self, is infinite, boundless, eternal. Free from the limitations of space and time."

I loved the word "boundless." I knew what it meant when I soloed in a Piper Cub. Like I'd burst through the rim of the universe and flown into freedom.

"Consciousness is our substratum," the monk went on. "It transcends the senses and mind. Without it, senses can't operate. Our senses don't perceive. Consciousness perceives through them. Consciousness sees through our eyes, hears through our ears, tastes through our tongue. That Witnessing Consciousness is the real 'I.' It is everywhere. Without, within, filling all space, expanding into all existence. Vast beyond knowledge.

"Consciousness illumines all. The world is its outward index. The entire visible mass is this formless essence appearing in form. God, in the framework of space and time. The ultimate reality, the unseen cause. The universe is not matter; it is a sea of Consciousness. We are waves in this sea. The realization of this universality, which we call *Brahman*, is the ultimate aim of life."

Brahman! The word jolted me awake like a loud alarm. *Brahman,* the Self.

"Our problem is mistaken identity," he said. "We identify with our bodies, age, gender, weight. We identify with our minds. Attachments, anger, lust. When identification goes, liberation comes. Liberation or Self-Realization is the goal of life. Liberated beings live beyond mind. This is freedom."

That's what I want! All my life I yearned for freedom. I thought it was freedom from the clutches of society, but this goes way beyond that. This is freedom from the illusion that I am just a body and mind, here today and gone tomorrow. I thought I was bound by a bag of skin. But the Self is boundless, formless, free.

I was sitting in the lecture hall, but I could see my parents' apartment in Queens. Gray shades on the windows. They zoomed up, suffusing the room with the light of a thousand suns. Catapulting me out of a deep sleep. How long had I slept? How long had I lived like a robot? Eating, sleeping, fornicating by rote. A machine performing mechanical functions. Eating when hungry, sleeping when tired, fucking when roused. Never questioning why.

I wanted to know the Self beyond my name and form. To feel and taste awareness. I wanted to set up headquarters in Consciousness instead of in my head so I wouldn't identify with lust, anger, or guilt. I'd witness them until they gave me up for want of nourishment. I didn't care how long the process would take. I didn't care how tough it was. I would stay until I got it.

How ironic! What I'd looked for all my life was *that* which was looking.

Karsta and I strolled the Ganges embankment in silence, turning right across the iron suspension bridge. Lepers squatting on both sides of the bridge held out their stump-like fingerless hands for our luncheon leftovers. They broke off bits of chapattis and tossed them into the river to feed the fish.

Two young Indian women clad in yellow saris with fresh marigolds in their long braids strode ahead, chatting in Hindi.

"They're so feminine," I said. "Makes me feel like a truck driver."

"Me, too," Karsta said. "KrishnaSwami once said that language is more than a medium of expression. He said that English is the only language in which the word 'male' is contained in 'female,' the word 'he' is in 'she,' and 'man' is in 'woman.'"

"What an insight!" I told Karsta about the night I chased Bedouins in the Jordanian desert with a fire extinguisher. "I wore jeans, a man's shirt and hat. Had I looked like these women, I might not have made it."

We turned right off the bridge, spread a blanket on a flat rock, and squatted.

"Amazing country," I said. "A few days here and my asthma attacks stopped. Another few days, and Scotch on the rocks stopped. Now I look in the mirror and don't recognize me. No makeup, no upsweep, twelve pounds lighter."

"India changes everybody," Karsta said.

"It's not just spirituality," I said. "It's mathematics, too. India gave the world the zero. And they invented chess."

"They have sex down to a science, too," she said. "Ever read the *Kama Sutra*?"

I grinned. "Never had to."

Our talk veered to KrishnaSwami. "He's sharp," Karsta said. "At one lecture, I was thinking about Hans, my lover. The swami pierced my thought. 'What is it that you love in that form?' he asked. In front of everybody! 'If that form were a corpse, would you love it? Of course not! You love the *Self* in that form.' Since that day, I think in German."

"It won't help if you think in Zulu," I told her. "He reads thoughts."

Monks in ochre robes, their eyes shut, sat poised like statues along the Ganges. If only I could sit like that and feel what they feel!

"What is meditation?" I asked Karsta.

"Stilling your mind."

"You think of God?"

"No," she said. "You can't *think* of God. You have to *relax* into God like you float in a pool. Meditation is the only thing you do that isn't 'doing.' It's 'being.'"

"Then why so much preparation?"

"Can you get *Voice of America* with a cheap radio? No. You need short wave. Yoga, breathing exercises, and light food make your mind receptive."

"What's wrong with meat?" I asked.

"Too heavy. Anchors you down. The aim is to rise above body consciousness."

"How long does it take?"

"Depends on where you start, and how much you want it. Intense yearning is half the battle. Maybe you're close because you're intense."

"Don't you want it intensely?" I asked.

Karsta looked away. "I want Hans more."

Evening shadows drew slowly over the hills like blankets over sleeping kids.

"We'd better go back," she said.

Musicians played harmonium, tablas, and strings at the evening program in the prayer hall. Players of unfretted stringed instruments sustained a single bass note called a *sruti*. The word means "underlying truth." The West has no *sruti* in philosophy or music. Our realities shift. Theirs are grounded.

A woman sang four bars; we repeated them. She sang again; we repeated. The tempo quickened. The rhythm didn't move the outside of my body like jazz did. It revved up the inside, unleashing an energy deep within. Whirling around an unknown core.

Karsta and I didn't utter a word as we returned to our rooms.

47

THE ASHRAM
1963-64

Heavy rain pelted the windowpanes at KrishnaSwami's lecture. He sat on a chair, pulling his saffron shawl over his torso and head. We laid our floor cushions around him.

"Science has come a long way," he said. "From materialistic theories to dynamic processes. Physics to metaphysics. Scientists once told us that we could reduce all constituents of the world to a hundred ultimate chemical substances. Later, someone discovered they weren't ultimate. They could be reduced to subtler elements called atoms.

"We've gone beyond that now. We recognize an immanent energy, a matrix of all things including our bodies. The bodies we thought belonged to us are part of a cosmic force. People accept this intellectually, but still think of themselves as individual bodies."

I adored the monk's wisdom. I'd never leave him. He told me that three weeks were enough for me, but they'd long passed, and he hadn't said a word.

Sister Agnes from Maine, teaching in a Catholic mission, asked, "Who is Christ?"

"Christ is the cosmic heart of the universe," the swami said.

"Then why is there so much conflict among Christian churches?"

"Because founders establish churches on the basis of differences, not similarities. Each doctrine presents an aspect of truth, so we shouldn't argue. The universe is like a crystal. Every facet has unique beauty."

A British professor asked what yardsticks could measure our progress on the spiritual path. And how far we had to go.

"Take paper and pen," the swami said. "List your desires."

"What desires?"

"All of them. What do you want in life?"

"Recognition. A good income. A home, car, kids."

"The longer your list, the further you are from the goal," the swami said. "Because desires are like itches. Scratching doesn't make you feel good. Getting rid of your itch does.

"Desires rise in our minds, demanding attention. We want an object; we get it, and feel peace. But peace doesn't come from the object. It comes from getting rid of the desire. To gratify desires is like throwing fuel on a fire to put it out."

My possessions on the floor of my room looked absurd after the swami's lecture. Why should I keep theatrical gowns and spike-heeled shoes? I'll never wear them again. They're incongruous with the Himalayas, the Ganges, the ashram.

But how will I perform without them? *Perform?* I don't want to perform anywhere for anybody. Then how will I make a living? I don't know and I don't care. I'm going to throw out everything that has anything to do with show business.

I dumped the gowns and spike-heeled shoes into a waste pit. Good riddance!

An hour later, small boys had gathered around the pit, doing something with my fishtail gown.

"What are they doing?" I asked a novice.

"Removing the twinkles."

"Sequins. Why?"

"To sell in the market."

"And that bottom part? The fishtail? What are they doing with that?"

"That little boy cut it off to make a blanket for his baby sister."

My hated fishtail, a baby's blanket. What irony!

We were six in my Land Rover, riding without the hard top. I'd stored it in a garage in the next village up. Karsta sat in front.

Four monks squeezed into the back. We headed north toward the cave of Vasishtha, a revered sixth-century sage who had authored the most profound guidance for the attainment of enlightenment.

Two cave guards greeted us as we pulled in. We removed our shoes and formed a queue outside the cave entrance, with me at the tail end. The monks warned Karsta and me. There would be no talking in the cave. No whispering. Not even thinking, if we were to profit from the sage's vibrations.

The monks and Karsta edged forward slowly into the utter darkness. I had never been in a cave. Surely it would be long and narrow, and too dark and bare to sustain any life. After all, what would a creature eat in a cave?

The others moved noiselessly with a slow, measured pace as though they were in a trance. I could barely discern Karsta's form in the murky distance. I felt cracks beneath my feet. And from the corner of my left eye, I caught movement along the fissured wall. My heart beat quickened. I dared not call out, not there in a silence guarded for fourteen centuries. *Steady, mind.* This is a cave. No creatures, no insects.

But what is that weird thing hanging from a crevice in the ceiling? Moving, yet there's no wind. It must be my imagination. Again it moved. An upside-down thing with wild ears and a foot-wide wingspan. *Oh, my God!* A bat! I hate bats. The look of them, the weird eyes, the clawed feet. It swooped over my head, darted toward the entrance, then back toward me. Clung to another crevice in the ceiling. Flew in circles above my head, zipped to the wall, clung to a fissure, darted back over my head. My heart thundered. I was alone, with a bat!

Vasishtha, help! I stood rigid, eyes shut while my mind repeated his words: *The universe is the eternal, effulgent, infinite consciousness.* But that thing clinging to a crevice above my head isn't eternal, and he's not effulgent. And he's picking on me. Why me? Why not the others? I wanted to scream. I couldn't think, let alone think of God. I turned around and made a bee-line back to the entrance. *So sorry, Vasishtha!*

An hour later, lunch was served outside. A large hand-woven

cloth to sit on, and giant palm leaves on which to eat our rice, lentils, vegetables, and homemade yogurt.

Karsta and I strolled around the cave after the meal. I didn't tell her about the bat or my bee-line to safety.

"The vibrations in there are so powerful," she said. "I wondered if Vasishtha had come back, and was sitting there."

"You believe in reincarnation?" I asked.

"I do," she said. "The law of Karma is like the law of physics: *Every action has an equal and opposite reaction.* It's Biblical, too. *As you sow, so shall you reap*. I don't think we're punished *for* our actions. We're punished *by* them. Like the way you throw a ball at a wall is the way the ball comes back. You believe?" she asked.

"Never did," I told her. "But now I have to answer your question like Eleanor Roosevelt answered when she was asked that same question. She said, 'It would be no more bizarre for me to show up in another lifetime than it was for me to show up in this one.'" We had a good laugh.

I yearned to meditate, but despite the classes I took and the books I studied, I couldn't do it. The theory is that if you can focus on anything for twelve seconds—an idea, a thought, a photograph, even the moon—without the mind jumping to anything else, concentration happens by itself. If you sustain the concentration for twelve times twelve seconds, meditation happens by itself.

The first time I tried to concentrate, I chose a simple object—the wooden door to my room. I loved it because a turn of the knob brought my world into view—the window that overlooked the Ganges and the foothills. The door was bright green teakwood with the numeral "2" painted in brown.

I focused my mind on it, but almost immediately my thoughts shifted to the weathered mahogany door of an old Catholic church in Copenhagen. Then to the door of the apartment where my parents and I lived in New York. To Timmy, our poodle, who barked when he heard my footsteps. When Timmy died, we got Queenie, a fawn-colored whippet that Dad loved. But why was I thinking of Queenie? I was focusing on a door when my mind took off. I couldn't concentrate on anything, even for twelve seconds!

My yoga teacher once told me that breath and mind are two sides of the same coin. That my breath was erratic, and therefore, so was my mind. Perhaps that was my problem.

I began to spend half an hour twice a day on breathing exercises. Inhaling slowly, retaining my breath, exhaling slowly. Then I'd focus my gaze on the crucifix hanging on my wall. As I understood it, it was the unwavering concentration on one single thing that would eventually bring my mind to its Source—the Self, Pure Consciousness.

The 6 a.m. yoga class ended. I climbed to the roof of my building with a mat and meditation pillow. Laid my diary and pen at my side, sat in a half-lotus pose facing east, and closed my eyes.

I focused on my wooden crucifix. After a while I saw every wound and crease in His garment. My thoughts ceased. The crucifix vanished from my mind, and I was sucked into the vortex of Christ's Being, catapulted into a sweetness I had never known. Ecstasy engulfed me. I lost awareness of time, my body and mind.

An hour passed before I opened my eyes. I'd sat immobile for an hour in an ecstasy of freedom. Freedom from involuntary thought.

Augustine Baker once wrote that when he meditated, he felt like he was all spirit with no body. St. Theresa of Avila said that in contemplation, she didn't know where she ended and Christ began because suddenly there was only One. Zen master Dogen wrote that his mind and body had dissolved into an ecstasy of release.

That morning, I understood what they meant. I understood what Emerson, Thoreau, Whitman and Blake meant when they described light and bliss, and the instant loss of the fear of death.

AnandSwami passed by as I climbed down the steps from the roof. "You're glowing," he said. "Must be meditation."

"Now I know what *ecstasy* means," I told him. "It turns the joys of the world to toys."

"That's the right way to put it. Many monks never had that experience. They try to meditate on God. Instead, they meditate on how marvelous it would be if someone invited them to America. They could lecture, taste freedom and fame. You tasted everything, and found the taste sour. The world could never satisfy you. Few people are that ready."

But a week passed, and all my bliss passed with it.

Relaxed in my room, I tried to clarify my goal. I didn't want temporary bliss. I wanted permanent bliss, and freedom from my mind. Not for an hour, but always. Freedom from guilt, anger, lust. Freedom to live in the moment instead of bemoaning the past and fretting the future.

The mail carrier brought a letter from my mother. She had enclosed the July twenty-first, 1963 edition of the *New York Sunday News*. The Brooklyn Section published my picture on the front page, perched on the hood of my new Land Rover in London.The reporter, who had interviewed me in New Delhi, captioned his five-column article, "Girl, Her Car & Jazz: Having a Global Ball." He wrote that I was on my way to become the first female New Yorker to drive around the world.

There I sat, perched on a cane chair in my room at the ashram, gazing at the Ganges, reading about myself like I were a character in a novel. Somebody who played jazz from Lapland to the Congo. Who studied malariology at the London School of Tropical Medicine. Drove through bandit-infested countries. Won a chess game that won her a cabin on a ship through the Suez.

I felt nothing. No pride, no thrill, no joy. Compared with the ecstasy of rising beyond mind, the article had no impact. Once meaning is discovered, the means mean little.

Karsta reclined on my bed as I sorted possessions, discarding what I no longer needed. "I won't need the map of Malaya anymore," I said.

"Why not?"

"No more traveling. I'll never leave India."

"What about your visa?" Karsta asked.

"I had a three-month visitor's visa, and got a three-month extension, which expires next month."

"And then?"

"I'll get a student visa for a year, and renew it every year after that."

I pitched sheet music in the garbage can.

"You're getting rid of that? What will you do when your money runs out?"

"Write articles," I said.

"How do you know you'll earn enough to live on?"

"I don't. I didn't know how I'd make enough money to get here, either. I had a hundred bucks when I left the States. When I left London in my Land Rover, I didn't have enough money for gas. The company filled my tank. I never planned, so why start now?"

"Since your rooftop experience, you act like you've seen God," Karsta said. "The challenge is to see God in everybody, not just in meditation. Can you see Him in the psychopath you told me about? Or the guy who tried to cut your throat?"

I sat quiet. "I'd have to be Saint Theresa."

Karsta and I drove to the local police station to file my application for a student visa, valid for a year. While I printed every word, two officers played cards at a corner desk. Another read *The Times of India.* Stacks of file folders bulged on the open shelves of cabinets. Hundreds more lay piled on cabinet tops, some touching the ceiling.

"You're sure they'll grant a visa?" Karsta asked.

"Positive."

"How can you be sure?"

"Because I'm not going. India is my home. I'm here to stay."

The officer in charge of visas said that an official response would be sent by special delivery.

At last, the long, thin, floppy brown envelope from the Indian government arrived. I signed under "Received," and opened it with a penknife. I dared not tear that precious document. I unfolded the tissue-thin letter.

> Your request for an extension of visa has been denied. You must leave India within forty-eight hours of receipt of this letter.

Forty-eight hours! No! No! No! I'll never leave India! "Karsta, Karsta!" I banged on her door.

"What happened?"

"Look!" I burst into tears. "I'm not going. I'm not going!"

"You can't fight the government. They'll order you out."

"I'll hide in a cave."

"An American in a cave will make headlines. And your car. How'll you hide it?"

"I don't care about the car. You can have it."

"You can't give a car away in India. It's against the law. The government will think you sold it."

"I'm not going, Karsta. They'll never get me out. Never!"

"Crying won't help. C'mon. Let's see AnandSwami."

My face confounded the monk. All my bliss had gone. He read the letter with no change of expression. "If you keep crying," he said, "you'll have to go. If you stop, I'll help."

I breathed in deep, and breathed out long.

"I'll write a letter to Gulzari Lal Nanda," he said, "the Minister of Home Affairs. You'll have to give him the letter personally at his office in New Delhi. I suggest you leave now."

48

THE HOME MINISTER, NEW DELHI

1963

Any chance of seeing the Home Minister was slim. I sat at the back of the waiting room. Every chair in front of me was taken. I wanted to stand and shout, *Only thirty hours left till I'm illegal! Please let me pass!* But who would care?

I dozed. The train ride from the foothills had drained me. I couldn't take the Rover because the detachable top was stored in a garage. I had no time to get it.

Now and then I pleaded with the receptionist. "Please, it's urgent!"

"Sit, Madame," he said, handing me another film magazine. He pointed to the others. "Their matters are also urgent."

"But they're Indian. They won't be illegal in twenty-four hours." He shrugged.

Even if I wanted to leave India, I couldn't do it in the time left. I'd have to update my Nepali visa, take a train back to the foothills, get the Rover's hardtop, pack, and drive to the border. But I won't go. If the Home Minister turns me down, I'll pack for a cave. Bats and all.

I checked my papers again. The swami's letter, my passport, entry applications, the government rejection letter, photographs, news clippings to show my bona fides.

Two p.m. I was hungry, nervous and beat. Lunchtime came and went. Still, a dozen Indians waited ahead of me. A door opened at the end of the hall. A tall man stepped out, and entered another door. "That's Mr. Nanda?" I asked the receptionist.

"That is the Honorable Home Minister, Gulzari Lal Nanda."

"He left?"

"He'll be back."

He didn't come back. The office was closing and people left. They'd return tomorrow. I couldn't.

"Excuse me, what's your name?" I asked the receptionist.

"Mahendra."

"Please, it's so urgent, can you tell me where he lives?"

"Who?"

"Mr. Nanda."

"The Honorable Home Minister's address is private."

I had no time to fool around. I opened my bag. "Would this do it?" I handed him a five-dollar bill. He closed his palm over it, tore a strip of paper from the margin of *The Times of India,* and scribbled the address.

The motor rickshaw swerved to a stop. I climbed in, and gave the driver the address. He peered at me through his mirror. "Home of Gulzarilal Nandaji, Memsaab?"

"Yes," I said, "the Honorable."

He fiddled with the picture of Mecca that hung from his visor, and snaked his way through late afternoon traffic.

"Drive safely, please."

He pulled up in front of a mansion. "Minister's home, Memsaab."

The home, surrounded by tall trees and a well-manicured garden, bore the stamp of British elegance. I pictured formal rooms where oil portraits of imperial heroes had hung before independence. An armed officer stood guard at each of the two entrance gates. The gates were open. My foreign face would surely get me in. I only needed five minutes with the man. Who would deny an American that?

"Excuse me, guard. I'm American. I have an urgent matter to discuss with the Honorable Home Minister. Here is a letter of introduction."

"No, Memsaab. Go."

That clean-looking kid of about twenty rapped the butt of his rifle on the ground. "You no visit. No see minister, you."

"Please, it's urgent. Just five minutes."

"Go!"

"Okay. Then take this letter to him, please. I'll wait here."

"No." He wouldn't touch it. "You go. Go!" he shouted.

No point in giving *him* five bucks. I dragged myself back to the main street, and hailed a rickshaw to the hotel. I'd have to find another way.

Twenty-two hours left. I napped, got up at dusk, sat on the edge of the bed. I opened the window in the stuffy room, but the light attracted horse flies. I turned the light off. What next? I would *not* leave India. I would *not*. Tears welled up. I lay down again.

Three a.m. I'd slept with my clothes on. Eleven hours to go before I was illegal. I washed my face, sent for a bucket of hot water, and bathed. Good thing I had clean *Punjabis* to wear.

Outside, the air was cool. Hot coffee at the corner café tasted good. I could think after that. What were my options? Just one. The Home Minister.

The sky was black. A rickshaw dropped me off a block away from his mansion. I took a fleeting look left, and kept moving. From the corner of my eye, I caught the guard smoking, his right leg bent at right angles, his foot on the open gate. Why keep it open, I wondered. VIP gates in America were always locked. I moved to the top of the street, turned left, and left again. From there, I could see the other gate. That guard sat on a stool, his rifle pointed down, his head on the butt. He was asleep.

Should I dare?

What can I lose?

The guard could wake up and shoot me.

But he'd see I was a woman, and foreign.

What are my options?

None.

In the shadows, I took off my sandals. I urged myself. *Don't think, kid, just do it. You've been in hot soup before. This is nothing. Keep going.*

I stepped through the gap between guard and gate, not daring to turn to see if I woke him. I headed for the trees and knelt between two bushes. The deed was done.

Only God knew what lurked there in the dark. Something bit my ankles. Ants, maybe. The shadow of the other guard was in view. Leaning, smoking, sometimes moving. I had to urinate. I pulled down my *Punjabi* pants and peed like a dog at the base of a tree. The drops didn't make a sound. Suppose I was caught on camera. A guard in the house, pulling a curtain aside, could have detected movement, shone a flashlight and clicked a camera. Headlines. "American Woman Pees In Home Minister's Garden."

That would fascinate the CIA. What a dossier they must have on me! Dates a Russian Intelligence agent in Ankara. Gets Embassy escorts to the Pakistan border. Pees on the Home Minister's daisies. What a reputation.

I pulled up my pants and knelt. I was twenty feet from the steps that led to the front door. Indians rise early. Before dawn, they wash themselves and worship God. Nanda wouldn't come out. A servant would open the front door to sweep and wash the steps. That's all I needed, an open door. I'd wait.

Dawn brought all things into sharp relief. Trees, bushes, flowers, insects, the house. The wooden door opened. A woman in a maid's uniform stepped out carrying a short straw broom. That was my chance. I leapt out of the bushes, raced to the steps, and bolted up. "Mataji, Mataji! Please, here, this letter, for the Minister." The guards ran toward me, rifles up. The woman dropped her broom and grabbed her chest.

"Please, Mataji!" She took the letter and slammed the door. The guards shouted in Hindi. It didn't matter. The deed was done. I walked down the steps. They stood at my sides, rifles pointed, howling in Hindi. My heart raced. I did what I had to do. Now it was in the hands of the gods. I sat on the bottom step.

"Off it, off it," the guards shouted. I stood, waited. It didn't matter. The door opened. The tall man with stern features, whom I had seen the day before, appeared in a robe of blue silk brocade. His eyebrows met. I'd stunned him. How did I pass the guards, he'd ask. When? But he didn't ask. He ordered the guards back to their posts, then asked the maid to bring his reading glasses. There, poised at the top of the steps outside his front door, garbed in silk, he read AnandSwami's letter.

"This says you want a year's extension as a student. Is that correct?"

"Yes, sir."

"But that's illegal. You didn't enter India as a student. You came as a tourist. We gave you a tourist visa for three months, and extended it for another three. Now you're suddenly a student instead of a tourist."

"Yes, sir."

"How can you come to India as a tourist and transform into a student?"

"That's what happened, sir. That's exactly what happened." Tears streamed down. "Had I known, sir, had I known what India was, what it would mean to me, I'd have asked for a student visa in the first place. But I didn't know."

"What you want is illegal. Suppose I went to your country as a visitor, and at the end of my stay, I decided to become a student. You think the American government would give me a student visa? Of course not!"

"Sir, I must stay here. That's all there is to it. I can't leave India."

Nanda descended the steps, handed me the letter, and climbed back up.

"Sir, please, sir! Tell me what to do. I've got to stay."

At the top, his hand on the doorknob, he glared down. "In that case, madam," he said with cutting sarcasm, "you can either see the Prime Minister, or marry an Indian." He turned, stepped inside, and slammed the door shut.

Seven hours left. The Minister had made it clear. See the Prime Minister or marry an Indian. He said it with sarcasm, but I had to take him literally.

I ambled along a busy street, not knowing where I was headed. Marriage wouldn't be a problem. Thousands of Indian men wanted an American wife to get to the States. But first, I'd try the Prime Minister. How can a foreign woman with no status see a Prime Minister? In less than six hours? Well, I got to the Home Minister. But I'd never get past the PM's guards. What now? I wondered.

The window of a sweets shop tantalized me. *Jelebees* dripping oil, honey and sugar. *Gulabjam*, small round balls fried in oil. Chocolate and almond *burfis*. I could have eaten them all. Maybe after a *burfi* I could think of a plan.

Two men exited the shop, one in an army officer's uniform. "Sir, how can I see the Prime Minister?"

He snickered. "Madam, how can I get to the moon?"

They turned away. I tapped his shoulder. He shrank back, brushing it off. I kept forgetting that India wasn't America. You don't touch men in India. If he were a Brahmin, he'd go home to bathe.

"I'm sorry, sir. It's urgent. Very urgent."

"I told you. It's easier to land on the moon than to see the Prime Minister."

"Someone, some official besides the Home Minister, must have access to the PM."

"Parliamentarians can see the PM anytime." He brushed his shoulder again and took off.

Parliamentarians, parliamentarians. I stepped into the shop. "Chocolate *burfi*, please." In five minutes, I'd eaten it. "Two more. And coffee. By the way, you know any parliamentarians?"

"Sorry Memsaab, no much English. You speaks to boss man."

The short, stocky boss was counting money in a small space at the back, separated from the café by a glass divider. The waiter pointed to me, and the boss came to my table.

"May I help you, Mataji?"

"I'm American. By noon, my visa will be invalid. I'll be in jail. I need help, sir."

"First, my name is not 'sir.' See there?"

"*'Sharma's Sweets,'* it says. You are Mr. Sharma?"

"*Shurrmuh*," he corrected. "Short 'a.' Your name?"

"Shirley."

"Sheerlee?"

"Right. I came here as a tourist but fell in love with India. The philosophy, the spirituality. I stay at ShivaSwami's ashram, and need to renew my visa."

"Mataji, see that wall."

Behind me was a portrait of ShivaSwami perched cross-legged on a rock along the Ganges.

"Oh, my! You knew him?"

"He was our family guru. He saved my brother's life when

Jeetu was six months old. AnandSwami visits our home when he comes to New Delhi."

"You know him, too! Here's his letter asking the Home Minister to help me, but it didn't work. The Minister said that only the Prime Minister could help. I need to see a parliamentarian who can contact the PM."

"Look how God guides you. My brother is in parliament. Stay here. I call him."

Uncanny! A day earlier, I was a boat without oars. Now, in a sweets shop, I'm about to meet a parliamentarian who has instant access to the PM. It happened in minutes, and I had nothing to do with it.

I recalled Karsta's remark: "Germans have a saying," she told me. "We know we don't control our entry into life. And we know we don't control our exit. But for some weird reason, we think we control the middle part."

Short like his brother and eight years younger, Jeetu appeared more Italian than Indian. He wore flashy gold rings and a wristwatch with an oversized dial. Instead of greeting me with hands folded at his heart, he shook my hand vigorously. The world fascinated him. I could see it from his open, inquiring eyes. Jeetu was the right guy.

"Tell me, tell me," he said. I went through the story.

"You got past Nanda's guards? Fearless woman you are!"

I showed him photographs and news clips of my Land Rover. He brought them to his brother. "This is the woman we saw in *The Times of India*. Sitting here!"

Jeetu pressed AnandSwami's letter to his forehead. "A saint," he said. "You're fortunate to have his testimony. If he recommends you, you deserve a visa."

"The Home Minister says it's illegal."

"Nanda's a clot," Jeetu said, "and he's second in the cabinet. If anything happens to Nehru, he'll be the acting PM. God help India. You know who gets visas here? B girls, that's right. B girls, prostitutes. That's who. If you can't get an extension to study Indian spirituality, I'll bring it up on the floor of Parliament.

"Here's what I want you to do. Give me your passport, official papers, Swami's letter, and press clippings. My driver will drive you back to your hotel. Go to your room and stay there. Don't move about because you have no proof of identity. Have all meals sent to your room. Understand?"

"Understand."

"*Teekha?*"

"*Teekha. Dhanyavaad.*" The only two words I knew in Hindi. Okay, and thanks.

Zucchini with lentils was the plate of the day. I ate it in my room, and ordered potato pudding for dessert. Full and relaxed, I leaned back in the worn upholstered chair beneath a whirring fan. My life whirrs like that, spiraling toward some summit undirected by me. Maybe everyone's life spirals, undirected by themselves.

The timing seemed awesome. When I arrived in Kashmir, I couldn't breathe. An illiterate servant took me to a *hakim*, and three days later, I breathed normally for the first time in sixteen years. One month later, I was doing breathing exercises in the Himalayas.

Delhi, too. With only a few hours left, I stroll along a street, walk into a café for sweets, and an hour later, the owner's brother tells me that if his government won't give me a visa, he'll bring it up in Parliament. If I'd written that scenario myself, I couldn't have done a better job. This *can't* be coincidence. Something, some *power* must be writing the script. So why should I worry? But I worried. What if it didn't work? Then I'd look for a cave. Then the government would look for me.

The small spiritual book I'd brought with me said that One Supreme Being manifests as many. KrishnaSwami put it another way: *Our only problem is the fictitious conceit of doership.* We think *we're* doing everything.

The phone rang. "Jeetu here. You have a forty-eight hour emergency extension."

My heart sank. "Forty-eight hours? That's all?"

"No, that's not all," he said. "You have an audience with Prime Minister Nehru tomorrow morning at 10 a.m."

"Oh, my God! An audience with the Prime Minister! Where does he live?"

"You don't need his address. My driver will pick you up at nine. He'll have your papers. Show only AnandSwami's letter to the Prime Minister. Understand?"

"Understand."

"Teekha?"

"Teekha."

"Don't move about. Stay in your room until eight-fifty tomorrow morning. *Teekha?"*

"Teekha. Dhanyavaad."

An audience with Prime Minister Nehru! I could see it. The two of us in a small reception room. I'd sit across from him, maybe for fifteen or twenty minutes. He'd already know about me, so what more should I say? We could talk about religion but I heard that he doesn't call himself religious. He wrote that in the name of religion, great deeds were done, but so were despicable crimes. I believe this, too.

I could say something funny since everyone knew that Nehru had a sense of humor. Once, when an American friend was shocked to see Indians eating with their hands, Nehru told him that using a fork was like making love through a translator.

America's blatant materialism had stunned Nehru when he visited the States. On return to India, he remarked that no one should ever go to America *for the first time*. I could tell him that I agreed. During the Indian freedom struggle, the British jailed him for political activism. I could say I resonated to his values. But would it matter?

Among all the celebrities he'd met in the West including Einstein, Kennedy, and Eleanor Roosevelt, he said that only Adlai Stevenson had impressed him. I could tell him that he impressed me, too.

Suppose he offered me tea. My hand might shake when I raised the cup. I'd decline. *No, thank you, sir.* I forgot to ask Jeetu how to address a Prime Minister. *No thank you, Mr. Prime Minister*. That doesn't sound right. "Sir" is better.

My brain buzzed like a beehive. I couldn't sleep.

49

PRIME MINISTER NEHRU

1963

Teen Murti, the name of the Prime Minister's residence, referred to the monument to three soldiers that stood near the front.

Activity near the entrance was feverish. Chauffeurs of Cadillacs, Ambassadors, Mercedes and Rolls Royce limousines dropped off dignitaries of every color and nationality. If all those people had an audience with the PM, I wouldn't get more than ten minutes with him. All carried something, a big thing or a small thing. Jeetu didn't tell me to bring a gift.

"I wait here," my driver said.

At the entrance door, uniformed men asked our names and checked their lists. That imperial mansion had been the home of British viceroys. The last of those to live in the mansion was Viscount Louis Mountbatten, the great-grandson of Queen Victoria. Sixteen years earlier, he had sworn in Nehru as India's first Prime Minister.

I followed other guests into the grand reception room, a palatial ballroom. Security guards were posted at every door and window, and along the back walls. The room had a high ceiling, Indian paintings, and busts of the famous. The most impressive, Mahatma Gandhi. A guard led me to the opposite side of the door to join a line of guests that had formed a U-pattern around the room. I was one person among fifty. *So this is what it means to have an audience with the Prime Minister!*

To my right, a man with Greek features carried a box with the Prime Minister's name engraved in gold. A European woman to his right held an oversized card. An invitation, maybe. To my left, a man garbed in flowing red and white robes with billowing sleeves and a matching headdress looked like royalty from West Africa. His gift was a map of his country printed on hand-woven cloth. Several guests looked American, all presenting impressive gifts. Paintings, busts, invitations in gold. And there I was, with a letter for a visa. I wanted to run, but it was too late.

No one spoke as Indira Gandhi, the Prime Minister's daughter, approached the first guest on my side of the room. Indira was in her mid-forties, slim and strained. Her hair was short and black, with a distinctive silvery white streak. Like traditional Indian widows, she wore a white sari. With a cursory nod, aloof, unsmiling and cold, she greeted each guest. They stated their mission and handed her their gift, which an aide carried off.

If I have to speak to Indira instead of her father, I'll be finished. But she stopped. Heads turned toward the stairs. A pin-drop would have sounded like thunder as the aging Prime Minister descended the steps. Nehru's face was lined and mellow, older than his pictures. A widower for many years, he'd given the duties of the Prime Minister's wife to his daughter. Chief hostess, chief assistant, head of the house.

Indira took her father's arm, and together, in clockwise movement, they addressed each guest, starting from where Indira had stopped. They appeared unmoved as they acknowledged gifts, exchanged a few words and carried on. When the Greek man to my right offered his golden lettered box to the Prime Minister, my stomach churned. My knees trembled.

Nehru turned to me. "What is the purpose of your visit?" he asked.

I wanted to say, *A visa, sir,* but nothing came out. My mouth had dried up. I felt the scrutiny of Indira's eyes as I handed him the three-paragraph letter from AnandSwami. He pulled his reading glasses from his vest pocket and read from the top. All eyes focused on me. The giftless guest.

To my dismay, Nehru frowned as he read it. Then he read it again. Didn't he understand? Was this a terrible thing to do? Outrageous?

"But this is not a matter for the Prime Minister," he said.

Oh, my God! I stared at the floor beneath my feet, willing it to open and swallow me. I'd sail straight down, suctioned into the pit like a dust mite in a vacuum. A lid would close forever on my head. No one would see me or hear me, ever. I stared at the pit. Open, open. Every ear was cocked my way. Eyes accused me. The gall of this woman, giving the Prime Minister something not meant for him.

"This is a matter for the Home Minister," he said.

"But, sir, I saw him. He said that only the Prime Minister could help."

Nehru folded the letter, put it in his pocket and took off his glasses. "Well, I'll see," he said. "I'll see."

"Thank you," I whispered. My face burned with shame. My eyes remained riveted on the floor beneath me until all was finished.

The driver showed me Jeetu's note. *Wait in your room for my call,* it said.

A zombie stared back at me from my bathroom mirror. Terror, dread, fear, and nothing. Empty, void. I lay down, too spent to sleep. Hours passed.

The phone rang. "Shirley, I'm downstairs," Jeetu said.

"Come up, come up, please."

"No. You come down." I should have remembered. This is India.

In the lobby, young men surrounded us, unashamed to gawk and listen. "You've got it!" Jeetu said. "A student visa good for one year from today!"

I longed to throw my arms around him. "Thank you, thank you, thank you!"

"Still some work for you. Our government auctions off cars kept longer than the original permit date, so tomorrow you have to see the Finance Minister. But he can't refuse an extension now that the PM sanctioned your stay. My driver will pick you up."

"Thank you, thank you."

"Now don't get the idea that you can do this again next year. That won't happen. This is it. One year and finish. Understand?"

"I don't understand, Jeetu. India is my country. I want to stay forever."

"No. Not possible. You'd have to become a citizen, and that's impossible."

"I can marry an Indian."

"No, no!" The men crowded us, hanging on every word.

"Look at them, Jeetu!"

"Scatter, scatter," he ordered in Hindi. They backed up, but edged forward again.

"Americans would have fits," I said.

"These chaps mean no harm. They're just curious."

"But we're not monkeys in a zoo."

"You mentioned marrying an Indian," Jeetu said. The men closed in. "Scatter, scatter," he ordered, but they giggled.

"What's wrong with marrying for citizenship?" I asked. "Many men want to go to America to live and work. A marriage like that would make two people happy."

"The ashram would kick you out."

"Why?"

"ShivaSwami's ashram has high standards, and marrying for a visa is shameful."

"Why call an arrangement 'shameful' that makes two people happy?"

"Because that's not the purpose of marriage," Jeetu said. "To us Indians, marriage is a sacred pact. A lifelong commitment between two people. In India, marriage is the beginning of a love affair. In America, marriage is the end of it."

On the train back to the foothills, I felt like two people. One relaxed, relieved that the Delhi ordeal was done, and I'd won. The other tensed, acknowledging for the first time that the day would come when I'd have to leave. Where would I go? What would I do? Now that show business was out, how would I make a living?

Not only did work worry me, but once I left India, I'd have no spiritual support. The masters say that we should live like a lotus, with our feet in the mud and our head up high. Easy to say, but few have done it. Early Christian saints renounced the world for the desert. St. Theresa, St. Benedict, St. John of the Cross lived in monasteries. Thomas Merton, the American Trappist monk, fought for solitude. If they couldn't do it in the world, how could I? Besides, in the West, I'd have to swim upstream alone.

A cartoon on my wall made the point. A long line of cars, some driven by Americans, others by Indians, stop at a junction. A sign reads, "*Drive right to be transformed. Drive left to be informed.*"

The Indians turn right. All the Americans turn left.

50

THE ASHRAM

1963-64

One year. That's all I had. A year to free myself from the baggage I carried. The illusion that I am a body and mind bound by a bag of skin. Here today, gone tomorrow.

I knew what to do, but didn't know if I could do it. Inner work differed from all the work I'd done. Performing, composing, driving around the world, learning languages. Inner work meant de-brainwashing. Stripping myself of judgments. A subtractive process like cleaning the dross off a light bulb. My worldly strengths—boundless confidence, obduracy, dogged insistence—wouldn't help. They hindered.

I needed to learn to surrender. AnandSwami told me that surrender is tough for Westerners because we're taught that when things don't happen, we have to make them happen. That doesn't work on the spiritual path.

"The universe is a cosmic operation," he said. "*Thy* will be done, not mine. Think of your life like a train ride. You're a passenger, so why carry your bags on your head? Put them down. The train will carry them."

Karsta could have helped me understand, but she'd gone back to Germany. I sat on the rocker she gave me, gazing through my window at the foothills across the Ganges. I should have been grateful for the extra year I got. Instead, I worried. How would I make a living when the year was over? Show business was out, so what would I do? I could place an ad in an international paper: *Lady with Land Rover wants a job. Any country within driving distance of the Himalayan foothills.* But what country would give me a work permit? It was tough enough to get a visitor's visa around there.

But why was I so preoccupied with the future? When I left America, I didn't think about "what next." When I left London in my Land Rover, I didn't know when or if I'd eat, or where I'd sleep. Why was I worried now?

As the winter months passed, meditation became effortless. When I first began to meditate, I felt like an outsider. An onlooker, ecstatic with rare glimpses of an inner sacred stillness. That changed. Now, I was on the inside looking out. I was the stillness in which movement occurred.

A strange thought crossed my mind. Why should I leave India when I'm making spiritual progress? Why should I be shackled by a one-year visa? If KrishnaSwami asked the Prime Minister for my citizenship, I could stay forever.

The monk's room was still. He scanned a letter while an aide at his side sat poised with a notebook and pen. I knelt. "I can't leave you, sir. Ever. And why should I, when I'm through with the world?"

His look pierced me. *"Because the world is not through with you!"*

I returned to my room, shattered. Hadn't I done enough in the world? What need did the world have for me? Why should I trade bliss for the world?

KrishnaSwami knew I was almost broke, but I could earn money by writing articles about my life, my travels. I'd tell him after his lecture. He'll say, "Yes, yes. Write! Tell the world about your experiences!"

A hundred guests filled the lecture hall that day. When everyone had settled into sitting postures, KrishnaSwami fixed his eyes on me. "*You* want to write? What makes you think that anyone would read what *you* have to say?"

I felt shredded, like he'd rung me through a washer. When the lecture ended, I tried to slip out before anyone spoke to me. But a French woman yanked my arm. "Don't feel bad. He does this to break the ego. Is compliment, not insult."

At his next lecture, I leaned on the entrance door where he couldn't see me. But he did. "Why don't you want to leave India?"

Why didn't he ask me that when I was in his room? Why does

he wait until a hundred people can hear it? I shut my eyes to block out their faces. "I'd have to relate to worldly people."

"Your problem," he said, "is that you separate the spiritual from the secular. You think that what's holy is spiritual, and the world is everything else."

I could barely hear my own voice. "Isn't it?"

"Secular life is no different from spiritual life. To think the world is divorced from spiritual life is flawed perception. Body and spirit are not isolated departments of human activity. Your task is to fuse them with your spiritual aim. Not divorce them from it. Why? Because the world is spirit in form."

But I've felt ecstasy, I told him mentally. *Doesn't that count? I don't want to give that up for a job in the world.*

"The proper measure of spirituality," he said, "is not the ecstasy you feel in meditation. It's how aware you are of universal truth as you interact with the world."

The monk was heartless. He'd exposed my most private thoughts.

Stillness settled quickly as I meditated in my room one balmy summer night. Two hours passed before I wrote in my diary:

Thoughts ceased. The "I" that sometimes loves and sometimes hates, that regrets the past and fears the future, was stripped of name and form. I became formless, sucked into an infinite mass of Being in which past, present and future coalesced into one. No up, down, right, left, yesterday or tomorrow. I had neither beginning nor end.

This was bliss. Not the bliss from objects that change, but bliss itself. The noun, not the adjective. Infinite freedom was no longer a future possibility, it was a present fact.

All the world's scriptures and sermons could not have taught what I'd learned in those two hours. About surrender, love, God. All the bliss in the world would not have yielded one iota of that ecstasy.

The rains had stopped in my final month in India, and cool, dry air settled over the foothills. I was nowhere near my goal of cosmic consciousness, but nobody can attain it in a year, the monks had told me. Not even in ten years. I thought I could do it. After all, I'd done almost everything else I set out to do.

One evening, I sat on a rock along the river, drawing my brown Kashmir shawl, big as a blanket, over my body and head. I had meditated for an hour when I heard footsteps. KrishnaSwami and a novice had descended the steps to the embankment.

They turned away from where I sat, moving slowly along the river toward the Ayurvedic pharmacy, a small building that stood apart. The Ganges was calm, the moon full. The swami and his aide exchanged a few words, the aide turned back, and KrishnaSwami entered the building where he would climb the steps to a room at the top. Perhaps he stayed there every full moon. The room had windows on every side. All were open, all was dark.

From my far-away rock, I gazed in silence for a long time. I would carry that monk in my heart for the rest of my life. He showed me who I am.

My room was bare, the Rover packed. I was off to Kathmandu. KrishnaSwami, AnandSwami, monks, novices, and foreigners—even the ashram dogs—gathered to see me off on that bright November morning.

I asked KrishnaSwami a question that had weighed on my mind.

"For a year, sir, you have taught me that all that we see, hear, and know are manifestations of the one universal Self. Suppose, on my solo drive to Kathmandu, I meet tribes trekking south for the winter. Suppose they see a woman alone in a car which surely must contain the riches of the earth. Suppose they attack. What should I do?"

"Get down on your knees," he said. "Put your head on their feet, and say, *'Oh Lord! So you have come to me in* this *form!'*"

51

KATHMANDU, NEPAL

1964-65

The Valley of Kathmandu. *Shangrila*, cradled by the Lords of the Snows. Buddhist temples everywhere. Multi-tiered pagodas and fierce fabled figures guarding entrances against evil spirits. Saffron-robed monks twirling beads on temple steps. Giant golden spires. Tiny wooden houses with teakwood carvings. Colors. Fragrance. Bells. *Shangrila.*

Peasants traded goats and sheep in grassy squares. Tibetan pilgrims strolled the streets in purple robes. Barefoot children flicked marbles on the road. Gurkha soldiers marched in groups. Coppered-skinned women chatted. Men sauntered in their tilted pillbox hats, tunics with Nehru collars, and flared pants. No hurry, no rush. A mountain ecstasy, four thousand feet up. Cool, clear air. *Shangrila.*

I came *here* to get a job? One goes to New York, Frankfurt, or Geneva to work. But Kathmandu?

Something tugged at my tunic. I was standing on a main street when I felt the pull. A kid, bright eyed and barefoot in short pants and a torn shirt with stubbed out butts in his shirt pocket. And the most incongruous thing pressed to his chest. A new Oxford dictionary.

"Missus, please. This dictionary, all I want in life. Ten dollars, missus, please." A tear dripped on the book as he gripped it.

I couldn't afford ten dollars. I couldn't afford five. But could I afford to ignore him? This kid with cigarette butts in his shirt pocket could become a prime minister if given the chance. I gave him ten.

"Tanks, missus!" He galloped down the street to the book store.

I checked into a backpackers' hotel, ate a cheese sandwich in the "eatery," and strolled down the street past Western backpackers, kids skipping home from school, a French travel agency, and the book store. There he was, the same kid, pleading with an elderly Western couple. Pressing that same dictionary to his chest!

The man pulled a bill from his pocket and handed it to him. That kid probably hooked ten people a day for that same dictionary. Gave the owner most of the money, and kept the rest for cigarettes.

Experienced woman that I am. World traveler. Had by a kid.

Joe Toner, a small man with a reserved manner and mellow voice directed the office of U.S. AID, the United States Agency for International Development. My life, portfolios, and Land Rover fascinated him. In his office, he guaranteed that by the end of that day, I'd have a job. "Meantime," he said, "let's have lunch."

The Royal Hotel was a converted palace near the center of town. Heads of animals hunted by royalty decorated the walls of the marble entrance hall. Deer, tiger, and bearskins covered floors. Ornate chandeliers hung from the ceiling of the dining hall. We chose the warm veranda, as did other Americans, British and French diplomats, businessmen and tourists.

"The hotel owner is famous," Toner said. "A White Russian expatriate who danced in ballet, ran nightclubs, and dabbled with imports. He's close to the royal family, knows everybody. I guarantee that when he sees your brochures, he'll book you on the spot."

"Oh, no!" I said. "I showed you my brochures just to share my background. I'm finished with show business."

"Finished? With your experience? You can make a fortune here."

"I don't want a fortune. I just want a job. Any job, but not show business."

"You'd turn down a job at the Royal? The hub of Kathmandu's elite?"

"I would," I nodded.

"Pity," he said. "In that case, the only other guy in town who can help is Father Moran, an American Jesuit. Everybody knows Father. Before he came, Nepali kids studied in India. Father founded all our local schools."

A portrait of Saint Ignatius of Loyola hung in the reception room of the Jesuit House. Below it was the Jesuit motto printed in Latin and English: *For the greater glory of God.* I sat on a comfortable brown chair with a high back, drinking English tea and relishing a slice of Swiss chocolate cake served by a novice.

Father Moran stepped in, shook hands, and sat across from me. A tall man with horn-rimmed glasses clad in a black cassock and stiff white clerical collar.

"Joe Toner said you need a job. What are your qualifications?"

His question wiped my mind clean. I couldn't think. Had I no qualifications?

"None, Father."

"The first woman to drive halfway around the world alone has no qualifications?"

"Well, I can drive a Land Rover."

"Toner read your clippings. Said you mix jazz with mechanics. Tell me about it."

"The Land Rover school taught me a few things. How to clean my air filter and spark plugs."

"They financed your trip?"

"Oh, no. I had to work."

"How did you find work in strange places?"

"Booked myself as an accordionist and singer on TV, radio, hotels, and military installations through Europe, Africa, Turkey, and Pakistan. In India, I booked into a five-star hotel, showed the manager my brochures, and got a month's contract."

"Very enterprising. Tell me about your education."

I told Father I'd gone to NYU for several years, but quit because night work left no time to study. "I studied at the University of Munich medical school for a short time, and took a course in Malariology at the London School of Tropical Medicine."

"Hmm. Why medicine?" he asked.

"I always wanted to work in a medical mission."

"Interesting. What languages do you speak?"

"German, French. Some Greek and Norwegian. A little Italian."

Father studied me as though he were trying to put the pieces of a puzzle together. His gaze moved to the portrait of St. Ignatius. Then he ticked words off his fingertips. "Pioneering. Leadership. Courage. Fearless. Medical mission. German. French. Initiative. Mechanics. Young lady, I've been looking for a special person to work with Tibetan refugees. I think that special person is you."

He told me that when the Dalai Lama escaped from Tibet in 1959 and was smuggled into India, eighty thousand Tibetans followed him. Half of them landed in Nepal, bringing only what they could carry on their backs. Many got sick since they weren't used to lower altitudes. Nepal had no resources to help, and no Red Cross. The Jesuits raised funds from the West.

"We got stretches of flat land where Tibetans could set up their tents and live like they did in Tibet. But their tents are too heavy for Nepal. Their woolen clothes are too warm. They can't adjust. Their red meat dries well in Tibetan sun, but rots fast here. They use cooking oil to fuel their altar lamps, and they think latrines are strange.

"The Swiss Red Cross took over the camps," Father said. The camp that needed me was Trisuli, seventy-two kilometers from Kathmandu.

"The road is bad, the accident rate is high. Beriberi is rampant at the camp, and the Swiss doctor comes out only once every two weeks. You'd have to give vitamin B injections, and dispense medicine, but he'd show you what to do. A Swiss couple manages the business end, carpet-weaving, and export to Switzerland. You'd work in the clinic, teach English and hygiene, inspect huts, and raise funds."

"For how long, Father?"

"Until the camp closes. Every day, a few more Tibetans head for the hills to climb into India and join the Dalai Lama. When the last one leaves, the camp will close."

Father paused, peering at me above his horn rims. "Well, what do you say?"

"When do I start, Father?"

Seventy-two kilometers. Forty-five miles northwest of Kathmandu. Six hours if I'm lucky.

I drove along a mountain dirt road, skirting tumbling rocks, backing up to slopes when vehicles approached. Around hairpin bends, inches from narrow ledges that looked like windowsills. At one point, when my right front wheel spun in soft mud on the cliff side of the road, I dared to glance over the edge. At the bottom of the four-thousand foot drop, a tractor-trailer lay upside down like a toy. But beneath it, a body or two must lay still, crushed, long forgotten.

I crawled in lowest gear. I'd left Kathmandu at 8 a.m. At 4 p.m. I saw the Trisuli refugee camp. Hundreds of men, women and children with long braided hair and leathery copper skin had come out of their tents to welcome me. Their long dark woolen robes were bunched up from belted waists, crisscrossing their chests. They waved, the late afternoon sun rays dancing like golden flames above their heads.

52

WESTWARD HO!

1965

A year passed. The last sixty refugees gathered before me on a bleak October morning. The others had already climbed the hills into India to be with the Dalai Lama. Hundreds of vacated tents surrounded us.

Lobsang, my interpreter, told me that the Tibetans wished to offer me a gift. The eldest, a shriveled ninety-year-old man with a long gray beard, edged toward me with outstretched arms. A pair of cracked, rimless eyeglasses lay in his withered hands.

"Oh, I can't take this man's glasses!" I said. "How will he see?"

Lobsang translated. The Tibetans roared with laughter. "This man can't see with or without his glasses," one said. Lobsang whispered, "To be kind, you must take them. They have nothing else to give."

Tears streaked the glasses that I cradled in my hands. I thanked them for the privilege of serving them, and stared mutely as they turned toward the hills.

The year that had passed taught me as much about myself as it taught me about Tibetans. I had driven to the refugee camp with the mindset of a Harvard "cum laude" graduate on her first job. Father Moran had warned of difficulties, but I was convinced that no challenge would disturb my equanimity. After all, I had tasted spiritual bliss.

I was sure of it until the day that yak butter arrived on my table replete with the hairs of a yak. Until I drank the buttery, salty liquid that tasted like soup but was called "tea." Until the night that rats the size of cats scuttled along the walls of my room, and

I jumped on my bed, screaming for help, forgetting to witness my fear.

In our makeshift clinic, Tibetans with beriberi rolled up their sleeves and thrust out their bronzed arms, wide grins on their faces as I prepared to inject them with Vitamin B. Every jab of an arm felt like I'd stabbed my stomach with a sword. I, who had craved an M.D. since childhood, sweating at NYU and the University of Munich. But it could have been worse. I might have gotten that M.D.

On a fund-raising trip to Kathmandu, I turned a bend and almost ploughed into a truck parked at right angles in front of me. One of its rear wheels dangled over the cliff.

But roads, rats, hairy butter and salty tea did not diminish the joy of working with Tibetans. Teaching English and geography to the children, orienting them with maps of Tibet, where they came from. Nepal, where they were. India, where they were going.

The Soviet tourist office was located at the top of an inclined street in Kathmandu. I waited outside for the Finance Minister's chauffeur to drive me to Gaucher Airport. The minister—the only man in Nepal with U.S. dollars—had bought my Land Rover for three thousand dollars in cash. The price I paid to buy it.

All my past efforts to visit Russia had failed. Now, the green Intourist tickets for travel to and within the Soviet Union filled my purse. Tickets for flights, trains, hotels, meals. Everything purchased in advance in case money changers on the street might tempt a tourist with an exchange rate ten times that of the bank rate. I'd visit Moscow, Leningrad, Kiev, Socchi, and Tbilisi.

I'd studied conversational Russian and compiled a list of sentences that I could rattle off with ease. A Russian climber in Kathmandu told me I sounded like a native Muscovite, as usual with foreign languages. But as usual, my vocabulary was poor. Still, I was prepared. If a railway ticket agent asked me a question that I couldn't understand, I would point to my left ear. "*Izvinite,*" I would say. "*Ya gluhaya.* (Sorry. I am deaf.)"

A long queue of passengers trudged across the tarmac toward the Indian Airlines plane. Climbers with their gear. Indians with their bedrolls and food containers. Germans and Americans with their cameras. I would get off in New Delhi, take a bus to the ashram for a short visit, and return to Delhi for the flight to Moscow.

The Lords of the Snows stretching to the east and west pulled my eyes to the windowpane. Our plane heaved and lifted, shadowing the valley of Kathmandu—the palaces and golden spires, pagodas and prayer beads, purple and saffron. *Shangrila.*

I leaned into my seat as we flew into the vastness of a cloudless, infinite sky.

53

AMERICA TO AFRICA

1966

In January of 1966, I returned to New York to visit my mother. Five months later, I boarded the *S.S. African Mercury*, a cargo ship bound for South Africa. Now was the time to do something for others. After all, I had realized my dreams: I'd seen the world. I'd found meaning. I had a long way to go spiritually, but I was firmly on the path.

The image of black kids' legs sticking out of drainpipes had festered in my mind since I'd seen them seven years earlier while performing in Johannesburg. Now was the time to help. I could work in a clinic, teach English, and raise funds.

We were twelve passengers on the *S.S. African Mercury*. The ship offered no movies or entertainment, so we stayed in our cabins and socialized only at meals. The liner made no provision for vegetarians. I brought my own protein: three dozen containers of flavored yogurt, a new item in American supermarkets.

And I brought three books on the lives of Christian saints—about their solitude and spiritual experiences. By the time I'd finished all three, I wondered why I planned to work. Why should I teach? Why raise funds? Why sweat in a clinic when all I wanted was the bliss that St. Theresa of Avila had? That the early Fathers enjoyed in the silence of the desert. That the monk, Thomas Merton had, in the seclusion of his meditation hut.

I began to image myself veiled in black. Aloof from society. Silent, eating little, meditating all day. Blissed out.

By the time the *S.S. African Mercury* docked in South Africa, I was convinced: my future lay not in an active life, but in cloistered solitude.

◆ ◆ ◆

The Carmelite monastery outside Johannesburg was silent, with a pervasive air of mystery. I entered a reception room and asked a nun if I could meet Mother Superior. She escorted me to a dimly lit room, bare but for a wooden chair. I sat facing an aperture in the wall secured on my side by vertical iron bars. On the other side, a slab of wood.

I heard a click. The slab slid sideways. There sat Mother Superior wearing the scapular and a black veil that covered her face. She asked why I came. I told her that I yearned for a life of silence and meditation. That St. Theresa of Avila, the Carmelite founder, had inspired me.

Mother said nothing. I asked her about the daily routine. She told me that the Sisters studied Catholic history for three hours a day.

"Three hours a day for *history?* How can that help them spiritually?"

Mother asked if I had any other questions.

"How many hours a day do the Sisters sit in silent contemplation?"

Her brittle voice snapped back. "Half an hour every morning."

"Just half an hour? Contemplation is the most crucial part of religious life. Even *I* sit for an hour in the morning and an hour at night."

Mother rose from her chair. "Madame," she said, in a voice like gray stone, "If I were you, I'd go to the desert, and start my own Order."

The slab slid back, and the aperture closed.

One week later, I was delivering food to poor families in Durban's Tin Town. Typing thirty fund-raising letters a day on a Remington manual typewriter. Packing pink pills into tiny bottles at a clinic serving Africans and Indians.

One year later, I was raising funds for Inanda Seminary, a boarding high school for African girls. Eight years later, I would begin to compile and write the first Who's Who of Black South Africans.

I had to face it. I was through with the world. But the world was not through with me.

A Note From the Author

Nothing I'd done in my life was as tough as writing this book. Where should I start? End? What should I include? Exclude? The task challenged me like no other, but I had to write it. I owed it to Life, a debt that wielded a force I couldn't defy.

If my parents could read this book, they would understand why I didn't pursue a "normal" life. Daughters of their friends had married doctors and lawyers, reared children, rose in social stature. Mom and Dad with only one child, always far away, had nothing to show. No son-in-law, no grandkids; just press clippings and odd stamps. But if they could have read my book, they would have grasped the strong sense of responsibility that I bore to myself, not to them or society. They'd have grasped my perception that the world was my home. This I believed, and by virtue of that belief, I felt entitled to see it.

I wasn't naïve. Rootless, itinerant living was fraught with dangers—poverty, hunger, loneliness and worse. But such suffering would not be senseless. I preferred the freedom of insecurity to the security of conformity. I wanted my inner decisions to direct my life, not outer expectations. To embrace inner triumphs, not outer success. A triumph over myself would grant meaning to my life that success in the world could not.

Something else urged me onward—something deep inside me that I could not articulate, that hankered to be realized. That inner dimension unfolded in the Himalayas, baring freedom, permanence, and bliss that yielded the strength to cope with the powers of apartheid in South Africa. Strength to accept the things I couldn't change, and to change my reactions to them.

I embarked on this memoir almost nine years ago. I felt like a courier on a sensitive mission that had spanned four decades, sixty-seven countries, and adventures I'd kept so secret that my closest confidantes could not dare to guess. A year later, I calculated that my book would total eight hundred pages. Too long for one book.

I rang my friend, James Ethridge, a founder of Gale Publishers in Detroit. "I'll have to write two volumes," I told him.

"Two volumes?" he roared. *"Who do you think you are—Winston Churchill?"*

A year passed before I began again. Despite having written and published two books—one in the late seventies, and one in the late eighties—I needed help, intelligent, objective help, and I got it. My close friend and attorney, Rod Enns, read it and suggested cuts—sentences, paragraphs, whole chapters. He noted words that confused, changes in time and place too abrupt to grasp. He complimented me on thematic consistency, on being explicit, on condensing and capturing the vital stuff and moving my story forward with good pace. He gave me choices: "Put the full version in or take the whole thing out." Sometimes he advised me to stop hitting the reader over the head with detail. "Just tell the story."

Despite his busy schedule, he made time to read my memoir because he believed that my story should be told. To Rod, the literary midwife and godfather of "An Unreasonable Woman," I owe profuse gratitude.

I am particularly indebted to Al Perry, literary guru and mentor, founder of Winston-Salem Writers, novelist and former journalist, for reading many sections of this book, and suggesting where and how to introduce more immediacy and vibrancy. Al's professional insights helped me to bring my memoir to fruition.

I extend appreciation to my brilliant writer friend, Martha Brown, who imparted invaluable literary guidance to me as I embarked on this book.

"An Unreasonable Woman" could never have become a reality without the unique energies, the editing and publishing skills, the artistic genius and extraordinary patience of Kevin Watson, founder, editor and publisher of Press 53. Thank you, Kevin, for your brilliant cover design. And thank you for all that you are!

I shall always be grateful to the trustees of the Who's Who of Black South Africans Board for their guidance, faith in me and courage in the face of the apartheid government's harassment: Dr. Ephraim Mokgokong, Dr. Conrad Strauss, and those who have passed on: Duchesne Grice (whose obituary is captioned "The

Ultimate Reasonable Man"), Rev. Enos Sikakane, Percy Thomas, Joseph Bhengu, Edward Moumakwa, and Obed Kunene.

Very warm gratitude to Professor Michaelle Browers, a specialist in Arabic studies who kindly translated my Arabic press clippings. And to my dear friend, Dr. Maria Sommer, who corrects my German so graciously and translated my German press clippings.

I owe the late Sri KrishnaSwami eternal gratitude for showing me who I am. And above all, I thank Lenita, my late mother, who made all things possible.

Photo by Paul M. Jackson

SHIRLEY DEANE was born in New York City and was given her first accordion at the age of eight. At 27, she left the United States to work her way around the world playing her own brand of jazz and classical music. She visited 67 countries, living in Pakistan for six months, Nepal for a year, India for eight years, and South Africa for 14 years. She studied music, psychology and philosophy, attending NYU and the University of Hawaii, and for a brief period studied medicine at the University of Munich. She was the first woman to drive a Land Rover from London to Kathmandu, and later managed a clinic at a Tibetan refugee camp in Nepal for the Swiss Red Cross, where she also raised funds and taught English. In 1967, she became public relations officer and fundraiser for Inanda Seminary near Durban, South Africa. She is the author of two previous books, *Black South Africans, a Who's Who* (Oxford University Press, Capetown, 1978), which she published under Dee Shirley Deane, and *Wisdom, Bliss, & Common Sense: Secrets of Self-Transformation* (Quest Books, 1989), which she published under her Indian name, Darshani Deane. Ms. Deane returned to the United States in 1998 and settled in Winston-Salem, North Carolina, where she now writes.

CPSIA information can be obtained at www.ICGtesting.com
Printed in the USA
269485BV00001B/8/P